War, Politics and Society in Early Modern China, 900–1795

In this new take on China's early modern history, Peter Lorge presents a fresh overview of the repeated recreation of the Chinese empire through military force. Emphasizing the relationship between the military and politics, and China's power as an empire, Lorge argues that the strength of the territorial claims and political impact of each dynasty were determined primarily by their military capacity rather than by their cultural characteristics.

Using a chronological narrative, *War, Politics and Society in Early Modern China, 900–1795* breaks free of the dynastic boundaries that shape much scholarship in this area, focusing instead on the growing power of local elites. This power eventually led to a system of loose central control – to the sacrifice of real, centralized power over local affairs.

Ideal for students of military and Asian studies, *War, Politics and Society in Early Modern China, 900–1795* is essential reading for anyone interested in the military history of China.

Peter Lorge is Senior Lecturer in Chinese History and Film at Vanderbilt University.

WARFARE AND HISTORY
Series Editor: Jeremy Black
Professor of History, University of Exeter

To my parents, and to Tracy and Aileen, who make it all worthwhile

War, Politics and Society in Early Modern China, 900–1795

Peter Lorge

Routledge
Taylor & Francis Group

LONDON AND NEW YORK

First published 2005
270 Madison Ave, New York, NY 10016

Simultaneously published in the UK
by Routledge
2–4 Park Square, Milton Park, Abingdon, Oxon OX14 4RN

Routledge is an imprint of the Taylor & Francis Group

Typeset in Bembo by RefineCatch Ltd, Bungay, Suffolk
Printed and bound in Great Britain by The Cromwell Press, Trowbridge, Wiltshire

British Library Cataloguing in Publication Data
A catalogue record for this book is available from the British Library

Library of Congress Cataloging in Publication Data
A catalog record for this book has been requested

ISBN10: 0–415–31690–1 (hbk)
ISBN10: 0–415–31691–X (pbk)
ISBN13: 9–78–0–415–31690–3 (hbk)
ISBN13: 9–78–0–415–31691–0 (pbk)

Contents

Acknowledgements

This book would never have been written without the support of Professor Jeremy Black. He not only suggested the topic, and allowed a then graduate student to take on the project, but also stuck with it through several years of publishing limbo, during which I had entirely given up on it ever seeing the light of day. Over the years, I have also benefited immensely from the advice, criticism and encouragement of David Graff on almost every academic project including this one.

Much of the research for this book was done while I was on a two-year post-doctoral fellowship at the Institute for History and Philology at the Academic Sinica in Taiwan. For that fellowship, and for most of my knowledge of Southern Song military history, I must thank professor Huang K'uan-chung. I must also thank the staff of the Fu Ssu-nien Library for their cheerful aid.

Finally, my wife endured my endless ramblings about this subject for many years. For that alone, she deserves my grateful thanks. For all the rest that she has done and continues to do, I can only say of her, *Yongyuan zai wo de xinli.*

Introduction

> For in war it's experience of action that matters. The so-called *Seven Military Classics* are full of nonsense about water and fire, lucky omens and advice on the weather, all at random and contradicting each other. I told my officials once that if you followed these books, you'd never win a battle . . . All one needs is an inflexible will and careful planning.
>
> The Kangxi emperor (1654–1772), Emperor of China[1]

There is no such thing as "China." In the same sense, there is also no such thing as "Europe." By this I mean that the terms "China" and "Europe" do not refer to specific, unchanging territories, or static, monolithic cultures. And while there are places and aspects of culture that are undeniably Chinese, in whatever sense we wish to understand this, there are also places, and aspects of culture, that have less clear pedigrees. This is not to say that the term is useless or meaningless, only that it is not neutral and needs to be defined. A given dynasty's territorial and cultural claims were political statements and must be understood as such. The extent to which those claims corresponded to what a government actually controlled was a military question. In every dynasty since the Qin (221–206 BCE), "China" was an inherently imperial term, defined politically and enforced militarily.[2]

The traditional Chinese state (after 221 BCE) has not been commonly characterized as martial or even imperial in the sense that it encompassed diverse lands and peoples who did not share its culture. It has most usually been portrayed as a civil-oriented bureaucracy, staffed by scholar-officials who qualified for their positions by passing rigorous exams, dominated by Confucian beliefs, and held together at the most basic level by a common Han Chinese culture which spanned most of the Chinese ecumene.[3] While this picture is substantially correct in its particulars, it is incomplete and does not explain how the Chinese empire was repeatedly reconstituted in the last millennium of imperial history. By contrast, empires were more sporadic in South Asia, as shown by the Mauryan (322–184 BCE), Gupta (320–550 CE) and Mughals (1526–1857);[4] or in Europe, where, after the Romans, no one was able to build an empire of

1

comparable territorial or cultural span for the lifetime of even a single conqueror. Rather than attempt to explain why South Asians and Europeans were so inept at South Asian and European empire building respectively, I will attempt to explain instead why the Chinese, Mongols and Manchus were so skilled at Chinese empire building.

First and foremost, all of the successful imperial Chinese dynasts were extremely skilled in the use of war in state formation and maintenance. Chinese empires were not created by the cultivation of virtue, a fundamental cultural orientation to political order, or ideological pleas for ethnic unity; they were created by decades of war and political strife. Organized violence was applied toward political goals intelligently and ruthlessly, with the targets of that violence almost exclusively the power elite, the men and women who held significant political, military, cultural or economic power. (The actual effects of that violence, however, fell most often upon the farmers and ordinary people in the path of armies.) Although this has been most apparent during the rule of "alien" conquerors like the Mongols or Manchus, it has been equally true of the Han Chinese dynasts as well. All imperial dynasties were conquest dynasties.

What Chinese dynasties did better than any South Asian, Middle Eastern, or European would-be conquerors was to centralize the control of military means under a single ruler, without leaving local strongmen the possibility of raising their own legitimate military forces. There was nothing like the feudal European nobility, who, at least originally, owed their king military service with a certain force of men for a certain time, in return for their lands. The Tang dynasty (618–907) had come to grief by delegating too much military and civil authority to border commanders; the Southern Song (1127–1279) border fell to Mongol entreaties aimed at the Lü family; the third Ming emperor (though he counted himself the second) usurped his position from his base as military commander on the northern border. These failures, though, prove the general rule, which kept legitimate military force in the hands of the central government. In dynasty building, this was reflected in strategic practices that directed attacks not only against a rival strongman or ruler personally, or against his political apparatus, but also against his army. To some extent this was coincident, as attacks against the political apparatus tended to be defended by the army.

Imperial Chinese history has been consistently de-militarized by both Chinese and foreign historians, downplaying the inherently violent nature of dynasty founding.[5] By contrast, the martial inclinations of the non-Han conquerors of Chinese territory have been emphasized and juxtaposed with the civil-centered and civilized Han Chinese. Like so many generalizations, there is some truth to this, but it is a simplification that leads to some profound misconceptions about Chinese dynasties and Chinese culture.[6] There is also a political and cultural agenda behind the de-militarization of imperial China, and the emphasis on violent, predatory foreigners. For the imperial Chinese historian of an established dynasty, it was an important part of imperial ideology to hide the value or coercive effectiveness of war as a political, cultural or social

2

tool. In post-imperial China, it has been equally important to establish the historical reality that a weak or fragmented China is subject to exploitation and even conquest by foreigners.

Established governments sought to maintain their monopolies on violence not only by forcefully suppressing anyone else who tried to use it but also by advertising that it was not effective.[7] This was not hard to justify during times of peace, but it created a good deal of tension between rhetoric and practice in times of dynasty founding. A dynasty tended to reach the point at which it made sense to downplay the value of violence just as it was most intensely engaged in using violence to establish itself. Imperial ideology was inherently hypocritical, or at least tautological, insofar as it argued that the social and political order the dynasty was imposing or had imposed led to the dynasty's social and political order. Violence against that order would lead to chaos, and violence by the dynasty in supporting that order was in the pursuit of peace and stability. Moreover, continued resistance by the remnants of a previous dynasty was also transformed into chaotic violence. It was not violence that created order, but order that created order. This was a pleasant fiction, often reiterated even today, but it was simply untrue. Political order was created by war.

It has also served the ideological needs of post-imperial Chinese governments to maintain that there is a natural Chinese territorial, ethnic and cultural polity with a long, continuous history, that social and political chaos is the worst possible societal condition, and that when China is not unified it is subject to conquest by rapacious foreigners. This continuous outside threat requires that unity and strength be placed ahead of individual or group rights. After WWII, outside threats, perceived or real, were intermittent, so a historical perspective based upon imperial ideology was a convenient prop. This is offered not as critique of current affairs but to explain the historiographical problem of looking at the past, and the stakes even for current governments and events in their interpretation. The interpretation of the past is very much a present occupation of the Chinese government. War's central role in shaping and reshaping the definition of China and its political order has been downplayed because admitting this reality would offer the possibility of radically reinterpreting Chinese history. This is not an attractive prospect for most Chinese leaders or academics (including foreign academics), and most studies of imperial China's history continue to portray the Chinese as non-military.

But the very imperial nature of Chinese dynasties argues that traditional Chinese culture was partly a martial culture, and that at least some segment of Chinese society maintained or regularly recreated a warrior ideology.[8] It is true that various steppe peoples were, person for person, more warlike, that more of their cultures were occupied with martial practice, and that Chinese dynasties often employed those more warlike peoples to enhance their armies. But Chinese men constituted the majority of the soldiers in most Chinese armies, including those of dynasties ruled by steppe people. The astonishing developments of traditional Chinese civil culture counterbalance but do not eliminate

Chinese martial culture. Systematic efforts were made to efface those aspects, but the Chinese always had some form of a martial ethos. It is only by understanding this that we can understand why Chinese are so proud of their martial accomplishments, chief among them a series of vast empires, and are so anguished by their martial failings.

The power elite

One of China's most distinguishing factors over the last millennium has been the extent to which membership in the elite has changed, not just from dynasty to dynasty but even within dynasties. Economic power, and with it political, social and cultural power, was more stable at the local level, with stability decreasing rapidly as one climbed the regional and national ladder. The safest long-term strategy was not only to develop a strong local power base but also to stay as close to that base as possible. Involvement on the regional and national level could be fabulously rewarding, but it was also increasingly unsafe in the last millennium of imperial Chinese history. Moreover, while at the beginning of the Song dynasty (960–1279) taking and passing the civil service exams was virtually a requirement for achieving the status of *shi*, literati, or later gentry, the growth of education and virtually static number of government positions made actual participation in the exams increasingly less important over time.[9] The trappings of education by themselves gradually became enough for a local gentleman with sufficient means to become respectable. Powerful local families became progressively less dependent upon a government's sanction for their position, and looked, rather, to defending against official intrusion. The problem was how to keep the state out, rather than how to join it. For its part, the state used the threat of intrusion to extract peace and some tax revenues.

The importance of a Confucian-based education to the Chinese elite is one of the most distinct aspects of imperial Chinese culture. Until well into the Tang dynasty, birth was the primary factor in determining entry to important government posts. Exams were used to determine competency among the ruling elite. During the Tang, however, demonstrable education through the exams allowed some men of lower birth into the bureaucracy. This trend accelerated and was institutionalized during the early Song, making the exams the main route into the civil side of government.[10] Yet even as the chances of passing the civil service exams and achieving real government power declined, education remained a key component of literati identity. Although it is tempting to ascribe this to an ingrained set of cultural values that esteemed education above financial and military means – the explanation favored by the literati – a more prosaic account would emphasize the financial means demonstrated by having an education and the access to government power it allowed. Education was conspicuous consumption like any other luxury good, and this was obvious to the vast majority of the population who could not afford to obtain it. Furthermore, an educated man could communicate with an official directly.

The obvious real power inherent in an education was scarcely mentioned by literati in favor of its function in cultivating and selecting the best men for government. Nevertheless, it was clear to most literati that the exams did not select the brightest and most moral men to serve in government.[11]

The emphasis on the exams and meritocratic selection also downplayed the role of women. Women were barred from taking the exams, though not from education. Women could be extremely influential in the court, however, through their access to the emperor. Aristocratic women among the steppe peoples had a much greater range of influence since they were not as physically restricted in their movements. Government officials frequently railed against the influence of court women, as well as eunuchs, but emperors were not necessarily unwise to seek a broader and less conventional range of opinion on matters of politics or policy. The literati had very quickly developed a group identity, as powerful as the elite identity of birth, which often placed their interests in opposition to the emperor's. These educated men claimed the exclusive right to determine right and wrong, and to remonstrate with straying emperors. Very few emperors accepted the literati's inherent moral superiority, but it was ideologically and politically useful to allow the self-righteous to voice their criticisms. In any case, most criticism was directed at other officials, since it was always dangerous, and even possibly treasonous, to criticize the emperor himself. Allowing officials to attack each other weakened all of them and strengthened the emperor's position. Of course officials might criticize palace women, but unlike officials the women were almost never dismissed from their positions.

The constellation of power seekers at the imperial court all revolved around the emperor. Emperors became increasingly autocratic within the compass of the court and government at the same time that government power reached less and less far down into the rural society where most of the population lived. The system could work well under a strong emperor who imposed his will upon the competing interests surrounding him to carry out needed policies. Under a weak emperor the competing interests degenerated into political war, paralyzing major policy decisions and leaving the dynasty vulnerable to rebellions and foreign invasions. Problems at the court, however, had little effect on the power of local elites. Imperial rulership demanded maintenance of a politically fragmented society that was only integrated in the forum of the dynastic court. Dynasties did not try to integrate their empires, but rather to block any unifying medium except the adoption of imperial culture and ideology. Those who followed that route to power were already co-opted by the time they were connected to the realm beyond their locality.

Gunpowder, technology and society

Changes in technology, and the introduction of gunpowder weapons in particular, would seem to be an obvious force behind Chinese military developments and their societal ramifications in the period under consideration. Surprisingly to anyone familiar with Western history, these changes do not appear to have played quite so important a role.[12] On the one hand, this may simply be a difference in the trajectories of Chinese and European history. On the other, the cultural and historiographical traditions differed to such an extent that the emphasis placed on technology by historians of the West has not been shared until recently by historians of China. While technology, particularly military technology, was almost always of interest to Chinese governments, it never appeared to traditional historians to be a driving force in events. Indeed, it is hard to argue with their perspective, since before the nineteenth century even European technology had a limited impact on China's social, political and military institutions. This is not to say that firearms did not play a major role in Chinese warfare after the fourteenth century, but rather that they were incorporated into the army and navy without dramatically changing their fundamental structure or producing any noticeable effects outside the military sphere. From the twentieth-century perspective, imperial China somehow missed the significance of technological development. In imperial times, however, it simply wasn't revolutionary. Historians did not fail to see the dramatic effects of technology; rather, there were none.

Chinese society did change from the tenth century to the eighteenth, and not always in a consistent direction, but this was driven more by developments in education, to which the growth of printing contributed, and economics than by technological inventions which overturned the social order. In China, technology reinforced, rather than weakened, the existing society. Tenth-century Chinese society was primarily composed of farmers living in various states of dependency or under the protection of local strongmen, who in turn had widely disparate relationships to the higher political authorities. The reach of any formal government down to the village level was never really that deep, and even by the end of the eighteenth century a Chinese farmer was fortunate to have little more interaction with his government beyond paying taxes. Justice existed in theory, and even sometimes in practice, but the well connected and influential were much more likely to obtain it. Private ownership of land was widespread, and most farmers were free, though subject to coercion by local strongmen. These strongmen were not hereditary, or in any way officially recognized as rightful power-holders, but held *de facto* power.

In real terms, local society was controlled by lineages that perpetuated their own power over generations in cooperation with similar lineages. Competition was continual, however, since the government did not recognize their power, and the struggle for economic resources, and the status and control of coercive powers to maintain that position, made all of these lineages unstable over time. Local Chinese society was thus free and competitive, if not subject to rapid social change. Extensive changes in agricultural practice and increased commercialization did not fundamentally change the power structure at the village level, even if it did change the person doing the exploiting. Poor farmers and landless laborers were always subject to abuse from the wealthy, whether they

6

were landowners, the managers of absentee landlords or even monasteries and temples. The imperial government could not protect the populace from such depredations.

Urban China was already highly developed in the tenth century, and became even more so in the following centuries. Eleventh-century Kaifeng was one of the largest urban centers in the world, with an estimated population in 1021 of 500,000 people within the walls alone, accompanied by a vast industrial, productive and transport system. This does not take into account the substantial population immediately outside the walls or the large unregistered population; in any case 1021 was not the peak of Kaifeng's growth.[13] Smaller and medium-sized cities also became widespread, and China was an urban empire compared to the rest of the world. Kaifeng is sometimes held up as a missed opportunity for an early industrial revolution.[14] It was close to something like that before it was overrun in the early twelfth century and its concentration of industrial, human and cultural capital dispersed. Setting aside speculations about such possibilities, what is clear is that the vast industrial and economic power of Kaifeng did not translate into overwhelming, or even dominating, military power for the Song dynasty.

China at the end of the eighteenth century had not been socially transformed from its tenth-century roots so much as formalized and categorized. The divisions between professions and occupations were clearer, even if the characteristics of the members of the groups might differ considerably from their earlier incarnations. Farmers were not soldiers, local gentry maintained the trappings of education, if not participating in direct government service, and imperial officials were recruited from a civil-service exam system. But some of these changes had already begun during the Tang dynasty, albeit without fully shifting thinking about society to accommodate those shifts. The rise of religious professionals and soldiers as clearly separate groups was contrary to the previous normative view of society divided into knights (*shi*, the term that would later be applied to the literati or gentry), farmers, artisans and merchants.

Two almost contradictory changes with respect to Chinese society and the military began early in the Tang dynasty with the collapse of the *fubing* system. The *fubing* system had originally preserved the Chinese ideal of the farmer-soldier, but after the early Tang soldiers became increasingly a separate, professional class. By the tenth century, soldiers, to the intense consternation of statesmen, were wholly divorced from any productive activities and earned their livings by skill at arms. Despite many attempts to replace this "mercenary" system, it remained in place until the end of imperial times. At the same time, however, local Chinese society became increasingly militarized. War had become more professionalized, but the need to defend one's community from bandits and marauders forced ordinary people to become increasingly competent in martial arts. Indeed, the government frequently encouraged these activities, either in the hope of forming a pool of farmer-soldiers to replace or support the professional, standing army, or simply as a bulwark of local social order. Farmers were no longer soldiers, but neither were they divorced from the means of war.

The problem Chinese statesmen had with the standing army was how to keep it out of politics and isolate its functions to a static, reliable instrument of dynastic stability. How could an inherently destabilizing, chaotic force be first transformed and then firmly integrated into a peaceful society? The Song dynasty simply maintained a large standing army at great expense with many complaints, but without ever finding an alternative. The answer for the Yuan, Ming and Qing dynasties was to feudalize much of the army into a hereditary class with attached lands that would support them in peacetime. In the case of the Yuan and Qing, the ethnic separation of the soldiers in garrisons was perhaps more logical, but just like the Ming armies, over time effectiveness suffered and the institution failed to maintain a functional military. New troops were then raised in times of crisis, adding new financial burdens to the government. No Chinese dynasty was ever able consistently to maintain an effective military within the social and political constraints of the imperial system for very long. Given time, imperial governments were able to react and reinvigorate their militaries, as the centuries-long rules of these institutions demonstrates, but they were still pre-modern structures.

Empire building and empire destroying

Chinese campaigns of conquest were frequently appallingly destructive, and Chinese and steppe military practice seldom took care to insulate the general population from the rigors of war. The trick for a would-be emperor was to transcend his regional power base and directly engage the higher order political structures. Not surprisingly then, the founders of the Song, Liao, Jin, Yuan and Qing dynasties did not begin their careers as regional strongmen, and even the founder of the Ming dynasty, the only one who might be considered to have started as a regional power, was connected to a larger religious group. This contrasts with the Tang dynasty, whose founders were closely tied to Taiyuan and the Guanzhong regions. And indeed, this explains many of the problems that Five Dynasties strongmen had in trying to recreate the Tang empire. Times had changed from the seventh century, and local ties hindered rather than helped.

The Five Dynasties and Ten Kingdoms period illustrates quite clearly the persistence of higher order political structures in the face of overall imperial political collapse. The Song empire was not created from scratch, but the regional powers also did not give up without a fight, or at least the Song army occupying their territory. Despite traditional imperial rhetoric and modern nationalistic historiography, the Song and subsequent empires did not reflexively or "naturally" condense into a large, territorially contiguous, culturally monolithic state following a period of disunity.[15] There was no dynastic cycle. Most obviously, the idea of the dynastic cycle does not fit the pattern of a divided China that persisted from the fall of north China to the Jurchen in 1127 until the effective destruction of the Song dynasty by the Mongols in 1272. Indeed, when we look at how long most conquests and consolidations took, the periods of disunion seem to take up a good fifth to a quarter of the period under consideration, depending upon when one draws the line and decides that a new dynasty has won and an old one has disappeared.

Regional power and patterns of interaction persisted and developed in widely varying relationships to the central imperial government. It is much easier to follow the changing imperial culture, what we have mostly accepted as the continuous, real Chinese culture, than it is to track the changing regional and local cultures. Regional culture comes to the fore in the available scholarship when it is directly drawn into or drawn upon by the central court, or when, as in the Five Dynasties and Ten Kingdoms period, the simplifying focus of a single imperial narrative is absent. By contrast, we know almost nothing about local and regional culture that did not connect to the central court, though more work is being done on this for later periods, or on interregional interaction. These disparate pieces made up any empire, but did not necessarily fit together smoothly. They were politically contained within the imperial structure without being homogenized or tightly connected. Indeed, I would argue that not only were no efforts made to unify local culture outside of imperial practice but also that the interregional connections and the homogeneity that they bred were actively discouraged.[16] This is most obvious in the realm of religion, where cults that spread outside of their locality had to be either imperialized, and thus removed as a possible threat to court power, or suppressed. The central court was always leery of anything like a spontaneous, interregional, grass-roots culture.

Empire building therefore required the ruthless use of force, canny political maneuvering, ideological flexibility, charisma and luck, none of which was unique to Chinese dynasts. The difference in China was the non-local character of the successful dynasts, who could lay claim to the non-local structures of imperial Chinese culture. This was not true in Europe, for example, where all would-be conquerors were tightly bound to their local cultures and the Western imperial model was too spottily available to entice local elites to join. The Roman ideal remained just that; it was not generally compelling in practice. In China, despite widely disparate local dialects and cultures, the imperial ideal worked. By the tenth century hereditary feudal rulership had not existed in China for over a thousand years, and the only higher-order political structure intellectually available was the imperial one. Perhaps the mentality produced by Chinese imperial rhetoric intellectually supported, or even compelled, the agglomeration of vast territory under a single government. In any case, there was no real alternative ideological system available by the tenth century: the actual operation of government was flexible enough to function effectively, leaving the rigid imperial rhetoric in place. Chinese empires did not reproduce the same institutional structure century after century, they reproduced the same language and abstract ideology. Functionally, however, they were quite different.

China has always painted its position as one of almost constant external threat, where the success or failure of outsiders to invade the country is dependent upon internal Chinese conditions. When China is united and strong, the external threat is at bay; when it is divided and weak, outsiders invade and interfere. As the Liao experience shows, this is not true: when they tried to take advantage of Chinese disunity, they won only a fleeting victory and actually lost influence over China. When the Song was fighting for control of China, the Liao stayed out of the conflict and only really became involved when the Song attacked it. The idea that the external threat always lurks is sinocentric: everyone always wants something from China. China is therefore possessed of something inherently valuable that must be protected from outsiders trying to take it. When seen with a less chauvinistic eye, however, it is clear that the external threat was variable, and what outsiders did want when they were there was not always the same.

Why then did dynasties fall? Most obviously because of military failure, though this proximate reason is too obvious to be wholly satisfying. The usual reason was failed leadership and bad policy choices. If we reject any notion of inevitability, the Song held out against the Mongols for half a century and fell for very specific, temporally limited reasons. Incompetent officials and poor emperors regularly made bad policy decisions based more upon internal political needs than military needs. The exam system clearly did not consistently select capable officials. One could well argue that it was the system for selecting among exam graduates that broke down over the course of a dynasty. But ultimately it seems clear that while dynasties, that is to say particular imperial courts, fell, the components of their empires did not. A Chinese dynasty was a political and military structure that cloaked the inherent disunity of the empire it ruled.

Military history and nationalism

Dynasties by their very nature as conquerors promote the idea that their military successes vindicate their claims to legitimacy. This is similarly true of modern nationalist narratives of states and cultures. In the Chinese case, the modern narrative exists in great tension with military history. Chinese military failures in the nineteenth and twentieth centuries at the hands of the Europeans and the Japanese prompted nationalistically minded men to wonder how a once-powerful nation could have met such an ignominious end. Men like Lei Haizong sought answers not in the nineteenth century, or even the eighteenth, but in the fundamental roots of Chinese civilization two millennia before.[17] It did not, and for some it still does not, seem ridiculous to trace the military and political failures of a recent century to essential cultural characteristics immutably set down thousands of years before. Modern Chinese nationalists assumed that Chinese culture was monolithic and unchanging, that culture and territory were virtually synonymous, and that the series of empires led directly to a Chinese nation. The powerful empires should have translated into a powerful nation.

The powerful Qing empire of the late eighteenth century did not become as powerful a Chinese nation in the twentieth century, and indeed, current Chinese nationalist sentiments often seem tinged with the anxiety that China is still not as powerful as it should be. As much as China today falls short of its projected military power, its cultural power, sophistication and dynamism cannot compare to imperial times. Much of what the government lauds as accomplishments are modernizations or economic advances given in Western terms. It is as if there is no Chinese nation any longer, just a developing modern state which lays claim to a glorious imperial tradition to justify its current borders. Those were the borders of late eighteenth-century Qing China.

Unfortunately, there were no "scientific" borders for the Chinese empire. Some have tried to interpolate such a boundary between the steppe and sown areas of north China, seeing an environmental divide no less profound for its uncertain location. The location of the Great Wall of China has been used as a concrete marker of that boundary; the unconscious acknowledgement of an environmental divide that marks a shift between the Han Chinese way of life, and thus people, history and culture, and the steppe way of life. Contrary to this view, however, is the history of that separation between "China" and the steppe. The imagined Great Wall line was not a "natural" border, and thus a reasonable northern extent for a native Han Chinese dynasty, outside of the claims of imperial ideology or later nationalism. A Han Chinese dynasty that went north of that successfully for any length of time was militarily strong, though probably overextended, and one that failed to reach it was militarily weak. What I hope to make clear here is how the attempt to transform a military equilibrium point into a natural separation is also a political play, an attempt to either rationalize a military and political situation or to support the separation of peoples.

Hence the unimportance of this imagined line during the Jin, Yuan and Qing dynasties is imputed to them being steppe, or "conquest," dynasties, and the inescapable fact of it during the Song and Ming dynasties because they were Chinese. While it was true that it was more difficult for Chinese infantry armies to campaign north than for steppe cavalry armies to invade south, the environmental and scientific border should more reasonably be placed at the Huai River. In any case, most Chinese armies employed steppe cavalry or followed their practice, and all successful steppe invaders employed Chinese infantry in their invasions. The real question of control of North China was political and then military: who could get politically unified enough to mount a successful invasion. In the late eighteenth century the Qianlong emperor harnessed China's commercialized economy to support his armies in far-ranging campaigns into the steppe, reversing fundamentally the flow of military power.[18] But the imagined Great Wall line had long been insignificant by then, and his northern invasions ranged much farther afield. The Qianlong emperor's political goals in Central Eurasia were more extensive than those of the Song or Ming, but not the Yuan, and his firearm-equipped armies operating with the support of an astonishing logistics system effectively enforced his political claims.

The Chinese imperial system did not create the basis of a modern nation-state because it was not designed to do so. Its design was in many respects opposed to any idea of an integrated polity of citizens who shared a common sense of national identity. The "common" written tradition was used to create an imperial bureaucratic class, and others who aspired to it, but it did not reach far down into the population, it was always strongly directed by the government, and – from any government's point of view – it had the unfortunate feature of an independent existence. There was an imperial ideological and personnel selection system based upon the written tradition, there was the tradition itself and then there were the men and women who engaged that tradition. Most history has focused on the relatively tiny minority of men in whom all three things coincided, and who mostly transcended their local affiliations as a result of that. These men, it would seem, would be ripe to be a nation, but they were the tiniest of minorities who, when forced to choose between nation and locality, almost always put their local interests first.

Breaking the dynastic paradigm

The late historian Robert Hartwell was wont to say that: "Historical periodization is a function of the job market." Despite the widespread rejection of the dynastic cycle among historians of China, most historians, both within China and abroad, still define themselves in terms of the dynasty they study. There are practical reasons for doing so, mostly with respect to the organization of the extant documents, and the institutions and the language consistent with the individual dynasties themselves, but this leads to a constant effort to define one dynasty or another as more significant to Chinese history than the others. In a comprehensive and extremely erudite survey of the attempts to periodize pre-modern Chinese history (primarily concerned with the Tang dynasty (618–907) and after), the historian Richard von Glahn states that: "All historical writing begins – implicitly, at least – from periodization."[19] Von Glahn even does the reader the service of including new ideas of world history into the question of China's periodization, though the picture that ultimately emerges is far too unsettled to allow for generalizations about a consensus view. Too many scholars have too much invested in their particular methodologies, and sometimes dynasties, to disregard regularly the dynastic boundaries in which they were trained.

Von Glahn's co-editor in the volume *The Song–Yuan–Ming Transition*, Paul Jakov Smith, precedes von Glahn's survey with an equally learned discussion of the continuities and developments that took place from the Song dynasty to the

Ming dynasty, and concludes with some remarks on the shift into the Qing dynasty.[20] Since Smith's description of China's society and economy is generally consistent with the views I have expressed throughout this book, I will not recapitulate them here. Rather, I would simply note that von Glahn and Smith were still forced to refer to dynasties even as they were spanning them. Yet Smith raises some important questions about imperial power versus the local effects of that power. He points out an apparent contradiction between the opinions expressed in the private writings of some gentry to the effect that the state was unimportant in their lives, and John Dardess's argument that the state became increasingly active. Smith acknowledges that the truth lies somewhere in between.[21]

The truth of imperial versus local power is that it was not a yes or no question. Imperial governments could be very important or not depending upon how interested they were in having an effect and what it was they were trying to do. Many aspects of culture developed entirely independently of the political center, and were often confined to a particular locality or class. These variabilities also demonstrate the dangerous inaccuracies that arise in viewing China and Chinese culture through the modern or even Qing dynasty lens.

The examples of queues and bound feet both demonstrate the complexities and problems of explaining the relationship between imperial political power and local culture. Footbinding started in the Tang dynasty and became more popular over the course of the Song, until it was ubiquitous among the Han Chinese elite of the Qing. Manchus and other non-Han peoples did not practice it, nor did the majority of the population, most of whom were too poor for it to be practical. The non-practicing poor no doubt understood its significance as a status marker vital for those hoping to marry into the elite, but did that understanding mean they shared elite values? Wearing a queue and shaving the front half of a man's head was instituted by the Manchus as a mark of submission. They initially had to relent in their insistence on its adoption, but soon after consolidating their grip on their empire they enforced it. It quickly became accepted practice throughout China. Thus, one practice developed over time outside the political sphere among a particular class, and the other was imposed as the idiosyncratic practice of a particular dynasty, yet both marked the modern Chinese and foreign impressions of pre-modern China. Bereft of a history of events, and floated in an abstract structure of periodization, China has become a reservoir of exotic cultural practices and a foil for the modernization theories of different scholarly camps. But the dynasties are still invoked in order to avoid mention of the events that occurred during them.

This book is not divided by dynasty, but by military and political events. In addition to making it clear that Chinese empires were built slowly at immense cost in blood, these divisions should emphasize that there was an important sequence of events that affected different parts of Chinese society differently based on their outcomes. Those outcomes were not certain, and the decisions individuals made led some to great fortune and power, and others to ruin and death. Chapter 1 ends with the Chanyuan Covenant that ended the Song–Liao war and concluded the formation of the Song empire. Chapter 2 finishes with the Shaoxing Treaty that temporarily paused the war between the Song and Jin empires. Chapter 3 brings the story of the Song dynasty to an end with the capitulation of the Song court to the Mongol Yuan dynasty. Chapter 4 stops at the sacking of Yuan chancellor Toghto as he was about to suppress the rebellions that would eventually destroy the Yuan itself. Chapter 5 discusses the creation of the Ming dynasty from its sectarian religious roots to the end of its territorial expansion. Chapter 6 covers the decline of Ming power, interrupted by its resurgence during Wanli's reign. Chapter 7 presents the rise of the Manchus, their conquest of China and creation of the Qing dynasty, and their consolidation of power. Chapter 8 focuses on Qing campaigns in Central Eurasia, and the Qianlong emperor's Ten Complete Victories.

Notes

1 Translated in Jonathan D. Spence, *Emperor of China*, New York: Vintage Books, 1988, p. 22.
2 "China" is, of course, a Western term. The first use of the term in English is 1555, and there is no consensus on its origins – see *The Compact Edition of the Oxford English Dictionary*, Oxford: Oxford University Press, 1971, vol. 1, p. 398. The Chinese term "*Zhongguo*" translated as "China" is similarly vague in its geographic meaning. In its earliest forms it may have indicated the lands of certain people who would become the Chinese, or the polity that occupied those lands in and around the Yellow River or the Central Plains. Since most imperial dynasties controlled considerable territory beyond that original area, the scope of *Zhongguo* became flexible. It is only with the modern People's Republic of China that a stable border corresponds to something called "China," and even there the current government lays "historical" claims to territories it does not actually control.
3 For an example of this see A.C. Graham, *Disputers of the Tao*, La Salle, Ill.: Open Court, 1989, p. 6.
4 Mughal power declined markedly after the death of Aurangzeb in 1707, initiating the period known as the "successor states." After 1803 the rulers were entirely beholden to the East India Company.
5 To date, there are only four published monographs in English on the founding of any Chinese dynasties: Edward L. Dreyer, *Early Ming China*, Stanford: Stanford University, 1982; Frederic Wakeman, *The Great Enterprise*, Berkeley: University of California, 1985; Hans Bielenstien, *The Restoration of the Han Dynasty*, Stockholm, 1953; and Woodbridge Bingham, *The Founding of the T'ang Dynasty*, Baltimore: Waverly Press, 1941. Despite the now classic status of the former two works, and several as yet unpublished dissertations on the founding of other dynasties, the military origins of Chinese dynasties have been generally neglected. The record is only slightly better if we include works in Chinese and Japanese, and then only for certain dynasties.
6 Hans Van de Ven has provided an excellent overview of the problems and importance of the study of Chinese military history in his introduction to *Warfare in Chinese History*, Leiden: E. J. Brill, 2000, pp. 1–32. I have necessarily covered some of the same ground in the discussion that follows for the reader unfamiliar with Professor Van de Ven's essay. As his quotes from John K. Fairbank's introductory essay to Frank A. Kierman and John K. Fairbank, *Chinese Ways in Warfare* Cambridge, Mass.:

Harvard University Press, 1974, pp. 1–26, attest, these points still require repeating. Hopefully this will no longer be necessary in the near future.

7   Alastair Iain Johnston, *Cultural Realism: Strategic Culture and Grand Strategy in Chinese History*, Princeton: Princeton University Press, 1995, has argued that the *Seven Military Classics* support two contrasting positions on war: that it is a failure of proper governing, and thus avoidable, and that is an unavoidable, regular situation that must be dealt with as necessary. Of course, court officials often argued for different military policies as much from political concerns as more fundamental strategic/philosophic orientations.

8   In more recent Chinese history it has been noted that, "the toughness of the PLA soldier and the martial spirit of the PLA go beyond the ideological to the larger intangibles of leadership, the sociology of small unit cohesion, and harnessed patriotic emotion." Mark A. Ryan, David M. Finkelstein and Michael A. McDevitt, "Introduction: Patterns of PLA Warfighting," in Mark A. Ryan, David M. Finkelstein and Michael A. McDevitt (eds), *PLA Warfighting*, Armonk, N.Y.: M.E. Sharpe, 2003, p. 12.

9   Peter Bol has argued that exam taking in the Song, at least, was crucial to literati status, though it is difficult to prove that this was the case. Peter Bol, "The Sung Examination System and the *Shih*," *Asia Major*, Third Series, vol. 3, part 2, pp. 149–171.

10   See John Chaffee's classic study on the social history of the exams during the Song, *The Thorny Gates of Learning in Sung China*, Cambridge: Cambridge University Press, 1985.

11   This is one of the underlying premises of Wu Jingzi's (1701–1754) sardonic eighteenth-century novel *The Scholars* (*Rulin Waishi*).

12   The importance of changes in technology, particularly improvements in cannon, in European history have been thoroughly debated. Kenneth Chase has convincingly answered the question of why firearms developed so much faster outside of China, particularly in the West, in *Firearms: A Global History to 1700*, Cambridge: Cambridge University Press, 2003. Recent debates over the significance of gunpowder in transforming European armies have been more extensive, involving many of the titans of the history field. Geoffrey Parker first revived and revised Robert Parker's thesis of a "military revolution" in *The Military Revolution*, Cambridge: Cambridge University Press, 1988. This stimulated a debate that culminated in the publication of Clifford Rogers (ed.), *The Military Revolution Debate*, Boulder, Colo.: Westview Press, 1995. As I read the debate, and the general direction of the field, though I'm sure many might not agree with me, technology is now considered less important than cultural factors in determining the course of military development. See, for example, John Lynn's *Battle*, Boulder, Colo.: Westview Press, 2003.

13   Edward A. Kracke, "Sung K'ai-feng: Pragmatic Metropolis and Formalistic Capital," in John Winthrop Haeger (ed.), *Crisis and Prosperity in Sung China*, Tucson, Ariz.: University of Arizona Press, 1975, pp. 65–66.

14   Robert Hartwell, "A Revolution in the Chinese Iron and Coal Industries during the Northern Sung, 960–1126 AD," *Journal of Asian Studies*, 12 (1962), pp. 153–162.

15   Peter Lorge, "War and the Creation of the Northern Song Dynasty," Ph.D diss., University of Pennsylvania, 1996.

16   A separate line of cultural imperialism was the introduction of Chinese education into parts of the empire populated by non-Chinese peoples. It was believed that educating non-Chinese in Chinese culture was both a civilizing duty and a means to make Chinese rule more acceptable.

17   Hans Van de Ven, *Warfare in Chinese History*, pp. 5–6, particularly footnote 22.

18   Peter Perdue, "Three Qing Emperors and Their Mongol Rivals," in Nicola Di Cosmo (ed.), *Warfare in Inner Asian History*, Leiden: E. J. Brill, 2002, p. 390.

19 Richard von Glahn, "Imagining Pre-modern China," in Paul Jakov Smith and Richard von Glahn (eds), *The Song–Yuan–Ming Transition*, Cambridge, Mass.: Harvard University Press, 2003, p. 35.

20 Paul Jakov Smith, "Introduction: Problematizing the Song–Yuan–Ming Transition," in Paul Jakov Smith and Richard von Glahn (eds), *The Song–Yuan–Ming Transition*, Cambridge, Mass.: Harvard University Press, 2003, pp. 1–34.

21 Ibid., pp. 21–23.

CHAPTER ONE

Unity through war, 900–1005

Alas! The rise and fall of states in the Five Dynasties was all due to soldiers, but their army regulations could not even be called such by later generations.

Ouyang Xiu (1007–1072), poet, historian and statesman[1]

On 27 December 901, Zhu Wen (852?–912), a former rebel commander, took control of the Tang dynasty capital at Chang'an.[2] The emperor was not in the city at the time, but that simply delayed matters. Zhu killed the emperor in 904 and set up his own short-lived puppet. By 907 Zhu threw off all pretense, ended the Tang dynasty and established his own Liang dynasty (conventionally referred to as the Later Liang to distinguish it from an earlier dynasty of the same name, like all of the other northern dynasties in the early tenth century). The Tang dynasty had been moribund politically and militarily for many years, and Zhu's demonstration of naked power, while unpleasant to many Tang officials, cannot have been terribly surprising. Although emperor Daizong managed to rescue the dynasty from extinction during the Anlushan Rebellion (755–763), the slow reconstruction of imperial power was almost completely undone by the Huang Chao Rebellion (875–884).[3] The last Tang emperor's abdication was merely a very clear acknowledgement that the vast Tang empire no longer existed. Form had caught up to reality.

Zhu Wen's Later Liang dynasty (907–923) did not simply replace the Tang imperial family in ruling the empire. By 907, there was no longer a unified empire to rule. Southern and western China broke up into a variety of smaller countries whose rulers claimed an assortment of titles up to and including emperor. To the north of what had been the Tang border, the Kitan had assembled their own empire, which stretched over the vast steppes and encompassed an extremely diverse collection of other nomadic tribesmen; with the official end of the Tang dynasty, the Kitan ruler also declared himself emperor. What the Later Liang dynasty had real control of was a more limited, but still quite large, territory stretching from the eastern seaboard to just north of Sichuan, and from the Huai River to the old Tang northern border. Perhaps most importantly, Zhu Wen controlled the cradle of Chinese civilization, that part of the Yellow River valley on the Central Plains of China where the capitals of every major imperial Chinese dynasty had been for over a thousand years. This proved, however, of no political or cultural value.

In a decisive break with the first half of imperial Chinese history, neither Luoyang nor Chang'an ever became the capital of a major dynasty again. Coupled with the destruction of the great aristocratic clans who had dominated Tang court life, this was a seismic shift in the political and cultural underpinnings of imperial Chinese society, at least at the elite level. Indeed, the centers of culture had shifted to the Shu court in Chengdu, Sichuan and the Southern Tang court in Nanchang, along with some of the other southern courts. After the Song court created an empire spanning northern and southern China, it had to form its imperial library and art collection from these southern and western courts. The shift of economic and cultural power to the south had begun during the Tang and has continued to this day. Military power remained in the north, however, now divorced from its previous connection with Chinese civilization.

Since the next large empire, the Song (960–1279), began from what, after several succeeding regimes, had started as the territory of the Liang, the political regimes that ruled that country are generally referred to as "dynasties," (*dai*) in the Chinese histories, whereas the countries in the south and west which were eventually conquered during the Song formation are referred to as "kingdoms" (*guo*). The period from 907 to 960 is thus referred to as "the Five Dynasties and Ten Kingdoms," or just "the Five Dynasties." This neat formulation, which tidies up a messy period with misleading simplicity, was put forward in the eleventh century by the Song statesman and moralist Ouyang Xiu (1007–1072).[4] Ouyang was a great prose stylist, but his historical writings served his didactic, explicitly Confucian, ends. Moreover, he was a Song court official and therefore driven to construct a legitimate transmission of the Mandate of Heaven from the Tang dynasty to the Song dynasty.[5]

Imperial ideology imposed certain organizing conventions on Chinese historians. Chief among these was the idea that a single regime should rule the Chinese empire. Deviations from this "norm" were unnatural periods of "disunion" between natural periods of unified empire. In these terms, the Five Dynasties was the last period of disunion in the final millennia of imperial Chinese history. Despite the fact that the Chinese empire was ruled by a clear succession of dynasties over the millennium from 907 to 1911, it is important to keep in the forefront of one's mind that the idea that this is or was the natural form of Chinese government is just that – an idea. Chinese emperors and their officials were continually engaged in a process of affirming and reaffirming the normative idea of a unified Chinese empire. This imperial ideology was both a non-violent way to exert control over the empire and an excuse for the violent means necessary when moral suasion failed. Even in modern English usage historians usually continue this practice, perpetuating the notion that the Chinese imperial model is correct, and that the fragmented parts of the Tang empire were not legitimate countries but sub-imperial polities waiting to be reunited under a single government.

If we accept that the Chinese ecumene in the first half of the tenth century was populated by perhaps a dozen countries of different sizes, and that they were not just pieces of an imperial puzzle waiting to be reassembled, then it becomes much clearer that each one of these sovereign countries had to be conquered to build an empire like that of the Tang. The military initiative remained in the north for the most part, so our focus will remain there, but the southern countries were not inactive in military affairs.[6]

A late Tang rivalry[7]

Zhu Wen's seizure of Luoyang and overthrow of the Tang dynasty did not end a rivalry with the Shatuo Türk leader Li Keyong (856–908), based at Taiyuan in northern Shanxi province, which had begun many years before. Both men had been appointed to important positions in 883 by the Tang court while it was putting down the final vestiges of the Huang Chao Rebellion (875–884). After cooperating to defeat Huang Chao, they fell out and Zhu Wen made a failed attempt to assassinate Li and his bodyguard in 884. The Tang court failed to act in response to this incident, losing credibility with both men and destroying its own power by allowing its two most critical commanders to oppose each other. Zhu Wen was then forced to deal with another rebellion by himself, which took three years to subdue and made him indispensable to the Tang court. He was also forced to build up his military strength, and develop an administrative system centered at his base at Bianzhou (Kaifeng). Bianzhou would later become the capital of the Song dynasty.

Despite Zhu's successes in expanding his own power, he failed to destroy Li Keyong in Shanxi. Zhu failed to capture Taiyuan, the capital of Shanxi, in 901 and 902, even while controlling the southern part of the province. Taiyuan was a key strategic city that held out against repeated attacks launched from the Central Plains during the tenth century, finally falling only in 979. Li was further bolstered in 905 when he swore brotherhood with Abaoji, the Kitan leader. This was a new and threatening force that would play an increasingly active role in northern Chinese politics. Zhu Wen was therefore unable to create a stable military situation in which to start his own dynasty.

When Li Keyong pushed south in 907 Zhu was induced to end the Tang and set up his own dynasty. This was militarily and politically premature, but Zhu felt he had no choice. He had struggled to construct a reliable governing system, tinkering with the Tang system to a greater or lesser extent, without fully stabilizing the structure into a regular, orderly set of power relationships. It was not simply a question of disloyal or overly ambitious subordinates; the elite society that the Tang institutions had originally been based upon had been destroyed. The aristocracy of the early Tang, a dynasty particularly noted for its aristocratic character, was mostly destroyed during the Anlushan Rebellion

(755–763). Nevertheless, remnants of those powerful clans continued to cling to power locally and within the central government, looking down upon the newly emerging, primarily military-based elites (though there was also a developing group of men who obtained their positions within the government based upon their learning). Without the distinction of pedigree or entrenched economic power, the new elites were less stable and harder to define. Zhu and his subordinates were almost unremittingly hostile to the old Tang aristocracy, often going out of their way to exterminate aristocrats. Seen in that light, Zhu's founding of the Later Liang was a desperate attempt to create a political reality that would trickle down to the then amorphous and volatile elite. The resulting social and political stability would then relieve his internal military problems and enhance his ability to deal with external threats, like Li Keyong and his Kitan "brother." The gambit failed.

Li Keyong died in 908, leaving command of his considerable forces in the extremely capable hands of his son Cunxu (885–926). Although Cunxu's relationship with Abaoji was not as close as his father's had been, he still proved formidable enough in his own right. Zhu Wen himself was assassinated by one of his sons on 18 July 912,[8] who was in turn killed by a younger brother on 27 March 913.[9] The rivalry between the Li family and the Zhu family continued without break into a second generation, however, reflecting the hardened geopolitical realities which had formed, or perhaps were formed by, their family conflict. Yet Cunxu still fought, as had his father, under the banner of Tang loyalism.

By 923 Cunxu's relentless onslaught had overwhelmed the Liang armies, capturing city after city despite brave and spirited defenses. The Liang dynasty did not simply crumble at the first shock, it was progressively worn down by the superior generalship of Li Cunxu, and a converse lack of cohesion and command ability among the top Liang army leadership. As the military situation deteriorated, political cracks in the court widened, leading to recrimination and suspicion; the Liang emperor even ordered his older and younger brothers murdered to secure his throne from usurpation. By November Cunxu's armies, led by his father's adopted son Siyuan (867–933), were closing in on Kaifeng. Feeling that he could not personally surrender to Cunxu, and realizing his rule was at an end, the Liang emperor had a retainer kill him on 18 November 923. Li Siyuan entered Kaifeng the following day at dawn, and Li Cunxu followed later in the day.[10]

Considerable Liang forces remained in the field, but with the fall of the capital and the death of the emperor they began to surrender, in one instance an army some 50,000 strong. A few former Liang officials killed themselves with the fall of their dynasty and ruler, yet most did not. This pattern would repeat itself throughout the tenth century; war was a political tool, directed at the capital and ruler of a country not at the apparatus of government or its non-belligerent officials. A particular regime was embodied in its ruler, who could maintain his position as long as he could maintain his capital. Any loyal forces outside of the line of an invading army's march were irrelevant to the political contest.

Li Cunxu had declared the re-founding of the Tang dynasty on 13 May 923,[11] so his entrance into the Liang capital did not give him the opportunity to use a particularly significant place to create his new, or reestablished, dynasty. Cunxu did move his capital from Kaifeng to Luoyang, and adopted a more Tang-style system of government, even to the extent of employing some of the remaining aristocrats. For the same reasons that had stymied Zhu Wen, this also failed to create a stable governing system. Nevertheless, the Later Tang began as a powerful country, prompting some of the other countries in the south to officially submit to the Tang court. This was symbolic, since neither Cunxu nor his successors were really capable of projecting power very far south. The Later Tang court, for example, recognized the ruler of Chu as the prince of Chu in 927, though this did little more than establish diplomatic etiquette. The story was somewhat different in Sichuan, where Cunxu sent an army in 925 to overthrow the emperor of Shu. After the campaign was successfully concluded, the commanding general was left to run Sichuan. He later took advantage of the death of Cunxu's successor, Li Siyuan, in 934 to declare himself emperor of a new Shu dynasty.

Li Siyuan's son-in-law, Shi Jingtang (892–942), overthrew the Later Tang in 936 with the help of the Kitan. This marked the beginning of direct Kitan intervention in Central Plains politics. The Kitan had been regularly raiding into Hebei for over a decade, undermining government authority there and impoverishing the populace, but they were looking for a more formal cession of positive ownership of Hebei from the Tang court. A steppe cavalry army was almost incapable of simply marching in and holding territory after seizing it. This was the basic weakness of steppe warfare: raiding a sedentary society could deny it peace and pressure a court to make political and economic concessions, but a steppe army could not easily capture territory. Just before his own death, Abaoji tried and failed to extort the cession of Hebei from Li Siyuan's envoy. Despite his frequent raids, he still clearly needed Hebei given to him by treaty, since he could not take it by force.

Steppe involvement in the politics of the Chinese Central Plains was obviously not anomalous in the tenth century. Direct Kitan intervention to help one Shatuo Türk leader overthrow another Shatuo Türk leader, thus overturning one "Chinese" dynasty and replacing it with another, seems not to fit the ideal conventions of Chinese historiography, but it was accommodated without undue difficulty. Given that the glorious Tang dynasty itself had been founded by a part Türkic family that maintained strong ties to steppe culture, this is less surprising. As long as the machinery of the central government was run on a Chinese system, at least minimally in literary Chinese, then a historical rupture was avoidable, even if the rulers themselves primarily spoke another language. Chinese history proved more resilient in the tenth century than any individual dynasty, though a severe rupture was not impossible. Shatuo Türk rulers frequently proved insensitive to the orientations of either Chinese imperial or written culture.

Shi Jingtang immediately paid off his debt to the Kitan for helping him found his Later Jin dynasty (936–947) by ceding the territory around modern Beijing, which had been the Lulong and Fanyang defense commands, to the Kitan emperor. This piece of territory, which would later be called the Sixteen Prefectures, contained the strategic north–south passes controlling travel between the steppe and the open plains of Hebei. Once through these passes, a steppe army had an almost unobstructed route to the Yellow River. Shi Jingtang was quite clear that this cession of territory rendered his dynasty vulnerable to his Kitan patrons, but he had little choice in the matter. He could not have known how significant the Sixteen Prefectures would become militarily, politically, diplomatically and historiographically long after his own dynasty had fallen.

Shi's successor, Chonggui (914–947), appears to have been less clear on the significance of the Sixteen Prefectures than his uncle and expelled the Kitan from his court shortly after taking the throne. The Kitan response was swift and decisive: in 946 a massive army invaded through Shanxi, captured Kaifeng in 947, and overthrew the Later Jin. This marked the high point of Kitan power in the Central Plains; having taken Kaifeng, the Kitan emperor declared his own dynasty, changing his empire's name from Kitan to Liao. He may well have imagined that he could simply take over the Later Jin, and add it to his vast territory. This proved militarily impossible however. His army was badly over-extended, and not only had his army left a trail of destruction behind it, the population of Hebei was already hostile after years of Kitan raids.

When the Shatuo Türk leader in Taiyuan, Liu Zhiyuan (895–948), decided to oppose the Kitan, now Liao, emperor, thus cutting off his original line of retreat, the Liao emperor had no choice but to abandon Kaifeng, taking as much loot with him as possible. This was the last time that the Kitan ever tried to capture the Central Plains, extend their direct power into what was unequivocally Chinese territory, or even destroy a Central Plains country.[12] The simple military truth was that the Liao army was not capable of taking and holding Hebei, let alone the Central Plains. Northern China was highly militarized and increasingly fragmented, making it difficult simply to behead a dynasty and take over. It was also logistically impossible for a large Kitan army to remain in one place for very long. This was particularly true in northern China, which had been impoverished by decades of war. Han ethnic identity and resistance to foreign rule was unimportant, particularly since the Kitan had displaced the second Shatuo Türk dynasty to rule, and it was another Shatuo Türk leader whose resistance was critical in undermining the Kitan position at Kaifeng.

The Liao emperor died on his way back to Liao territory, leaving Kaifeng open to the opportunistic Liu Zhiyuan. Liu rushed in and established the fourth of the five dynasties, the Later Han (947–951). The Kitan were temporarily preoccupied with their own imperial succession, though they retained the Sixteen Prefectures. Kaifeng had just been looted, major pieces of territory, like

Sichuan, had broken free, and the control exercised by the court claiming authority over northern China was questionable, but Liu was now emperor. He had little time to enjoy the possibilities of this position, dying in 948.

Northern Chinese warlords' continued ambition to seize the central government, despite its tenuous control over its claimed territory in the early tenth century, clearly indicates that there was something valuable there. Having shifted the capital from the well-established Luoyang and Chang'an, Kaifeng presented very little in the way of a legitimizing location, though the Kitan ruler seems to have felt it important enough to have declared his own dynasty there. This was probably, however, an indication of his intentions to take control of the territory which was formally subordinate to it. Kaifeng may have generated sufficient wealth by itself to be a worthwhile prize. Its function as a transport center also made it a center of trade and industry.[13] But in the tenth century the city was not nearly the economic powerhouse it became in the eleventh, nor was it particularly strong militarily, beyond its logistical value. Perhaps Kaifeng had achieved some measure of political value by virtue of its intact imperial palaces and remaining bureaucratic machinery.

The first step to creating a larger empire similar to that of the Tang was to destroy the incumbent dynasty and take control of the center. Both of these acts, destroying the old regime and holding the tattered remnants of the central government, made a would-be empire builder the man of the moment. It was now up to him to try and establish control over the Central Plains by whatever political and military means necessary, and so create a true political center, or central court. This process repeatedly foundered on the strength of the Shatuo Türks at Taiyuan, and the Kitan in the steppe, and disunity within each dynasty. Liu Zhiyuan's Later Han dynasty was the penultimate burst of Shatuo Türk power on the Central Plains, and when it was displaced in 951 by Guo Wei (904–954), one of its own, non-Türk, generals, the power of the Türkic leader at Taiyuan was already waning.

Given that Guo Wei, the founder of the Later Zhou (951–960), was a Later Han general before he was an emperor, it is perhaps unfair to downplay the power of Taiyuan in Central Plains' affairs. In effect, a part of the Shatuo Türk army remained in control of Kaifeng, while displacing the Liu family and its Later Han dynasty. The remnants of the Later Han dynasty then formed the rump Northern Han regime back at Taiyuan. The split between Taiyuan and Kaifeng during the first half of the tenth century was virtually an internal Türkic conflict, with various Chinese players scattered throughout. Ethnicity was occasionally important, but not consistently, particularly since one was more likely to be at odds with a member of one's own ethnic group than with someone from a different one. It was sheer accident that an ethnically Chinese general emerged from a Türkic faction to seize power in Kaifeng, which led to the emergence of another ethnically Chinese general overthrowing the Later Zhou in 960. There was no assertion of Han ethnicity throwing off Türkic oppression, nor even the gradual formation of a solid, unified government through institutional reform. The struggle for the emperorship was conducted amongst a large, non-exclusive group who nonetheless had pre-existing relationships before entering into hostilities.

While northern Chinese warlords and steppe leaders contended for power over the Central Plains, the rulers of the countries in southern China followed an entirely separate course. Some, like the Southern Tang, maintained erratic relations with the Kitan and whichever regime happened to hold nominal power over the Central Plains. This was mostly for defensive purposes, though the Kitan proved unwilling to act in concert with any of the southern countries against the Later Zhou or Song dynasties during their southern campaigns of conquest. The internecine struggle in the north neither concerned the southerners nor presented them with opportunities to seize power there. There were effectively two separate spheres of political and military activity, with the southern one being considerably more stable, and peaceful. This political chasm had more to do with the nature of the southern versus northern military means than with cultural inclinations.

The southern Chinese countries were extremely weak in cavalry, strong in infantry and particularly strong in naval forces. Since no functioning waterway led directly north–south into the Central Plains, the Bian canal would be repaired to assist Chai Rong's (921–959) southern campaigns after 955; even so, the comparative advantage in naval forces did not allow the projection of power north. The north was also poorer than the south, presenting the same problem, if somewhat less severe, that vexed Chinese regimes trying to campaign into the steppe with an infantry army: the logistical tail was too great to allow either much mobility or staying power. More open terrain favored the cavalry against the infantry, and the south's relative peace left its armies less conditioned for war. In sum, military conditions argued against southern participation in the Central Plains. Conversely, when the Later Zhou attacked the Southern Tang, although its field forces repeatedly defeated the Southern Tang's armies, it was badly hampered by its lack of a navy.

Southern China was safe from the Central Plains regime as long as it was occupied in simply staying in power. That began to change in 950 when Guo Wei, occupied defending the Later Han's border, returned to Kaifeng with his army in response to reports that his wife and family had been killed, and that a faction hostile to him was gaining control over the young emperor. He met little resistance as he marched south, until he neared Kaifeng. One army melted away before him during the night, and the commanders of a second, arrayed facing his army on 1 January 951, either left or joined him after a brief skirmish leaving scarcely more than a hundred dead. Guo still maintained that he was not seeking the throne and that his only intention was to disperse the evil ministers around the emperor; nevertheless, the emperor himself was murdered the following day.

Guo's transition to emperor was still to come, however, and he briefly took control over the government while awaiting another member of the Liu family to come to Kaifeng and take the throne. But before that could happen, a report arrived that the Kitan had invaded, and Guo was sent north to defend the dynasty. While en route, his troops demanded that he take the throne himself. Guo returned to Kaifeng with his army again, forced the abdication of the Later Han house and announced the creation of the Later Zhou dynasty (11 February 951).[14] This wonderfully constructed piece of political theater was repeated a decade later, in startling similar terms (a reported Kitan incursion, troops demanding the commanding general take over), when his own dynasty was overthrown and the Song dynasty created. For the moment, however, a new, vigorous ruler was in power, who had taken the throne with relatively little bloodshed. Guo's main efforts over the next few years were in consolidating power, and it fell to his successor, Chai Rong, to take advantage of a fairly stable political situation to expand the Later Zhou's territory.

On his deathbed in 954, Guo Wei ordered his top generals to swear allegiance to Chai.[15] We should not disregard the emotional force of such an act for a tenth-century general too casually, since, while many such men did disregard such oaths or find ways around them when they felt it necessary, the act itself was meaningful. At a minimum, it provided Chai Rong with some time to get himself established before someone else's ambitions overcame their sense of loyalty to the dead emperor. Once again, however, the immediate threat to the ruler in Kaifeng came from Taiyuan. And this time the Türk regime, which was now called the Northern Han, was assisted by its newly close patron, the Kitan.

The Battle of Gaoping, 954[16]

The Battle of Gaoping in 954 was the most important political event of the tenth century. More than any other single event, the battle changed the course of Chinese history, and broke the cycle of chaos that had hitherto characterized tenth-century Chinese political life. Moreover, a handful of commanders' actions during the battle laid the social foundation of what would become the Song dynasty imperial clan. This social foundation would have profound political consequences for the second Song emperor, and through him for the formation of the Song bureaucracy, the civil service examination system, the literati, and the next millennium of imperial Chinese culture.[17]

The Northern Han ruler, Liu Chong, took the opportunity of Guo Wei's death, and the succession of his adopted son Chai Rong, to launch an invasion of Zhou territory. Liu's mixed army of infantry and cavalry, some 30,000 strong, backed by an additional force of 10,000 Kitan cavalry under the command of Yang Gun, marched southeast from Taiyuan. Chai Rong, after overcoming an initial no-confidence vote from his civil officials at court, and having determined that Liu was proceeding southeast and not southwest, rushed to meet the invasion with whatever forces he could gather. The two forces ran into each other near Gaoping and arrayed for battle.

Liu Chong had the initial advantage because his army was more concentrated, but this led him into a fatal error. Believing that the Zhou army he faced was considerably smaller than his own, Liu ordered Yang Gun and his Kitan cavalry not to come up to the battlefield. Liu clearly wanted to defeat the Zhou army without his patron's assistance, and thus be less beholden to the Kitan emperor if he should take the Chinese throne. With heights to his rear and a well-ordered army, Liu waited for Chai Rong to rush his cobbled-together force to the battlefield. By the time the battle began, however, the two sides may well have been equal, at about 30,000 men each.

The battle quickly went awry for Chai Rong, as his right wing collapsed: the cavalry fled the field entirely after the initial clash, and the infantry line behind them threw off their armor and surrendered to the Northern Han. There may even have been treachery involved in the right wing's collapse, though there is no proof of this, which would also help to explain Liu Chong's confidence in his ability to win the battle without Kitan assistance. Chai Rong, who had taken up a position close by the battle behind the center, saw his right wing collapse and personally rode into the breach. Backed by his bodyguard force of several thousand men, this temporarily shored up his line. At that point, a 4,000-man Zhou cavalry force partly commanded by Zhao Kuangyin swept around the now stabilized Zhou line and rolled up the Northern Han line. The Northern Han army collapsed and went reeling back to the north. A brief stand by Liu Chong was quickly overrun by the Zhou rearguard, which had come up too late to take part in the battle and was sent in pursuit of the Northern Han remnants. Yang Gun and his Kitan cavalry simply rode off in disgust.

Chai Rong emerged from the battle a legitimate emperor, one who had proved himself in war after overcoming his own court. Of even greater political significance, however, was his execution of 72 senior military officers from the units which had fled the battle, and the promotion of his own corps of loyal commanders into the imperial army's highest ranks. Chief among those men was Zhao Kuangyin, who would soon found his own dynasty with the help of those self-same loyal commanders after Chai's death. Chai now had more control over the imperial army than any emperor since perhaps 755 and, just as significantly, the army itself was an effective military, and thus political, tool. The professional soldiers of the Zhou imperial army were veterans of numerous battles and campaigns, who were used to living outside of the bounds of ordinary Chinese society. Chai's execution of senior officers, as well as some 2,000 rank and file troops who surrendered to the Northern Han, was an effort to improve military performance and obedience to his orders, not to change his army into a civilian-friendly force.

After a brief, unsuccessful attempt to capture the Northern Han capital at Taiyuan,[18] Chai turned to the serious business of recreating the Tang empire. He was most concerned with his northern border, and the threat that the Northern Han and Kitan posed, but the time was clearly not ripe for a campaign against such powerful, and closely allied, opponents. Only in hindsight is it apparent that the Türks were a spent force after Gaoping. That left two major targets for Chai, who was both bold and ambitious: Shu, in Sichuan, or the Southern Tang, across the Huai River. Chai feinted at Shu, capturing four of its northernmost prefectures, and then launched a major offensive across the Huai.[19] His military objectives can only have been limited, as the Southern Tang was too large, and its military too strong, to be carried in a single campaign, but he may have hoped that the political effects of his invasion would have extended well beyond his army's immediate reach. If so, he was much disappointed, as neither the Southern Tang, nor any other country, relinquished any part of its sovereignty without fear of military reprisal. The individual polities of the early tenth century had been born in war, and they were conditioned to respond only to force. However compelling the idea of a unified empire was in the abstract, it had no effect on the ground beyond shaping the language of diplomacy.

The Huainan campaign, December 955 to April 957[20]

The first step in the Zhou campaign was to establish a secure foothold across the Huai River by capturing the city of Shouzhou. The unexpectedly stubborn 15-month resistance by Liu Renshan completely warped the original campaign plan, however, and endangered all of the Zhou army's gains until it was finally captured. A second unexpected aspect of the campaign was the importance of the navy. The Zhou began its invasion without a fleet of any kind, but depended upon the security of the pontoon bridge across the Huai River for communications and supplies. After repeated attempts by the Southern Tang navy to sever that link, and the success of the Tang navy in re-supplying and maintaining contact with cities along the river, Chai Rong realized that he needed his own navy. It is clear that the Zhou court badly underestimated the difficulties of launching a major campaign against the Southern Tang, and, perhaps because almost all of the planners and generals had spent their careers fighting in northern China, failed to even consider the importance of a navy. The Huainan campaign was a very *ad hoc* affair, but also forced the Zhou military to become a force capable of conquering an empire in southern China.

Chai Rong's campaigns against Shu, Huainan, and the Sixteen Prefectures, were land-grabs, rather than political duels aimed at destroying or forcing the capitulation of other regimes. This was most obvious during the Huainan campaign, where the Zhou army was badly overstretched in its limited theater of operations; the much greater reach and force it would have needed to overwhelm the Southern Tang court at Nanchang was far beyond its capabilities in 955. Nonetheless, it was still capable of waging a far-ranging campaign for nearly a year and a half, capturing dozens of cities and forts, and dealing a resilient and tough adversary repeated defeats in the field.

The campaign did not start out well. Even as Chai was setting out to take the field personally, the Zhou vanguard was forced to retreat from its foothold across the Huai River because an approaching Southern Tang fleet headed for the pontoon bridge spanning the river. As long as the river level was low during the winter, the bridge could be defended from the banks. The vanguard commander correctly determined that it was vital to preserve the bridge itself, rather than his position deeper in Southern Tang territory, and so fell back to concentrate his forces on the river. Chai reversed this conservative strategy, sending an army to attack the Tang land force and another to attack the fleet at anchor. Both attacks were successful, in the former killing more than 10,000 enemy soldiers, and in the latter not only defeating the enemy force but also capturing 50 warships. The Zhou would continually exploit the need of fleets to anchor regularly along a bank to attack them with land forces.

Now dug in around Shouzhou, the Zhou army began to attack and destroy Tang forces wherever they concentrated. It quickly became apparent, however, that the Tang strategy was to retreat into their fortified positions and try to wait out the Zhou army, while also trying to cut the bridge across the Huai River. This was not the sort of strategy Chai had expected or prepared for, and he could not remain in the field for an extended period of time. Even so, he rejected the Southern Tang emperor's initial diplomatic feelers exactly because he referred to himself as the "Tang Emperor." He relented somewhat and entertained a second feeler, at which point he demanded that the Tang ruler simply capitulate to him. Chai's military and diplomatic boldness did begin to yield immediate results.

Chai received a third Tang envoy, and this time the Southern Tang emperor explicitly accepted Chai's claim to possessing the Mandate of Heaven, and offered to subordinate himself to Chai formally, in return for ending the campaign. A limited political concession without a territorial gain was insufficient for Chai, who still had great confidence that his army would soon win him something greater. The Tang court was clearly panicking, and soon made another offer, this one containing cession of the six prefectures of Huainan, a million units of gold and silk in annual indemnity, and the Tang ruler abolishing his own title as emperor. A more calculating man would have wisely accepted this offer, since it would have placed the Zhou in an excellent position for future campaigns without further military cost or risk; but Chai refused again.

After more than four months in the field, Chai's luck began to turn. Not only was Shouzhou still holding out, he suffered diplomatic and military setbacks as well. The Southern Tang envoy Chai had convinced of the overwhelming superiority of the Zhou army was impeached and beheaded at the Tang court for selling out the country. This undermined Chai's program of bluff and intimidation. More seriously, a Tang relief army had approached the edge of the Zhou army's captured territory, threatening its position without advancing and giving the Zhou a chance to defeat it in the field. Chai was just then planning to return to Kaifeng, having been away from his capital too long. He dispatched a force to clear the Tang relief army, declared Shouzhou virtually fallen, and returned to Kaifeng.

The Zhou emperor's skilled generals saved him from his diplomatic blunders, but even so they could not prevent the campaign becoming a war of attrition. Despite almost unrelenting defeat, the Southern Tang continued to throw tens of thousands of troops into the fray and build up positions near Shouzhou. Losses in the Zhou army from disease and battle mounted, and the Southern Tang court had broken diplomatic contact. A Tang request for Kitan aid was turned down, however – a decision the Kitan court must have regretted when the Zhou attacked them in 959.

After eleven months, Shouzhou's food supply was almost exhausted, but the Tang positions nearby were beginning to threaten the siege. Two months later, Chai returned to the field, this time with a new navy and some rested and refitted troops. He overran the Tang positions near Shouzhou, and then swept the Tang troops from the river for 70 miles, inflicting over 50,000 casualties on the Tang army. In a series of smaller battles, the Zhou army destroyed any possibility of relief for Shouzhou. It finally surrendered some 15 months after first being besieged. Chai returned to Kaifeng again, this time on a more triumphant note, but also needing to rest and refit his army to continue the campaign.

The final push came six months later, with a much greater emphasis on naval warfare. And this time Chai quickly accepted the Southern Tang's concessions of territory, title and annual indemnity. He had gained a lot from the campaign, but the cost had been high and the outcome uncertain. The Zhou army was forced to attack cities and forts to pry loose the Tang hold on its territory and to inflict tens of thousands of casualties on the Tang army to convince the Tang court to give in politically. At no point did anyone, even after accepting that Chai Rong held the Mandate of Heaven, simply capitulate to the man bent on recreating the Tang empire. No one saw vision of empire as either inevitable, or obviously configured as a centralized bureaucracy.

The Sixteen Prefectures campaign[21]

Chai Rong's last campaign was an attempt to capture the Sixteen Prefectures from the Kitan in 959. Interestingly, he prepared for the campaign by repairing and opening up the waterways heading northeast from Kaifeng. The Zhou army was transported at least part of the way to the front by boat. In short order, the army bloodlessly captured the Kitan positions in the southern part of the Sixteen Prefectures called the Guannan region. When Chai raised the idea of proceeding on to try to take the whole area, his generals unanimously opposed it. Overriding their concerns, he determined to press on, even as he himself fell ill. It was too late for Chai, however, and the campaign aborted as his condition worsened. He died leaving an infant son to succeed him, a vastly expanded territory, and a coterie of accomplished and ambitious generals in charge of a powerful army.

The Song conquest

Although the Song dynasty was officially brought into being in February of 960, it would take some 45 years to reach territorial stability and peaceful relations with its close neighbors. The conquest can be divided into two parts: the first, until 979, was a two-decade-long expansion; the second, ending in 1005, was a struggle to resolve the Song–Kitan border and relations between the two empires. Even in modern Chinese, however, the Song conquest is described as the recovery of territory, despite the fact that the Song dynasty as a political entity never controlled the lands in question until after it defeated the governments which did rule them. The campaigns of conquest were tremendously bloody and destructive affairs, inflicting hundreds of thousands of casualties within the respective armies and an unknown number among the civilian populations caught up in the conflict. Historians since the Song have searched, successfully to their minds, for more institutional reasons for why the Song did not become the sixth dynasty in the succession of northern dynasties. Whatever the value of institution-building, political processes and an emphasis on civil accomplishment, these all followed military conquest. The Song, that most civil and cultured of the great dynasties in Chinese history, was just as much founded upon war as any other dynasty.

Expansion, 960–979

After Zhao Kuangyin overthrew the Zhou dynasty and established his own Song dynasty, he focused on two interrelated problems: how to expand his empire and power, and how to secure his position. Zhao, posthumously known as Song Taizu, could not expand without consolidating, and could not consolidate without expanding. But before he could even do that, he had to overcome several internal political problems that, because they concerned generals, were also military problems. The first was the loyalty of the regional military governors. Two of these rebelled in succession in 960, and both were quickly crushed by the Song army.[22] The other military governors took note of this and decided to cooperate with the new dynasty. The second political problem was how to reward his co-conspirators in overthrowing the Zhou. This was done in a mutually beneficial exchange of imperial intermarriage and comfortable retirement for stepping down from the top of the military hierarchy and ceding power to Taizu. This deal, known as "Dissolving military power over a cup of wine," was only possible because of the personal relationships between Taizu and the other former close servants of Chai Rong.[23] By the middle of 961, Taizu had firmly established himself in power; even the Southern Tang ruler had congratulated him on defeating the rebellion of Li Yun.

Taizu was an opportunist rather than a brilliant grand strategist, but he also seems to have learned from Chai Rong's mistakes. The Northern Han–Kitan problem continued to concern him since, unlike the southern states, they could actually threaten the Song dynasty's existence; but the easiest military targets were to his south. His policy, which in retrospect appeared to be a strategic south-first plan, was to secure the northern border and snatch southern states before any of his other opponents could take advantage of his diversion of force.[24] In this, he was helped immensely by the Liao court's lack of interest in fighting the Song. Although the Liao would soon be forced into a 25-year conflict with the Song, over the longer course of their relations with the Song it was clearly their policy to maintain peaceful relations, a point which usually escaped the Song court.

The first to fall were the tiny neighboring states of Chu and Jingnan in 963.[25] Chu requested Song aid against a rebellious general, whereupon the Song army "borrowed passage," a classic spring and autumn period ruse, through Jingnan, capturing it in a *coup de main*. Chu offered slightly more resistance before it too fell. The following year Taizu launched a series of mostly ineffective and uncoordinated attacks against the Northern Han that revealed an unexpected rift between the Liao court and its Northern Han client. A more coordinated Song invasion forced the Northern Han ruler to patch up his relations with the Liao, bringing desperately needed military assistance. The contest coalesced around the city of Liaozhou, which the Song initially captured with a force of 10,000 infantry and cavalry, and even beat off a Northern Han relief army before being forced to withdraw in the face of a 60,000-strong Northern Han–Liao army. The Song army quickly returned with an army of equal size, and severely defeated the Northern Han–Liao force before Liaozhou on 16 March. This important tactical victory stabilized the northern border overall, though the Liao court's renewed firm support of the Northern Han returned the strategic balance to a stalemate.[26]

In December of 964, Taizu launched the most strategically brilliant campaign of his career, unexpectedly sending two columns of 30,000 men each into Sichuan to conquer the state of Shu. Conducted in the dead of winter, with the northern column traversing steep mountains and the eastern column forcing its way up the Yangzi River, the Shu ruler capitulated a mere two months after the Song commanders left Kaifeng. It was a virtuoso display of military power, deftly executed and surgically aimed at the Shu court.[27] All of the campaign's brilliance was soon overshadowed by a mutiny in the Song army caused by the imposition of new discipline, and a rebellion incited by the depredations of the Song army (hence the new discipline) and fueled by demobilized Shu soldiers. Although the mutiny was soon suppressed, the rebellion took until 967 to be fully resolved. Only after Sichuan was settled did Taizu return to campaigning, this time personally taking the field against the Northern Han in 968. The Song emperor was frustrated a second time, despite flooding the Northern Han capital at Taiyuan and repeatedly defeating Liao relief armies, and had to withdraw his enervated army in July of 969.[28]

Taizu waited until the fall of 970 to launch another campaign, this time against the Southern Han. The Southern Han court was badly factionalized and its army poorly prepared, but it still took six months of fighting, virtually all of it one-sided, to subjugate the state. The Song army, again critically supported by its river fleet, inflicted repeated, bloody defeats on the Southern Han army without causing it to collapse. Only the defeat of the Southern Han army before its capital induced the Southern Han ruler to surrender.[29] The fall of the Southern Han simplified Taizu's strategic options, leaving him a choice between the Southern Tang, and the Northern Han and Liao. From 971 to 974, however, he was absorbed in governing his now much-expanded empire and consolidating his control over the new territory and his own court.

The Southern Tang court resolutely refused to accept the "inevitable" Song reconstruction of the Tang empire, despite increasing diplomatic pressure to do so. Whatever the conventions of Chinese historiography, or even our own perspective over the long span of imperial Chinese history, it is vital that we understand that none of the tenth-century polities believed that a unified Chinese ecumene was so natural or inevitable that they willingly gave up a shred of their sovereignty without a fight. This was why Taizu relied upon his army to create the Song empire, since he could not induce anyone to surrender by mere moral suasion. In the face of Southern Tang intransigence, Taizu put out peace feelers to the Liao in 974. After an exchange of envoys, a stable enough political arrangement was worked out to satisfy Taizu that his northern border was now reasonably secure. He was now free to attack the Southern Tang, which he did in October 974. This was Taizu's greatest campaign, and it took until January of 976 to induce the Southern Tang ruler to capitulate. Just as before, the navy played a critical role, and it took the Song army surrounding the capital, having defeated every field force, to convince the Southern Tang that he had no choice in the matter.[30]

Taizu's final campaign was another invasion of the Northern Han.[31] Apparently his deal with the Liao had left the status of the Northern Han open to a military decision. The campaign began in September of 976, but Taizu died on 14 November, very possibly poisoned by Kuangyi, his younger brother, post-humously known as emperor Song Taizong. The army was soon recalled. Taizong took the throne under a cloud, not only suspected of having his brother killed but also that he had usurped the throne from his nephew. His first solution was to prove his legitimacy, or at least fitness to rule, by attacking the Northern Han in 979. He succeeded where his older brother and Chai Rong had failed, but then decided to continue on to attack the Liao position in the Sixteen Prefectures.[32] This not only violated whatever earlier agreements had been made with the Liao but it proved to be a military disaster. The over-extended Song army was badly beaten at the battle of Gaoliang River, and Taizong himself was wounded and had to flee the battle in a donkey cart. While the Song army fell back, Taizong only narrowly avoided a coup, which would have placed his nephew, Taizu's son, on the throne.[33]

The Song–Liao War

Taizong's response to his failure, humiliation and near deposition was to murder his nephews and younger brother on the one hand, and to dramatically increase his reliance on bureaucrats recruited through the civil service exams on the other. The latter policy had profound effects on the nature of subsequent Chinese society, most particularly the way in which local elites interacted with the central government. It was during Song Taizong's reign that the characteristic pattern of an exam system as virtually the sole means of entry into the government's civil service, without regard for family background (with the exception of a few prohibited occupations), became the norm. This structured much of the intellectual life of national elites, local elites and local elites wishing to become national elites for the next thousand years. Although the exam system had been around in one form or another since at least the Han dynasty, and had received a greater significance socially and politically during the Tang, it was during the early Song dynasty that it contributed to the creation of a new class of professional bureaucrats and those trying to enter that class.[34] Studying for the exams was a defining activity for those claiming literati or gentry status (which had various legal, social and political uses), and soon created a basic tension between exam success and true learning, or, in other words, between competence in imperial ideology and real education.[35]

Although exam takers and graduates stressed the government's desire to recruit the most talented and moral men for service, the exam system also functioned to place all elites in competition with each other for the favor of the emperor. This latter aspect was particularly important for Taizong, since he was politically weak throughout his entire reign. His family was completely intertwined through marriage with his older brother's generals and former comrades, men who apparently neither liked nor trusted Taizong; the bureaucrats were a mixture of former Five Dynasties officials and his brother's men; the army was also controlled by his brother's men, and his own power base was limited to the capital city. Taizong came to the throne with a large group of retainers he had recruited while governor of the capital, and the clearest sign that his efforts to broaden his political base over the three decades of his rule failed, was that he was still ruling through those retainers at the end. The civil service exam provided Taizong with the opportunity to not only recruit badly needed competent administrators into the government but also to bring in men who would be loyal to him personally. To that end, Taizong personally met with every exam graduate. What he did not expect was that the man who had passed a difficult, objective series of exams would not feel that he had received his degree purely due to the emperor's grace. While these men were loyal to the emperor, whomever that might be, they also felt empowered to disagree with him when they judged him morally, politically or functionally wrong.

If Taizong's efforts to infuse the government with a large cohort of men loyal to him personally failed, he fared no better in his military efforts. Not only did his unprovoked attack on the Liao begin 25 years of hostility and chronic warfare, a second campaign to capture the Sixteen Prefectures in 986 also failed miserably, further diminishing his legitimacy.[36] Taizong was able to maintain stability after his second major failure because he had made sure to kill his nephews and younger brother before beginning the campaign. To make matters worse, the Tanguts became restive on the northwestern border, raising the possibility of a Tangut–Liao alliance. These problems on the northern border then prevented the Song army from immediately responding in force to a rebellion in Sichuan that broke out in 993. The rebellion continued to smolder even after the initial uprising was put down with immense brutality by one of Taizong's retainers. It would ultimately take until 995 before peace was reestablished. Coupled with the deteriorating military situation on the northern border, the rebellion further undermined Taizong's rule and convinced him to emphasize strongly the civil side of his reign.

Taizong's son, posthumously known as Song Zhenzong, took the throne in 997 without any cloud over his succession, but with serious military problems caused by his father's inept policies. While Taizong cannot be blamed for the rise of the Tangut leader Li Jiqian and his grand ambitions, his blunders with respect to the Liao hobbled the Song army's ability to deal effectively either with the Tanguts or with the rebellion in Sichuan. In effect, Taizong's failed campaigns to capture the Sixteen Prefectures exacerbated every other problem he had, and induced him to take some of the political and cultural choices that would so affect later Chinese history. Whatever force of will Zhenzong might have been born with had been intentionally wrung out of him by his father, who always feared that his heir-apparent might undermine his rule. The third Song emperor was indecisive, and occasionally belligerent, but also quite interested in ending the confrontation with the Liao. Incapable of making a positive decision, Zhenzong hoped to mitigate the effects of Liao raids so his policy became one of strong, passive defense without any diplomatic effort to establish peace.[37]

Zhenzong's passive defense was, through no fault of his own, the most problematic policy he could have taken from the Liao court's point of view. The Liao court's goal was to establish a peaceful border with the Song and to reestablish trade. Its only tool for bringing pressure to bear on the Song court to reach a political settlement, since a purely military one was clearly impossible, was through raids and invasions. Following Taizong's failed 986 campaign, however, Song defenses began to harden considerably by the creation of a network of canals, paddy fields and dikes running east–west across Hebei, just south of the Song–Liao border. Work on this hydraulic defense system accelerated under Zhenzong, dramatically blunting the force of Liao incursions into Song territory.[38] Beginning in 999, the Liao launched increasingly desperate campaigns into Song territory, often defeating the Song army in the field, but being forced to withdraw after failing to capture fortified cities. There were clashes every year until 1004, with major Liao invasions led by the Liao emperor in 1001 and

1004. As the hydraulic defense line neared completion, the Liao court saw the window on negotiating from a position of strength closing, and the possibility of the Song retaking the initiative. It was now desperate for a settlement.

The Chanyuan Covenant, 1005

The Chanyuan Covenant (Treaty of Shanyuan) in 1005 was the most important political event of the eleventh century.[39] Like the Battle of Gaoping, the Chanyuan Covenant was an event of far-reaching importance, well beyond the ability of the participants who negotiated and concluded it to understand. Few peace treaties in world history have ever been so successful, creating 120 years of peace, yet so disliked by at least one of the signatories, the Song. Eleventh-century China was one of the high points of Chinese and world culture in almost every human endeavor, whether artistic, intellectual, or technological, and this grand century of achievement was founded on the long peace that the Chanyuan Covenant created. On a more prosaic level, the covenant marked the end of Song empire building, at least in the expansionistic external sense, and the beginning of the military's retreat from political prominence. The end of fighting and large-scale military mobilization, coupled with the increasingly important civil bureaucracy, led to an unprecedented takeover of the government apparatus by civil service exam graduates, and a concomitant rise in the value of education for the ambitious.

Notes

1 Ouyang Xiu, *Xin Wudaishi*, Beijing: Zhonghua Shuju, 1974, 27.297.
2 I have been greatly aided in my discussion of the Five Dynasties by Naomi Standen's unabridged draft chapter for the Cambridge History of China, which will be included in an abridged form in the forthcoming volume on the Song dynasty. Due to my commitment to Professor Standen not to quote directly from her draft, I am unable to demonstrate fully throughout the text just how deeply indebted I am to her work. I am very grateful to Professor Standen for making her draft available to me.

   Richard Davis also made available a draft of his translation of Ouyang Xiu's *Xin Wudaishi* to me on disk about two years before its publication. Lack of time and computer problems prevented me from justifying his kindness, and I was unable to take full advantage of his astonishing work. The translation has now been published: Ouyang Xiu, *Historical Records of the Five Dynasties*, Richard Davis (trans.), New York: Columbia University Press, 2004.
3 David Graff, *Medieval Chinese Warfare*, London: Routledge, 2002, pp. 217–223 (Anlushan), and p. 238 (Huang Chao).
4 Johannes, Kurz, "The Five Dynasties and Ten States in Song Times," *Journal of Sung–Yuan Studies*, 33 (2003), pp. 190–191.
5 Richard Davis, *Historical Records*, introduction xliii–lxxvii, provides an excellent overview of Ouyang Xiu's view of the Five Dynasties period, and the conventions of history writing that he engaged while writing it. In sharp contrast to Davis, however, I do not think much of Ouyang Xiu as a historian. Indeed, I would go so far as to say that Ouyang Xiu's *Historical Records of the Five Dynasties* is frequently

worse than useless in its coverage of many events. Ouyang's prose is far superior to the *Jiu Wudaishi* or even Sima Guang's *Zizhi Tongjian*, but his strongly didactic bent and poor historical sense regularly led him astray. The work is extremely valuable as an example of the views on the history of the period immediately preceding the Song by one of the eleventh century's towering figures. It is highly unreliable as a history of the time.

6 For example, the Southern Tang campaigns began abortively in 940, and then with greater vigor under a new emperor in 945, described in Johannes Kurz, "The Yangzi between the Southern Tang and Its Neighbors," Wiesbaden: Harrasowitz Verlag, 1997, pp. 30–35.

7 This section follows Wang Gungwu, *The Structure of Power in North China During the Five Dynasties*, Stanford: Stanford University Press, 1967 (first published by the University of Malaysia Press, 1963).

8 Sima Guang, *Zizhi Tongjian*, Beijing: Zhonghua Shuju, 1992, 268.8759.

9 Ibid., 268.8767.

10 Ibid., 272.8898–99.

11 Ibid., 272.8881–82.

12 Traditional Chinese historiography assumed that the Kitan always wanted to conquer China, even after their retreat in 947. It is only recently that this assumption has been called into question. Christian Lamouroux, "Geography and Politics: The Song–Liao Border Dispute of 1074/75," in Sabine Dabringhaus and Roderich Ptak (eds), *China and Her Neighbours*, Wiesbaden: Harrassowitz Verlag, 1997; Peter Lorge, "War and the Creation of the Northern Song," Ph.D. dissertation, University of Pennsylvania, 1996, pp. 260–262.

13 Robert Hartwell, "A Revolution in the Chinese Iron and Coal Industries during the Northern Sung, 960–1126 AD," *Journal of Asian Studies*, 12 (1962), pp. 153–162.

14 Sima Guang, *Zizhi Tongjian*, 289.9447–290.9450.

15 Ibid., 291.9501.

16 The Battle of Gaoping, 24 April 954, is discussed in ibid., 291.9504–06; *Jiu Wudaishi* 114/3a; and Ouyang Xiu, *Xin Wudaishi*, 12.28. See also Peter Lorge, "War and the Creation of the Northern Song," pp. 80–89.

17 Peter Lorge, "The Entrance and Exit of the Song Founders," *Journal of Sung–Yuan Studies*, 30 (1999), pp. 43–62.

18 For the follow up campaign against the Northern Han (3 May–30 July 954), see Sima Guang, *Zizhi Tongjian* 291.9513–292.9516; Peter Lorge, "War and the Creation of the Northern Song," pp. 89–92.

19 For the campaign to capture the four northern prefectures of Shu (24 May–30 December 955), see Sima Guang, *Zizhi Tongjian*, 292.9524–33; Peter Lorge, "War and the Creation of the Northern Song," pp. 96–101.

20 For the Huainan campaign (17 December 955–8 April 957), see Sima Guang, *Zizhi Tongjian*, 292.9532–294.9581; *Jiu Wudaishi*, 115/5b–116/5b; Ouyang Xiu, 12.120; Peter Lorge, "War and the Creation of Northern Song," pp. 101–131.

21 For the Sixteen Prefectures campaign (29 April–27 July 959), see Sima Guang, *Zizhi Tongjian*, 294.9594–9602; *Jiu Wudaishi*, 120/4b; Ouyang Xiu, *Xin Wudaishi*, 20.124; Peter Lorge, "War and the Creation of the Northern Song," pp. 132–135.

22 For the Rebellion of Li Yun (10 May–15 July 960), see Li Tao, *Xu Zizhi Tongjian Changbian*, Beijing, Zhonghua Shuju, 1979, 1/12b–15a, Toghto (ed.) *Songshi*; Beijing: Zhonghua Shuja, 1995, 1.6; Peter Lorge, "War and the Creation of the Northern Song," pp. 137–142. For the Rebellion of Li Zhongjin (15 October–2 December 960), see Li Tao, *Xu Zizhi Tongjian Changbian*, 1/20a–24a; Toghto, *Songshi* 1.7; Peter Lorge, "War and the Creation of the Northern Song," pp. 142–145.

23 Sima Guang, *Sushui Jiwen*, in *Zhongguo Yeshi Jicheng*, Chengdu: Ba-Shu shushe, 1993, 8:526, and repeated in Li Tao, *Xu Zizhi Tongjian Changbian*, 2.49–50. Nie Chongqi

first drew attention to this importance of this anecdote in 1948 in "Lun Song Taizu shou bingquan," *Yanjing xuebao*, 34 (June 1948), reprinted in *Songshi Congkao*, Taibei: Huashi chubanshe, 1986, pp. 263–282, esp. 263–271.

24 On the south-first strategy, see Leung Wai Kei, "Xian nanzheng, hou beifa: Song-chu tongyi quanguo de wei yi zhanlue (960–976)?," *Zhongguo Wenhua Yanjiusuo Xuebao*, 8 (1999), pp. 73–100. Mr Leung's discussion convincingly supersedes all previous studies.

25 Li Tao, *Xu Zizhi Tongjian Changbian*, 3/10b–4/6a, Toghto, *Songshi*, 1.13; Peter Lorge, "War and the Creation of the Northern Song," pp. 151–156.

26 Li Tao, *Xu Zizhi Tongjian Changbian*, 4/14b–5/4b, Toghto, *Songshi*, 1.14–17; Peter Lorge, "War and the Creation of the Northern Song," pp. 156–158.

27 For the conquest of Shu (8 December 964–11 February 965), see Li Tao, *Xu Zizhi Tongjian Changbian*, 5/16a–6/2a, Toghto, *Songshi*, 1.18–2.21; Peter Lorge, "War and the Creation of the Northern Song," pp. 159–167.

28 For Song Taizu's first campaign against the Northern Han (10 September 968–3 July 969), see Li Tao, 9/6a–10/11b, Toghto, *Songshi*, 2.27–29; Peter Lorge, "War and the Creation of the Northern Song," pp. 167–177.

29 For the conquest of the Southern Han, see Li Tao, *Xu Zizhi Tongjian Changbian*, 11/8a – (*Yongle Dadian*), 12306/1b, Toghto, *Songshi*, 2.32; Peter Lorge, "War and the Creation of the Northern Song," pp. 177–183.

30 For the conquest of the Southern Tang see Li Tao, *Xu Zizhi Tongjian Changbian*, (*Yongle Dadian*), 12307/2b–12308/1a, Toghto, *Songshi*, 3.42–46; Peter Lorge, "War and the Creation of the Northern Song," pp. 185–202.

31 For Song Taizu's second Northern Han campaign (9 September 976–3 January 977), see Li Tao, *Xu Zizhi Tongjian Changbian*, (*Yongle Dadian*), 12308/9a–16a, Toghto, *Songshi*, 3.48–51; Peter Lorge, "War and the Creation of the Northern Song," pp. 202–204.

32 For Taizong's conquest of the Northern Han (6 February–19 June 979), see Li Tao, *Xu Zizhi Tongjian Changbian*, 20/1a–10b; Xu Song, *Song Huiyao Jigao*, Tarbei: Xinwenfeng chubangongsi, 1976, *Bing*, 7/5a–7b, and Toghto, *Songshi*, 4.60–62; Peter Lorge, "War and the Creation of the Northern Song," pp. 207–214.

33 For Taizong's first Sixteen Prefectures Campaign (26 June–1 August 979), see Li Tao, *Xu Zizhi Tongjian Changbian*, 20/10b–13b; Xu Song, *Song Huiyao: Bing*, 7/8a–9a; Toghto, *Songshi*, 4.62–63; and Toghto (ed.), *Liaoshi*, Beijing: Zhonghua Shuja, 1996, 9.102; Peter Lorge, "War and the Creation of the Northern Song," pp. 214–217.

34 Robert Hartwell, "New Approaches to the Study of Bureaucratic Factionalism in Sung China: A Hypothesis," *The Bulletin of Sung–Yuan Studies*, 18 (1986), pp. 33–40.

35 Peter Bol, *This Culture of Ours*, Stanford: Stanford University Press, 1992.

36 For Song Taizong's second Sixteen Prefectures campaign (20 February–18 June 986), see Li Tao, *Xu Zizhi Tongjian Changbian*, 27/1a–14b; Xu Song, *Song Huiyao: Bing*, 7/10a–b, and Toghto, *Liaoshi*, 11.120–122; Peter Lorge, "War and the Creation of the Northern Song," pp. 226–235.

37 Peter Lorge, "The Great Ditch of China," in Don Wyatt (ed.), *Battlefronts Real and Imagined*, Palgrave, forthcoming.

38 Ibid.

39 The terms of the treaty or covenant provided for annual payments by the Song to the Liao of 100,000 taels of silver and 200,000 bolts of silk; a clearly marked border between the two sides; enforcement of a peaceful border; extradition of criminals; and a ban on new fortifications or canals along the border. A fictive kinship relationship was established for the forms of address between the Song and Liao emperors. Christian Schwartz-Schilling, *der Friede von Shan-yuan (1005n. chr.): Ein Beitrag zur Geschichte der Chinesischen Diplomatie*, Wiesbaden: Otto Harrassowitz, 1959; Denis

Twitchett and Klaus-Peter Tietze, "The Liao," in Herbert Franke and Denis Twitchett (eds), *The Cambridge History of China*, Volume 6: *Alien Regimes and Border States*, Cambridge: Cambridge University Press, 1994; David C. Wright, "Song–Liao Diplomatic Practices," unpublished Ph.D diss., Princeton University, 1993, pp. 65–100; David C. Wright, "The Sung–Kitan War of AD 1004–1005 and the Treaty of Shan–yüan," *Journal of Asian History*, 32 (1998), pp. 3–48.

CHAPTER TWO

Empires at peace, empires at war,
1005–1142

> For thirty-three years there has been peace. All the soldiers who
> have had any experience of war are either dead or decrepit.
> Those who have been recruited later know nothing of actual
> warfare.
>
> Ouyang Xiu in 1040, poet, historian and statesman[1]

After the Chanyuan Covenant, the Song empire experienced a period of prolonged peace in the eleventh century, marred only by a few periods of intense
warfare with the Tanguts in the northwest. In sharp contrast, the twelfth century was a time of intense warfare during which the Jurchen destroyed first the
Kitan empire and then nearly destroyed the Song. The Song's military failures
were surprising given its immense economic strength, but cannot be explained
as they have been by the rise and dominance of an overwhelmingly civil society
and culture. Rather, its failures were the result of poor Song policy choices
made for political reasons, and the development of Jurchen political and military
power. These prosaic and incidental causes have not satisfied the desire of many
Chinese historians, beginning in the Song, to make overall generalizations
about the nature of Song rule and society, and to find fault in the fundamental
institutions of the dynasty. Unfortunately, these characterizations have tended
to obscure the real causes and results of the wars, and warped our view of Song
society.[2]

The Chanyuan Covenant itself became the first episode in a narrative of
Song military weakness, followed by two wars against the Tanguts on their
northwest border from 1038–1045 and again from 1081–1085 which went
poorly, and finally by the Jurchen capture of Kaifeng in 1127 and the subsequent retreat of the Song court to southern China. Because the Sixteen
Prefectures were not "recaptured," and Kitan ownership was officially recognized by treaty, all of the successes of the Song army in the tenth century were
forgotten, or simply written off to the extraordinary military capabilities of
Song Taizu. Most of this narrative of weakness was written for political reasons
in the eleventh century as part of a series of efforts spread over several emperors'
reigns to convince the ruler to give one faction or another control over the

government. Since several of the political figures involved wrote histories of the preceding Tang dynasty, and of the Five Dynasties and Ten Kingdoms period, they justified the now assumed weakness of the Song by demonstrating the chaos caused by emphasizing military affairs. If the Song was weak, it was a reasonable trade-off for stability and peace.

Kou Zhun (961–1023), the official who had urged the emperor to go to the front in 1004, emerged as the hero of the defense of the empire. The Chanyuan Covenant was initially seen as a success, particularly since the Song court imagined that the existence of the dynasty had been at stake. Kou's opponents attacked him politically by convincing the emperor that the Covenant had been a dynastic disgrace, a treaty concluded under military duress. Three decades later, after the Tanguts attacked and the army performed poorly, a new group of officials were able to argue, with some reason, that the dynasty's problems could only be solved with serious reform. Another three decades or so later, Wang Anshi was able to convince a young emperor that the military power to defeat first the Tanguts and then the Kitan could be developed by building up the empire through government reforms. Each wave of political argument reinforced the previous one, creating a consensus among Song historians and those who followed them that the dynasty had, in fact, been militarily deficient.

The source of this weakness was clear, if the cause and effect relationship has yet to be proven more than tautologically: the dynasty emphasized civil values over military values, and subordinated the army to civil bureaucratic control. This was originally done in reaction to the problems of militarism and the dominance of military men who tore apart the Tang dynasty and kept China in chaos during the Five Dynasties period. Song Taizu understood this problem and saw that the only way out of that chaos was to subordinate the military to civil control. Unfortunately for this interpretation, Taizu was not responsible for the creation of Song civil culture beyond the desire of any conqueror for peace in his subjugated lands, and the key policy for fostering that civil culture, making the exam system the primary means of entry into the bureaucracy, was taken by Taizong for his own political reasons.[3] At no point was there a desire to emphasize civil values as a means to reduce the chaos of the preceding period. That chaos had been effectively reduced through the violent destruction of the lesser military players. Indeed, much of the chaos had been caused, not reduced, by the desire of a series of emperors in north China to recreate the Tang empire. The divided ecumene was no more violent than the united one.

The Song army was a powerful force in the tenth century, as it had to have been, having conquered an empire and fought the formidable Kitan army to a standstill, but it declined markedly in the eleventh century. Experienced generals and veteran troops retired or died, and several decades of peace intervened between the 1004 invasions, the late 1030s Tangut war, and the early 1080s Tangut war. When the Jurchen first invaded in 1125, the Song army had not gone to war for 40 years. It is not surprising that the army was neglected during extended periods of peace, regardless of the military values of the court or government elite. There were soldiers and generals who could easily have spent their entire careers in the Song army without participating in a major campaign. Under such circumstances, the possibilities for advancement were extremely limited. Civilian bureaucratic control failed even to maintain troop numbers within individual units, leaving open great opportunities for corruption when commanders collected salaries for non-existent troops.[4]

War with the Jurchen eventually compelled the Song army to reconstitute itself as an effective fighting force; had it failed to do so the dynasty would likely have fallen soon after 1127. The immense political and psychological dislocation caused by the loss of north China and the reconstituted court's flight to the south took some time to sort out. In parallel to this, the military situation was extremely fluid with old military units shattered, never to reform, and new units appearing, only vaguely under the command of the central authorities. As these new formations became more organized and defeated Jurchen armies in the field, the military balance stabilized with the Song erecting a solid defense along the Huai River. The temporary military equilibrium allowed the negotiation of a treaty in 1141.

The political split between north and south China mirrored the larger cultural split that had been developing since the Tang dynasty. Even during the eleventh century the increasing economic strength of the south was translating into increasing political power at court. The exam system did have geographic quotas to ensure regional representation in the government, but southerners did better on the exams and began to dominate the upper reaches of the bureaucracy. This split would develop into a chasm after the loss of the north, as southerners monopolizing the court and civil administration argued for survival, and refugee northerners dominating the military urged a campaign to retake the lost territory.[5] The military–civil split that emerged in the twelfth century was anachronistically projected back to the eleventh century and explained by decisions made in the tenth. This is not to say that southerners and civil officials did not wish to retake the north, only that they were more likely to point to the risks and difficulties of carrying out such an effort. In practice, this meant that the court was unable to decide upon aggressive action until Han Tuozhou's disastrous campaign in the years 1206 to 1208.

A second problem with aggressive military action emerged almost immediately after the fall of Kaifeng: a powerful army might interfere in government affairs or directly threaten the emperor's position on the throne. Unlike Song Taizu, the imperial prince who became emperor on 12 June 1127, posthumously known as Song Gaozong, was not a general, and had neither expected nor been trained to become emperor. Gaozong became the embodiment of the Song dynasty, but for a number of years that meant running from Jurchen armies rather than ruling the Song government. The Jurchen had expended great effort to capture all of the members of the Song imperial clan in order to cripple the dynasty politically. Gaozong's escape and the gradual coalescing of a government around him proved the wisdom of their policy. Had they succeeded in capturing him on one of their attempts, the Song dynasty might well have ended in the twelfth century. The emperor was a military objective because he was politically critical to the continuation of the dynasty. Whatever form the Song army took, it had to protect the emperor, and anyone who could do so would therefore have tremendous political influence. Gaozong had to rely upon the army while trying not to fall under its influence.

Armies loyal to the Song emerged across north and south China in response to the Jurchen invasion, but they remained uncoordinated for several years. Partly this was due to the instability of the Gaozong's court, but perhaps even more as a result of the lack of clear goals. Although these forces fought against the Jurchen and any opportunistic bandits who cropped up, a position easily pursued for simple self-preservation, it was unclear what or who they were fighting for. With the capital fallen, the emperor, retired emperor, and most of the imperial clan captured, and reports of a new emperor of questionable legitimacy enthroned, what exactly was there to be loyal to? Local security certainly required an armed response, which provided opportunities for new, more martially accomplished men to exploit if the existing local power-holders did not take up the task. On a larger scale, Gaozong had not ordered all forces to fight to retake north China. The emperor put his own safety first, though there were good political reasons for this, and forces fighting for the Central Plains could not also defend his person. The natural incoherence of the "loyalist" armies proved what the Jurchen and Gaozong knew: that without the emperor there was no Song empire.

Throughout the twelfth and thirteenth centuries the Song court drew local forces into its imperial armies both to fill the desperate need for troops and to diminish the threat of local resistance to the center.[6] This had been Song practice in the tenth and eleventh centuries as well, but it was done for individual soldiers who proved themselves worthy of becoming imperial guardsmen, not for entire units. Gaozong's struggle was to establish that there was a central Song court which local forces could be loyal to, and that this central court was legitimate even if it did not insist on an all-out military effort to retake the Central Plains from the Jurchen. These two goals were in opposition to each other, particularly for those loyalist forces based in north China. Those forces faced the choice of either accepting Jurchen rule (through the temporary puppet state of Qi), or abandoning their homes and moving to the south. Many people, even those not involved in armed resistance to the Jurchen, chose to flee with the Song court, though whether this was a demonstration of political loyalty or simply the desire to avoid a chaotic environment is unclear. And while we have many notices of elite families going south, more probably remained in the north. Their ties to their locality were stronger than their connection to the Song.

Song society in the early eleventh century

Song Taizong's dramatic shift to relying almost exclusively upon the civil service exams to fill the ranks of the Song government gave rise to a professional bureaucratic class. This class was open to anyone able to acquire enough education to pass the exams, a threshold that effectively limited the candidates to people of a certain minimum economic means.[7] Still, this vastly expanded the opportunities for government service and, as the dynasty wore on, the cost of books and education decreased, and the general wealth increased. In the first half of the eleventh century, however, most of the prominent statesmen not only knew each other but also intermarried with one another's families. Factional politics became nastier as more new men entered the system, though it did not become violent during the Song.[8]

An individual's chance of exam success also diminished with the spread of education, as did the chance of a family, nuclear or extended, being able to hold office in successive generations. Office holding therefore became more episodic than regular, something which confirmed a family's status as of the literati class without needing a member actually in office all the time to maintain that distinction. Consequently, locally prominent families had to rely upon maintaining their power and position through local activities. This tied them to their hometown, and many families remained locally prominent across dynasties. At the same time, the education they pursued as part of the trappings of literati status was independent of the particular exam system knowledge a man needed to attempt to enter government. Imperial ideology as expressed in exam questions was a particular subset of literate knowledge, and a man could be known for his learning without being able to pass the exams. Nevertheless, a family's standing was not connected to a particular dynasty.

The fastest way to power in a man's own lifetime, assuming he did not have the advantage of a good education, was through the army. Success in battle could send a man from the ranks to the upper reaches of government in a few decades. Such dramatic success was the exception rather than the rule, of course, but even modest advancement was possible in the army for a man otherwise without prospects. There were few opportunities for dramatic advancement in the eleventh century because of the extended period of peace. All that changed in the twelfth century, placing newly risen generals in direct competition for political power with desperately competitive exam graduates. The generals who yielded to the political system survived, and those who did not, like the great patriotic hero Yue Fei, were destroyed. Good generals emerged from war, not peace, a fact that frustrated statesmen as they tried to maintain military effectiveness in preparation for conflict. It was only after a war began that the army could reinvigorate itself, by which time it might be too late.

Unlike the bureaucrats who emerged from locally prominent families, however, army officers usually owed their status to the dynasty they served. This was particularly true of the descendants of the Song founding generals who formed a military aristocracy through intermarriage with the imperial clan, and from whose ranks empresses were drawn. It is therefore not surprising that the shock of the Jurchen invasion and its shattering of the Song government had a direct social impact on the officer corps and military aristocracy on a scale far beyond its effect on the civil elites. The military was much more strongly connected to the Song political structure until 1127, and so the Jurchen strike that nearly beheaded the dynasty completely devastated the old military elites. When the dynasty was reconstituted in the south, the new military elite were scrupulously excluded from establishing close ties with the emperor and dynasty, leading to their alienation from the court. This split would ultimately lead to the dynasty's fall, when the Lu family surrendered to the Mongols in 1273.

The first Song–Tangut war, 1038–1045

The previously peaceful Tanguts came under the sway of a new and ambitious leader in Li Yuanhao (also known as Weiming Yuanhao). Li Yuanhao determined to make himself a leader on par with the Song and Kitan emperors. Neither court was willing to recognize these claims to emperorship, so he determined to force them to concede by invading, with the Song the first target. Although the Song army performed quite poorly against the Tangut army, Li Yuanhao still failed to achieve his aims. He could wreak havoc on the northwestern border, but he could not truly threaten the Song court's existence or legitimacy. The Tangut army simply did not have the power or reach to be more than a border problem. What concerned the Song court was the possibility that the Kitan would attack in concert with the Tanguts, an eventuality that would have threatened the dynasty's existence. The Kitan court took advantage of this fear, though they had no real intention of attacking the Song, to extract increased annual payments from the Song. The Song court was relieved to avert what it believed to be a serious threat, though this further contributed to the deep, underlying hostility to the Kitan. While maintaining the position that they were always ready, willing and able to invade, the Song was good for negotiations – it fostered an adversarial relationship that made it easy for the Song court to see an alliance with the Jurchen against the Kitan in the twelfth century as a great opportunity rather than a betrayal.

The Tanguts had previously fought the Song in the late tenth century under their ambitious leader Li Jiqian. His death in 1004 brought the Tanguts back into a peaceful relationship with the Song. Song–Tangut relations were extraordinarily personality driven, rather than developing out of inherent geopolitical clashes of interest. Indeed, from the point of view of the Tangut people's welfare, war hurt rather than helped them. Li Jiqian's successor, Li Deming, maintained peaceful, subordinate relations with the Song, to his and his subjects' great economic benefit. His son, Yuanhao, argued that a ruler should pursue power, wearing furs and herding cattle were native customs, and that silks were useless.[9]

Yuanhao opposed a comfortable, sinified and subordinate existence, preferring instead a rough Tangut nativist independence. What he did not understand was how limited his own military means were, and, perhaps most importantly, that his personal political interest in reordering the Song–Kitan–Tangut relationship did not coincide, and was even in opposition to, Kitan interests. Yuanhao assumed that the Kitan would support an increase in his own status if it diminished that of the Song. The Kitan court felt it was much more in their interests to maintain their own parity with the Song court, and extract economic concessions to keep the Tanguts in line. When peace was finally reestablished in 1045, almost nothing had changed politically, though the Song increased their annual payments to the Tanguts and Kitan.

Li Yuanhao (who changed his surname to Weiming when he succeeded his father as king of Xiping) assumed the title "emperor" in 1038, and sent an envoy to the Song court the following year to inform them. The Song court refused to recognize Yuanhao's new title, breaking diplomatic relations. For the moment, since it was caught completely by surprise, the Song court could only close the border market, revoke Yuanhao's Song-bestowed titles, and post a reward for his head. Song border forces were in poor shape after 30 years of peace. Effectives typically made up only one-quarter to one-third of most battalions' strength (500 men),[10] and in one battalion only a quarter of the men could use the heaviest-draw crossbows. Officials also complained that the soldiers posted to Kaifeng, about half of the entire army's total manpower, were poorly disciplined and unready for war. In theory, soldiers in the capital should have been the best trained. These sorts of complaints are typical of most armies during peacetime and may well have been exaggerated since not all Song troops performed poorly during the subsequent war. Almost the entire army, from soldiers to officers, had never been in battle.

Without experienced, successful generals to call upon for leadership or advice, it fell to the civilian statesmen to decide upon strategy, organize the armies in the field, and even sometimes command them. They performed poorly on most counts, at least initially. Just as significant for subsequent history, no general emerged from the war with the sort of unalloyed success that led to political power. There were some successful commanders at the tactical level, but they were quite subordinate to the civilian leaders. The Song army's poor initial performance was not due to civilian control, however; it was due to mundane management and planning problems – indecisive and ill-informed leaders, unclear objectives, divided command, poor coordination and overall lack of strategy. The generals were no less susceptible to these problems than the civil officials, though some were skilled at individual combat.

When Yuanhao first invaded in 1039, the Song army was dispersed in scattered forts of varying sizes configured to provide local security rather than withstand a major invasion.[11] Concentration was difficult because the region was poor and transportation difficult in the mountainous terrain. Without an overall strategy or a supreme commander, however, no one was able to coordinate these widely dispersed troops into a more coherent defense. The Song thus ceded the initiative to Yuanhao, who exploited their indecision with great skill. Yuanhao invaded in the winter of 1039, quickly overrunning three dozen forts under the control of a single commander (which may well have been due to bribery rather than military acumen) and besieging Yanzhou. He then ambushed a Song relief force of about 9,000 men at Sanchuankou, destroying it piecemeal and capturing its two commanders. It must have been a costly battle for the Tanguts as well, since the battle continued into the next day and went back and forth. In terms of men lost, it was not particularly significant, the Song had several hundred thousand troops in the region, but it was a devastating loss psychologically. A snowstorm undermined the Tangut siege or any further operations, and Yuanhao was forced to withdraw.

The defeat at Sanchuankou prompted a strategy debate in 1040 that led to a reprisal against the Tangut forts at Jintang and Baipao in early 1041. Both forts were overrun, their supplies destroyed, and nearby tribes annihilated. For the moment this seemed to vindicate the strategy of concentrating troops against the Tanguts, but Yuanhao was already planning his campaign for that year. His plan was remarkably similar to his previous one, in that it consisted of luring a Song force into an ambush. A Song army of about 18,000 men was marching through the mountains to outflank an approaching Tangut force. At the Haoshui River it encountered and defeated a small enemy force, encouraging the commanders to advance quickly and surprise the larger Tangut army. After engaging the Tanguts in a fierce battle, Yuanhao sprang the trap, catching the Song army in the rear with another force. Most of the Song commanders were killed in battle, and only a part of the original army was able to escape. This was a much more costly defeat for the Song since it destroyed some of the best troops and commanders. Once again the Tanguts must have sustained serious casualties themselves in the drawn out battle, and once again Yuanhao was not able to exploit his battlefield success for much territorial gain.

Later in 1041, the third player in this struggle entered the game when the Song detected a Kitan military build-up on the border. The Kitan envoy arrived at the Song court in early 1042 with demands for territory, specifically the Guannan region captured by Chai Rong in 959, a marriage alliance, and an increase in the annual payments to the Kitan court. Desperate to avoid a two-front war, offended at the prospect of a marriage alliance, and clear that the territorial concession would cripple the Hebei border defenses thus leaving them open to further political pressure, the Song were relieved to settle the situation by increasing the annual payment. Part of the increase in payment was also supposed to be for the Kitans reining-in the Tanguts, something the Kitan emperor felt confident he could do. The Kitan emperor thus gained economically without actually going to war and incurring the expense or risk of campaigning.

The Song–Tangut struggle was more even in 1041, with the Song winning several smaller engagements and frustrating several Tangut attempts to capture forts and prefectures. Yuanhao's political position was itself eroding as the war continued and his own people suffered the consequences of military service and lack of trade. He invaded again in 1042, initially winning a crushing victory at Dingchuan Fort, inflicting 9,400 casualties on a force of perhaps 19,000 men. The Song response was much better coordinated this time, however, with one force threatening the Tangut rear and a second actually defeating the Tangut vanguard. Yuanhao was forced to withdraw. Now militarily frustrated, he proposed an alliance against the Song to the Kitan in 1043.

The Kitan court rejected Yuanhao's proposal, so the Tangut leader turned on the Kitan. Much of the struggle between the Tanguts and Kitans seems to have gone unrecorded, but hostilities had clearly broken out by 1044 when a Kitan envoy arrived at the Song court to press the Song not to make peace with the Tanguts. The Song were under no obligation to do so based upon their earlier agreement with the Kitan, nor were the Kitan ready to renegotiate the agreement in order to form an alliance against Yuanhao, so the Song took advantage of the situation to hasten peace talks with the Tangut leader. Song–Tangut peace was established in early 1045, with an increase in annual payments to the Tanguts, but without recognizing Yuanhao as an emperor. The Kitan emperor personally led a massive invasion of Tangut territory to bring Yuanhao in line, but was defeated at a battle on the banks of the Yellow River. This time Yuanhao wisely took advantage of his victory to make peace with the Kitan emperor.

Although the Song lamented their own inability to subdue a minor power like the Tanguts, Li Yuanhao's war demonstrated the military limitations of all three powers. The Tangut leader utterly failed, despite some battlefield successes, to advance his political status in the eyes of the Song and Kitan courts. He impoverished his country in pursuit of a fairly pointless personal goal, one which was simply impossible to accomplish without first establishing a real military alliance with the Kitan. Of course, such an alliance would have also been impossible because the Kitan were not interested in either the expense or risk involved in war with the Song. The Kitan clearly did not want to destroy the Song empire, a policy they held to consistently. Yuanhao's goals were completely quixotic in that his military means were simply inadequate to his political goals. The Song can perhaps be excused for doing so poorly against such an accomplished general as Li Yuanhao, since even the Kitan, with their vast steppe army, were also unable to defeat the Tanguts. Yet the Song army did not totally fail once its commanders fixed upon a strategy and overcame many of the initial command and control problems. The Tanguts never seriously threatened the existence of the Song dynasty, or even did much damage to Song finances. Very much like the Kitan leading up to the Chanyuan Covenant in 1005, Yuanhao's ability to create political pressure through military action was diminishing as the Song army's defenses hardened up and its superior numbers and finances began to tell in what was becoming a war of attrition. The Tangut leader made peace in 1045 because he could not longer sustain a war, and because he finally realized that his ambition to be recognized as emperor placed him in conflict with both larger empires, a position which might have resulted in an alliance against him. Ultimately Li Yuanhao's war changed almost nothing, at a great cost in human lives. He did not even live very long to enjoy the extra payments he'd acquired; his son assassinated him in 1048.

Several innovations in the Song army during the Tangut war transformed the army's structure, armament and tactics. The most important change was in the creation of "legions" (*jiang*) of from 2,500 to 4,000 men (on rare occasions as high as 10,000 men) as permanent maneuver elements. The success of these legions in the latter stages of the war not only discredited the older system, in which armies were created by drawing disparate battalions of 500 men from larger garrisons, but also created a distinction between field or border forces and the garrison forces in the capital. The legion was more formally introduced throughout the army during the New Policies reforms of Wang Anshi during the reign of Song Shenzong (1067–1085). At the same time, more and better crossbows (particularly the Divine Arm Bow), heavier, bladed shields, fewer spears and more axes and long bladed swords, transformed the army's tactics. Gunpowder-enhanced arrows and catapult projectiles were introduced, primarily to improve city defenses, in increasing quantities by the imperial arsenals.

Wang Anshi's New Policies were sold to Emperor Shenzong as a means to increase the empire's power, which would ultimately allow the Song to defeat the Kitan and capture the Sixteen Prefectures. Wang argued that the empire first needed to increase its wealth through a series of government reforms and economic policies; this increase in wealth would translate into an increase in military power. At the same time, Wang promoted the *baojia* system, which would organize all of the empire's subjects into local militias. These militias, he believed, would both return society to the ideal Confucian state where farmers served as soldiers when needed, saving a great deal of money, and harness the Song's far larger population into a force which would easily overwhelm the Tanguts or Kitan. In reality, the *baojia* sanctioned preexisting militias in some areas, created new ones in others, militarizing local society, but never produced any effective troops capable of replacing the imperial army.[12]

The second Song–Tangut war, 1081–1082

While Wang Anshi gained control over the government by promising a revitalized empire leading to military conquest, he was notably reluctant to go to war. He did support Wang Shao's extension of Song territory in the Xihe region in 1070, and a campaign against Vietnam in 1076 and 1077, but he had to argue to an impatient Shenzong that the empire was not yet strong enough to attack the Tanguts, let alone the Kitan. Wang's larger program was extremely controversial, however, and he was forced to step down from his position permanently in 1076. Shenzong was no longer constrained after Wang's departure, so when it was reported that the Tangut king had been overthrown and some Song officials proposed a military campaign to take advantage of the presumed political chaos to destroy the Tangut state, the emperor readily agreed.

The expeditionary army was divided into five separate forces: the first with 60,000 soldiers and 60,000 porters; the second with 93,000 soldiers; the third with 87,000 troops and 95,000 porters; the fourth with 50,000 soldiers; and the fifth with 30,000 troops. Their operational objectives were to capture the cities of Lingzhou and Xiazhou, which would have effectively destroyed the Tangut state. Extraordinary logistical efforts were made to support these massive armies, since they had to assume that there would be little or no sources of supply for them along their respective routes. It was estimated that even with these extraordinary efforts – specifically the provision of equal numbers of porters to soldiers – an army of 100,000 men could campaign for only 31 days. Speed was of the essence, though the likelihood of being able to besiege two sizable cities successfully under such narrow time constraints should have alerted the planners to the weakness of their designs.

The campaign began in late 1081, with separate Song armies soon winning convincing victories over major Tangut formations of 80,000 and 20,000 men, and continuing on to capture important Tangut forts. Another Tangut army of 30,000, strongly situated on a high ground defending a pass, was dislodged in a fierce frontal assault that shattered the Tanguts' morale and opened the way to Lingzhou. In the face of this series of severe defeats, the Tanguts contemplated a strategy of protracted war to wear the Song army down. The discussion was moot, however, since the Song army's victories had already driven the main Tangut armies from the field and the Song army's logistical window was closing fast. On the eighteenth day of the campaign, two Song armies reached Lingzhou, only to find that the Tanguts had destroyed a nearby dam, flooding the area around the city. They had no choice but to withdraw. With the failure of the attack on Lingzhou, the other Song armies, who were much farther from Lingzhou or Xiazhou, also withdrew.

Although the initial invasion had failed in its objective to destroy the Tangut state, the Song army won the major battles and wrought considerable destruction on their enemy's country. Unlike the earlier Tangut attacks on the Song, the Song invasion had raised the real prospect of destroying the Tangut ruling house and its government. The logistical problem remained, however, and the considerable desert that lay between the immediate Tangut border and its main cities presented an insurmountable barrier. Song attacks then turned to Tangut territory immediately adjacent to the Song, but poor coordination and remarkably inept generalship on the Song side, and a maximum effort by the Tanguts, dealt the Song a severe reverse in 1082. Shenzong's enthusiasm for war was blunted by his campaign's failure, and particularly by the human cost he had paid for it: some 600,000 men on the Song side alone.[13]

If Shenzong's war against the Tanguts had not succeeded, it had also not entirely failed. The Tanguts were clearly on the defensive afterward, subject to another victorious Song campaign in 1099, and continued exhausting fighting for both sides in the early twelfth century. The Song empire could afford a protracted war much more easily than the Tanguts, though the limits of the

Song army's reach seemingly made it impossible to deliver a knock-out blow. Still, the Song army's performance in Shenzong's Tangut campaign was impressive, demonstrating the value of improvements in army organization and military technology made since the first Song-Tangut war. Those improvements were squandered through protracted war with the Tanguts in the early twelfth century, and a general neglect of the Song empire's military preparations. Even a wealthy empire had limited material and manpower resources, and continued hostilities with the Tanguts not only diverted attention from the looming threat of the Jurchens, but also left the Song army a diminished force from its 1081–1082 incarnation. This would prove to be a near fatal mistake for the Song dynasty.

The Song–Jin war against the Liao[14]

As the Song court became aware of the rising Jurchen power threatening the Kitan empire, the dream of capturing the Sixteen Prefectures began to seem within the realm of possibility. Despite over a century of peaceful relations, the Song court was almost unrelentingly hostile to the Kitans, and actively sought an alliance with the Jurchen to destroy them. The Kitans were as responsible for this hostility as the Song, since they had always maintained that they were ready, willing and able to invade. Even though the Song court recognized in the 1060s that both the Kitan and Tanguts were no longer serious threats to the dynasty's existence, and in that light discussed the strategic function of continued annual payments, there was no move to end those payments or renegotiate the diplomatic status quo in the absence of a dramatically changed military situation. The rise of the Jurchen, and their rapid destruction of the Kitan regime, provided the necessary conditions.

The Song court first heard of the Kitan's Jurchen problem in 1115, and soon sent envoys to the Jurchen leader, Aguda. Despite his steppe upbringing, Aguda was well informed about Chinese imperial practice, and conducted his diplomacy with the Song court with justified suspicion. He understood that it was temporarily in his and the Song's interests to attack the Kitan jointly, but was uncertain about what the Song's longer-term objectives were. What he could not really grasp, or believe, was that Song statesmen and emperors were actually so fixated on the Sixteen Prefectures that their ambitions could be limited to gaining that piece of territory. This seems, in fact, to have been the case, though particularly from the perspective of a steppe leader it made no real sense. The control of territory was always predicated on political control, which relied upon alliances backed by force. Stable territorial control was therefore a follow-on effect of military and political dominance; temporary occupation of territory without broader military and political dominance was meaningless. If the Song wanted the Sixteen Prefectures, then it must have really aimed for a dominant military and political power relationship with whatever steppe power would remain after attacking the Kitan.

An agreement was reached between the Song and Jurchen that they would jointly attack the Kitan in 1122. The Jurchen would attack the Kitan Central Capital while the Song would attack the Southern Capital, Yanjing, in the Sixteen Prefectures. This would also leave the Song in a position to take control of the Sixteen Prefectures when the war was over. The Jurchen captured the Kitan's Central and Western Capitals in 1122, forcing the Kitan emperor to flee west. Some of the Kitan emperor's relatives then established a new emperor at the Southern Capital, and sent an envoy to the Song court to announce this and demand the Song's annual payment. Pursuant to the Song–Jurchen agreement, and about to launch its own attack on the Kitan Southern Capital, the Song court refused. A Song army of 150,000 men under the eunuch general Tong Guan launched a two-pronged invasion in June of 1122.

Kitan forces quickly defeated both prongs of the Song army, and the terrified Song emperor Huizong ordered the army to pull back and camp. Huizong ordered another advance in August, and two Kitan officials surrendered with their prefectures. In November, a 200,000-man Song army advanced on Yanjing. The advanced guard quickly took control of the city and massacred the Kitan inhabitants. The inner city remained strongly defended by the remaining Kitan troops, who sent an urgent message to a nearby Kitan army to rescue them. Having failed to capture the inner city, and with the main army still distant, the Song force was forced to withdraw; it was ambushed by the Kitan relief army about seven miles from Yanjing. The main army burned its camp and fled in confusion when it heard of the advance guard's defeat, and was chased back to the Song border with heavy losses in men and equipment.

Having failed to capture Yanjing, Tong Guan then solicited Aguda's aid. In January of 1123, a Jurchen army stormed down and the Kitan defenders fled. The Jurchen carried off the city's remaining inhabitants, and thoroughly looted the city. When the Song envoy went to Aguda to request that he turn over the Sixteen Prefectures to the Song, Aguda demurred, citing the Song's inability to hold up its end of the agreement. A new agreement was concluded which increased the Song annual payment to the Jurchen from 500,000 units of silver and silk, to 600,000. When the Song army entered Yanjing in May they found a completely empty city, denuded of residents or goods. They took this as a sign of Jurchen duplicity, particularly in light of Aguda's changes in the original agreement. This would soon lead to open hostilities between the erstwhile allies.

The fall of Kaifeng, 1126–1127[15]

While the Jurchen pursued the remnants of the Kitan court, the Song court congratulated itself on finally "recovering" the Sixteen Prefectures, despite its army's poor performance. The destruction of the Kitan empire was similarly gratifying, and it seemed to most statesmen that the empire was not only now complete but also more secure. Several seemingly minor disputes between the

Song and Jurchen obtruded into this complacent view without alerting the Song court to the possibility of a looming crisis. While much of the responsibility for this failure to understand the true political and military situation rests with Emperor Huizong and the high officials he selected, blindness to the Jurchen threat was widespread, though not universal. The Jurchen had now seen how weak the Song army was, and must have suspected that the Song court was similarly incapable.

Several Kitan officials who had surrendered to the Jurchen urged Wuqimai, who had succeeded Aguda as Jurchen ruler after Aguda's death in the summer of 1123, to attack the Song, both to ingratiate themselves with the Jurchen ruler and to exact a measure of revenge for Song complicity in the destruction of the Kitan empire. In November of 1125, Wuqimai launched a two-pronged invasion of the Song, with one army driving south through Hebei and the other through Shanxi via Taiyuan. Wuqimai had a variety of reasons for launching the campaign, though the demonstrated military weakness of the Song army paired with contentious diplomacy was probably enough to convince him that applying military pressure might net him a good return for a low risk. The Jurchen invasion in 1125 was similar to the Kitan's escalating campaign at the beginning of the eleventh century, only far more successful. Hebei's hydraulic defense line, which had contributed so much to blunting the Kitan invasions, was long gone, as were the veteran troops and commanders who had stood ready to defend against expected incursions. The invasion caught the Song army completely by surprise. Tong Guan, who was in Taiyuan at the time, first heard of the impending campaign when the envoy he sent to discuss the Jurchen hand-over of two prefectures was told that the Song had broken the agreement, and could only seek peace by ceding Hebei and Shanxi to the Jurchen.

Tong Guan was shocked by the sudden turn of events. Completely at a loss as to how to respond or what action to take, he simply retreated from Taiyuan. In January of 1126, the Jurchen army overran Song defenses and besieged Taiyuan. The other Jurchen army captured two Song prefectures in December, smashed a Song army in January – effectively retaking control of the Sixteen Prefectures – and then drove straight down through Hebei to the walls of Kaifeng. Emperor Huizong was persuaded to abdicate in favor of his son, something that had never been done before, but which seemed necessary if the dynasty was to be saved. The new emperor, Qinzong, named his first and only reign period "Jingkang," a title forever associated in Chinese history with the Jingkang Disaster. Huizong left for the south.

Li Gang, a minister who would soon play a critical role in reestablishing the dynasty in the south, convinced Qinzong that he should defend the city firmly. They opened negotiations with the Jurchen commander. Since the Shanxi army was still hung up besieging Taiyuan, and because Jurchen commanders were given great latitude in decision-making in the field, the Jurchen general was willing to treat. He demanded 5 million taels of gold, 50 million taels of silver, 1 million bolts of satin, 1 million bolts of silk, 10,000 head of cattle,

10,000 horses, 10,000 mules, 1,000 camels, and the cession of Taiyuan (in Shanxi), Zhongshan and Hejian (both in Hebei), the three northern border defense centers. The political demands were equally onerous, including delivering an imperial prince and the prime minister as hostages, and that the Song emperor should acknowledge the Jurchen emperor as his overlord.

Given the immense size and strength of Kaifeng's defenses – her walls alone were almost 27 miles in circumference – it seemed ridiculous to give in to the Jurchen general. But then a Song detachment led by a veteran Song commander was defeated outside the walls. A shaken Qinzong sacked Li Gang and ceded the demanded territory. The Jin army withdrew. The siege had begun on 31 January 1126 and lasted until 5 March, a total of 33 days. Qinzong almost immediately began to regret his actions, soon brought Li Gang back into government, and dispatched troops to relieve the Jin siege of Taiyuan and to rescue Zhongshan and Hejian.

In June, the 90,000-man Hebei relief force was intercepted and scattered by the Jurchen en route; its commander died fighting. The 60,000-man Taiyuan relief army was also intercepted and defeated en route, but its commander fled. A second attempt to relieve Taiyuan with a three-pronged attack was defeated as well. Taiyuan finally capitulated after a 260-day siege. On 15 December, both Jurchen armies arrived under the walls of Kaifeng.

After the defeat of the various relief forces, Qinzong cancelled his order to gather the remaining Song troops to defend the capital and dispersed them to defend the various prefectures. The emperor had decided on peace talks rather than war, and so made a fatal mistake that left Kaifeng with somewhat less than 100,000 men to defend it. Qinzong simply failed to recognize the critical importance of the capital and his own person, or understand that army units scattered over the northern landscape were effectively useless. The Song emperor cannot be faulted for his army's battlefield defeats, since he dispatched what he believed to be his best commanders at the head of massive forces to rescue Taiyuan, Zhongshan and Hejian, and the operational details of the army were reasonably beyond his responsibilities. He can, however, be faulted for the strategic decisions he made, which were just as responsible for the ultimate disaster which followed. The fall of Kaifeng was not a given; it resulted from weak political leadership and astonishingly bad military decisions.

On 9 January the Jurchens took advantage of a great snowfall to overwhelm the city's defenders. In an initial assault on the walls with three siege towers, the Jurchen suffered more than 3,000 dead and the defenders only about 300 killed and wounded. But the Jurchens collected and concealed their dead, while the Song left their dead and wounded atop the wall. The remaining defenders were completely demoralized, and when the Jurchen renewed their assault, they broke. The Jurchen now entered Kaifeng searching for loot, mules, horses and young women. Qinzong hastened to provide them with all of these things, emptying the imperial coffers, the imperial stables, gathering common people's wealth and daughters, and including palace women. Many palace women drowned themselves rather than be given to the Jurchen invaders.

Qinzong, the retired emperor Huizong, the empress, various imperial princes and princesses, and much of the imperial clan were transported back to Jurchen territory in the north. The commanders of the two Jurchen armies set up a puppet dynasty, called Chu, under a former Song official, to govern the Central Plains and provide an annual payment to the Jurchen. This was an *ad hoc* measure designed to relieve the Jurchen army of the responsibility of trying to suppress opposition to their presence. Jurchen depredations far more than loyalty to the Song had created a vast pool of armed resistance to the Jurchen. It was also unclear to the Jurchen commanders what they were supposed to do politically with the results of their military success. The fall of Kaifeng and the capture of the Song emperor was as unexpected for the Jurchen as it was for the Song court. Their aim had been to extort wealth and territory by threatening the dynasty's existence, not to actually destroy it. Once Kaifeng was captured, however, it was hard to see an alternative to trying to behead the Song politically and render the entire empire prostrate. Their effort proved imperfect, since there was at least one imperial prince at large.

Having now mortally wounded the Song, it seemed wise to try and administer the *coup d'grâce* to diminish resistance and avoid the possibility of a resurgence. Jurchen forces now anxiously sought to capture Prince Kang, the imperial prince who had served as a hostage during the attempts to negotiate a peace settlement. This younger brother of Qinzong narrowly escaped capture on several occasions on his flight to the south, where he formed the center of a reconstituted dynasty. The case of Prince Kang, who would take the throne and continue the Song dynasty as Song Gaozong, demonstrates all of the strengths and weaknesses of the Chinese imperial system. A vast empire could be ruled by a small group of men because it was fragmented and connected only at the center. If that center collapsed or was destroyed, however, the empire would fall apart. The Jurchen failed to prevent the reestablishment of the Song center, which created a focus for the otherwise incoherent "loyalty" of the anti-Jurchen military and political forces that sprang up across north China.

Peace, and the death of Yue Fei

Between the fall of Kaifeng and the Shaoxing Peace Accord (1142), Song Gaozong had to steer his way through a dauntingly complicated and frequently changing political and military field to reach some kind of stability. If he often appeared vacillating or weak-willed, it was probably because he was a rather ordinary man faced with an extraordinary and unexpected situation. His first priority was his own survival and freedom, followed by preservation of his position as ruler of the remaining Song empire. These interests argued for making peace with the Jurchen as soon as possible, under whatever conditions would allow him to remain as emperor of the Song empire. Gaozong could not openly adopt this position, however, since it would have undermined his legitimacy in the eyes of many people. He therefore initially brought the belligerent Li Gang back into government to reassure the officials and generals of his intent to resist the Jurchen and perhaps recapture the north, and then sacked Li and brought in officials more concerned with Gaozong's personal authority. The emperor would swing between peace and war repeatedly, changing officials as his position changed, in response to military events, political struggles and social conditions.

Not only did Gaozong have to balance his desire for peace with the need to appear belligerent, he also had to credibly seek the return of Huizong, Qinzong and his own mother, now Jurchen captives. The return of either Huizong or Qinzong would have undermined his position on the throne, a factor that the Jurchen exploited in negotiations, and which rendered any peace agreement that did not secure the return of the former emperors suspect. Any negotiation would proceed from the military situation, something that changed repeatedly and dramatically. The Jurchen were initially unwilling to negotiate because they believed their military position was so dominant that they could simply destroy the Song, obviating the need for political compromise. Gaozong shared the Jurchen evaluation of the situation at that time, and made rather abject offers to the Jurchen court in the pursuit of peace.

The military situation began to change, however, as Song loyalist forces became more coordinated and competent generals emerged to deal the Jurchen several defeats. Jurchen armies also began to run into the usual operational problems that diminished the power of steppe armies on extended campaigns. Even in economically developed areas, an army that lived off the land could not return through the same place it had just looted. As Jurchen soldiers became more encumbered with loot, they became less mobile and less interested in further campaigning, though they might be more willing to return in the future. Southern China was also much less favorable for cavalry than northern China, and the Jurchen had to cross not only numerous small rivers and canals but also the Huai and Yangzi rivers.

Having failed to capture Gaozong or destroy the newly formed Song court, Jurchen raiding became less a positive instrument of policy and more the reflexive continuation of a tactic by an uncertain leadership. Jurchen raiding was destructive, and did serve for a time to keep the initiative, both military and political, in Jurchen hands, but the Jurchen court was simply unable to conceive of what stable, long-term result it wanted from its attacks. Although the puppet Chu regime had quickly failed and been replaced by the puppet Qi regime, which was ultimately very useful in stabilizing north China, there seemed to be no strategy for dealing with the new Song court beyond attempting to pummel it into submission. Only as the military balance shifted more in the Song's favor was the Jurchen court forced to formulate at least a temporary political solution to the war. This brought about the Shaoxing Peace Accord (named after the reign period in which it was concluded) in 1142, which placed the Song in a ritually inferior position to the Jurchen, and required annual payments to the Jurchens like those that the Song had previously paid to the Kitan and Tanguts. Still, the Jurchen were no more satisfied with the settlement than the Song.

It was also in 1142 that the Song court executed one of China's greatest patriotic heroes, a general by the name of Yue Fei. Yue's career followed the trajectory of Song military fortunes in the first half of the twelfth century. A northern Chinese from a humble background, he participated in the Song's attempt to capture the Sixteen Prefectures in 1122, and defended Kaifeng after the Jurchen withdrew in 1127. Yue moved south with the other loyalist forces in 1129, and took an active part in driving the Jurchen advance back across the Yangzi that year. He continued to advance in rank, and to increase the size of his army as he repeatedly led successful offensives into north China and put down bandits within Song territory. Several other generals were also successful against the Jurchen, and their combined efforts secured the survival of the dynasty. Yue, like most of them, was committed to recapturing north China. He saw the strengthening Song army not as a chance to achieve peace with what remained of Song territory but as a chance to defeat the Jurchen outright and recover what was lost.

Gaozong was as concerned to control the military as to strengthen it, however, and Yue and his radically irredentist colleagues threatened the emperor's peace plans. Although the emperor had personally written letters to Yue Fei thanking him for his efforts and telling him how important he was,[16] Gaozong installed Qin Gui as his chief councilor to make peace with the Jurchen and rein-in the generals. The more politically astute generals saw the signs and did not protest their reassignments to central government jobs. Yue tried to resign instead, and his intransigence made it clear that he could not coexist with a peace settlement. He was jailed, and then poisoned in 1142, thus bringing efforts to recapture the north to an end.

Notes

1 Quoted and translated in Henry Raymond Williamson, *Wang An Shih*, Westport, Conn.: Hyperion Press, 1973 (reprint of Arthur Probsthain edition of 1935), pp. 186–187.
2 For a recent example of this sort of characterization, see Frederick Mote, *Imperial China, 900–1800*, Cambridge, Mass.: Harvard University Press, 2003, pp. 112–118. Mote's discussion of a "war faction" and a "peace faction" is somewhat deceptive, since it elides the overriding importance of Song Taizong's political problems with respect to the dynasty, the government, and the army. It was Taizong who wanted to go to war for his own political reasons, and he was supported in this idea both by his own retainers and some generals, most notably Cao Bin. Cao believed, correctly, that the Northern Han could be conquered. After it fell, none of the generals supported the idea of continuing on to capture the Sixteen Prefectures, except for one sycophant. Moreover, one of the most direct critics of Taizong's second failed campaign was Zhao Pu, the architect of Song Taizu's conquest of China. Once again, the politics behind these policy positions were extremely complex.
3 John Labadie, "Rulers and Soldiers: Perception and Management of the Military in

Northern Sung China (960–ca. 1060)," Ph.D. dissertation, University of Washington, 1981.

4 Only one document attesting that units were under strength is extant in Bao Zheng, *Bao Zheng Ji*, ch. 8: "Qing yi ji, bo, shen, san zhou bingma," cited in Wang Zengyu, *Songchao Bingzhi Chutan*, Beijing: Zhonghua Shuju, 1983, pp. 29–30. Bao was requesting that several battalions be moved back to their original posts because of difficulty supplying them. He notes that the battalions in question had strengths of 358, 449, 473, 471, 462, 470, 439, 375, 425 and 450 men. Taken as whole, at least some of these units were close to their full strength.

5 Huang K'uan-ch'ung, "Cong Hezhan dao Nanbeiren," in *Zhongguo Lishishang de fenyu He Xueshu Yantao hui Lunwen Ji*, Taibei: Lianhe baixi wenhua jijinhui, 1995, pp. 169–189.

6 Huang K'uan-ch'ung has done a series of studies on individual local forces. These articles are now conveniently collected in his *Nansong Difang Wuli*, Taibei: Dongda tushu gongsi, 2002.

7 Robert Hartwell, "Demographic, Political and Social Transformation of China, 750–1550," *Harvard Journal of Asiatic Studies*, 42, no. 2 (1982), pp. 365–442; Robert Hymes, *Statesmen and Gentlemen: The Elite of Fu-chou, Chiang-his, in Northern and Southern Sung*, Cambridge: Cambridge University Press, 1986.

8 Robert Hartwell made this argument in his last paper given before he passed away. He never published it, and to my knowledge no copy of it is extant.

9 Toghto, *Songshi*, p. 13993

10 Wang Zengyu, *Songchao Bingzhi Chutan*, pp. 29–30.

11 This account of the Song–Tangut war follows Shui-lung Tsang, "War and Peace in Northern Sung China: Violence and Strategy in Flux, 960–1104," Unpublished Ph.D. dissertation, University of Arizona, 1997, pp. 221–239.

12 The literature on Wang Anshi's New Policies is enormous, particularly because his attempts at political reform resonate so strongly in modern China. A useful short biography of Wang that covers the New Policies is Zhang Xianghao, *Wang Anshi Pingzhuan*, Nanning: Guangxi Jiaoyu chubanshe, 1997. See also James T.C. Liu's *Reform in Sung China: Wang An-Shih (1021–1086) and His New Policies*, Cambridge, Mass.: Harvard University Press, 1959.

Liang Gengyao has argued strongly that the main point of the New Policies was increasing revenues, "Shiyifa shu," *Songdai Shehui Jingji Shi Lunji*, Taibei: Yunchen wenhua shiye gufen youxian gongsi, 1997, pp. 104–260.

As an example of the pro-reformist bias that informs much of the modern attitude about Wang's reforms, see Frederick Mote, *Imperial China*, who, on p. 142, describes the opposition to Wang in 1074 as "a cabal composed of the empress dowager and some court eunuchs who disliked Wang and resented his interference in practices from which they benefited." Since Professor Mote knows very well that the opposition Old Party was led by Sima Guang, and filled with the entire pantheon of Northern Song luminaries from Ouyang Xiu, to Su Shi, to the Cheng brothers, his characterization is odd. Following K.C. Hsiao, Mote maintains an overall positive view of Wang's efforts, though admitting that some specific policies were poorly considered, and attacks modern scholars who have attacked Wang Anshi. Since time and the partisan politics of the period have made it impossible to evaluate the real effects of most of the New Policies, it is impossible to judge the need for, or effects of, the New Policies fairly.

13 Bi Yuan, *Xu Zizhi Tongjian*, Shanghai: Shanghai Guji chubanshe, 1987, ch. 77, p. 398a.

14 Lin Ruihan, *Songdai Zhengzhishi*, Taibei: Zhengzhong shuju, 1989, pp. 293–299.

15 Ibid., pp. 300–312.

16 Peter Lorge, "Song Gaozong's letters to Yue Fei," *Journal of Sung–Yuan Studies*, 30 (2000), pp. 169–173.

CHAPTER THREE

Three empires and a century of war, 1142–1272

> I'd rather be a southern Chinese ghost than serve as a Jin official.
> Li Quan (d. 1231) a bandit of Shandong[1]

The Southern Song (as this period of Song rule is usually called) military situation in the twelfth and thirteenth centuries accelerated and deepened the growing split between the imperial government and local power-holders, a progression which has often been misunderstood as a civil–military split within Chinese society. Local military forces were larger, more important, and more powerful in southern China than they had ever been in the eleventh century, but civil officials were far more dominant at court. The court, which had never been much populated by generals, either on the throne or among the ministers, was extremely suspicious of the army and desperately dependent upon it. Military men, who arose from local militias that the government assimilated into its regular armies, or from northern Chinese who immigrated south, were shifted to the highly militarized border with the Jurchen and then Mongols. Civil officials were drawn from the southern local literati through the exam system, a system they had increasingly come to dominate even before the fall of Kaifeng, and tended to be less emotionally tied to north China. Southern literati understood the importance of retaking the north for the dynasty's political credibility, but they weighed the risks of failure more heavily. Since the court could never explicitly abandon the idea of recapturing the north, there was an inherent split between the "national" interest of the court and local interests of its officials.[2]

Civil officials had already taken over control of the Bureau of Military Affairs in the eleventh, which was the perhaps inevitable outcome of extended periods of peace, the need for a high level of literacy in administering a large bureaucracy, and the fierce competition for positions among exam graduates and other civil officials. In the Southern Song, the initial instability of the court made it highly suspicious of the military. Generals like Yue Fei (1103–1141) gained their authority from success in battle, not by the court's dispensation, something that was a fundamental threat to the court's power. Moreover, the military men who stubbornly pressed for a more belligerent posture made the court look dovish, also undermining its legitimacy. Civil officials like Li Gang (1083–1140) were simply sacked when they were on the wrong side of a debate; attempting to displace generals was much more dangerous. One such attempt in 1137 resulted in more than 40,000 troops mutinying and going over to the state of Chu across the Huai River. Managing the army and its generals was thus more dangerous than managing civil officials.

Subordinating the generals to civil control, which had been Song policy after Song Taizu's rule, kept control of war policy in the court's hands but structurally alienated the military from the government. This weakness in the Southern Song system would ultimately bring down the dynasty in the face of Mongol military pressure; it worked reasonably well during the Song–Jurchen relations. Civil dominance at court did not mean that Jurchen relations were always handled dovishly. There were quite enough hawkish men of letters, even southerners, who advocated war. Many hawks subscribed to a particular brand of Confucianism, sometimes called Neo-Confucianism, which was morally and ritually intolerant of the sort of political compromises the Song court had made to survive.

Southern Song literati culture was highly developed, but abstracted from the cradle of Chinese civilization in the north. In a similar vein, the literati were strongly connected to China's literate culture, but somewhat ambivalent about their relationship to a particular dynasty. Literati identity had developed early in the Song with the "objective" sanction of the exam system to designate those learned enough to be officials. While an official of the dynasty clearly owed it loyalty to the death, someone who did not pass the exams or serve the government did not. And like so many literati families, one's local ties were more important than theoretical ties to a dynasty. This pattern developed in the Song, and continued to the end of the imperial age.[3]

Matters were less stable on the political level in the Jurchen-controlled north.[4] Although the Jurchens had declared themselves to be a dynasty, the Jin, even before they had destroyed the Kitan empire, a basic tension remained between tribal institutions and Chinese imperial institutions. This was a problem which all steppe ruling groups faced. Tribal institutions were less hierarchical, less centralized, more dependent upon the particular relationships of a given leader to his peers and subordinates, non-bureaucratic and not literacy dependent. Chinese imperial institutions were extremely hierarchical, highly centralized, formally abstracted from a given individual, bureaucratic and run by paperwork. The Kitan solution had been a dual administration, with a northern chancellery to handle steppe affairs and a southern chancellery to handle the Chinese parts of its empire. The Jurchen progressed through a similar solution, before shifting almost entirely to a formal Chinese system, and then adding a few Jurchen flourishes to somewhat disguise that structure with nativist references. Generally, the Jurchen ruler preferred to be a Chinese emperor far above the other Jurchen leaders, while the Jurchen and other tribal leaders preferred the less hierarchical "native" traditions. Once the Jurchen did away with the puppet state of Qi in 1137, however, it was clearly easier to administer the former Song territories in a way similar to the manner they had been run. That required officials trained in Chinese bureaucratic institutions, whatever their putative ethnic background.

At the local level, the Jurchen were transferred en masse into northern China between the 1120s and 1140s, already divided into population units that supported particular field armies. Leadership of these units was hereditary, and, in theory, the Jurchen immigrants would retain their traditional values, skills and loyalties. That they did not is hardly surprising, though characterizing it as "sinification" is misleading. It has often been argued that steppe peoples have conquered China and then been "conquered" by Chinese culture, swallowed up by its richness, dominance and greater power. This is a sop to Chinese pride injured by military defeat (why can't such a great culture support a powerful military? – it doesn't need to since it ultimately defeats everyone), which tries to create a hegemonic narrative out of a practical choice. Ordinary Jurchen living in north China had much more in common with their Chinese neighbors, families who were living the same lifestyle and subject to similar problems, than with their Jurchen overlords at the Jin court. If they had some privileges their Chinese neighbors did not, they also had military responsibilities that could be considerably more onerous. Thus for ordinary Jurchens their process of assimilation was not so much one of sinification as localization.

Elite Jurchens, by contrast, now forced to operate within the Chinese imperial system favored by their emperor, pursued the literate tradition that would allow them to advance. By the time that the Chinese classics were translated into Jurchen, however, Jurchen interested in advancement through literacy could read Literary Chinese. There were thus two separate processes of assimilation or accommodation operating on the Jurchen, as they would on other steppe peoples in contact with China: localization and imperialization. In localization, a minority group gradually found itself more closely tied to the place and people it was living with than to more tenuous ties to a larger ethnic group. Of course, ethnic identification could sometimes be successfully called upon to reinvigorate those sorts of ties, but those sorts of efforts were hard to sustain for long because they simply made little sense in a day-to-day economic and personal sense. Over time, most of the ordinary Jurchen living in north China became part of local society, indistinguishable from the people who lived there before them.

Imperialization was confined to the elite, and much better represented in the written record. The Chinese imperial system was extremely well articulated by the tenth century, and attractive to paramount rulers. Steppe traditions were similarly well articulated, but much more dependent upon personality, and less given to long-term, stable political structures. Some might argue that these very different political systems were reflections of the lifestyles and cultures of the different peoples, sedentary versus steppe, but such unprovable assertions can just as easily be seen as tendentious rationalizations. What cannot be questioned is that there were different political systems, and that different people preferred different systems based upon their own power interests. Imperial systems run better with a unified written system to connect the governments that make up a given empire. The usefulness of a written language was clear to steppe rulers trying to keep control over their constructed polity, and all of the dynasts – Kitan, Tangut, Jurchen, or Mongol – had written versions of their spoken languages created. Some were more successful than others, but all faced over-whelming competition from the vast Chinese written tradition. There was simply more to read in Classical and Literary Chinese.

Rather than invent a new imperial system, steppe dynasts availed themselves of the Chinese one. The Mongols, who would soon rise to destroy the Jurchen, Song, and most of the ruling houses of Asia, went through a process similar to the Jurchens as they sought a stable political system that transcended an indi-vidual. Also like the Jurchens, it could be argued that the Mongols never really achieved political stability because the political founders of their campaigns of conquest did not conceive of what the ultimate political form of their empire would be. Both Aguda and Chinggis were skilled at consolidating political control over disparate and often hostile steppe tribes, and exploiting the military power of those unified groups, but neither laid a functional groundwork for an imperial system. The Jurchen Jin dynasty and the Mongol Yuan dynasty were relatively short-lived for Chinese dynasties. It is an open question whether localization of their steppe populations, with a consequent loss of steppe mili-tary skills, was more responsible for their respective demises than the political instability caused by the tension between the interests of imperialized elites and non-imperialized elites.

Chinese society at the local level changed very little with the change from Song to Jurchen and then Mongol rule. Most farmers were equally oppressed by their local elites, whether they cloaked their thuggery with higher learning or not, and the imperial government remained a predator regardless of the eth-nicity of its ruling house. The wars were extremely destructive, of course, and a community in the path of a major army would suffer immensely. Wars did offer opportunities for poor, uneducated young men to advance themselves, though most simply got killed, maimed, starved to death, or wiped out by disease. Cities were not safe places during wars, as they became the main targets of campaigns aimed at destroying a government's control over an area. It was the elites whose fortunes were most subject to changes in government, particularly those who had direct ties to a given dynasty. Imperial governments could not waste the effort on subduing every individual town and village, however, and readily settled for displacing the incumbent dynasty's control of the higher order political centers.

Northern China suffered repeated military incursions as the Mongols pounded the Jurchen empire apart.[5] Mongol warfare under Chinggis Khan was particularly destructive. Strategically, he was patient enough to wear down his opponents by what amounted to large-scale hit-and-run raids, which grad-ually eroded a government's revenues and legitimacy. Tactically, the sudden arrival of fast-moving cavalry armies denied an opponent time to mount a concerted defense, forcing them to prepare everywhere, and thus be weak everywhere, in anticipation of future raids. Mongol troops were intentionally destructive of the local population and goods, destroying what they could not usefully carry off. Since the Mongols did not present a political or military center within reach of the Jurchen armies, they had no response to these raids other than to prepare for more. This was a disaster for the Jurchen court as well as for the residents of northern China. The destruction of the Jurchen conquest, followed by that of the Mongol conquest, further exacerbated the north's already diminished economic fortunes.

The economy and society of southern China continued to thrive and develop despite the threat on its northern border. While the northern defense line was highly militarized, the rest of Song territory was not subject to direct disruption. Southern Song society was still extremely localized, and the diversion of most imperial forces to the border forced communities to develop their own defense capabilities against banditry.[6] These developments within the diminished Song empire were overtaken by the rise of the Mongols as a consolidated political and military force. In sharp contrast to their rapid success against the Jurchen and many other kingdoms in Eurasia, the Mongols took half a century of enervating war to conquer the Song. This protracted war exacerbated the preexisting north–south split in Chinese culture and society.

The Jurchen failure and the Mongol success in conquering the Song demonstrate once again the importance to a would-be Chinese empire builder of developing a powerful enough riverine navy to achieve control of the rivers. The Jurchen simply failed to create such a navy, imagining that they simply needed to get their troops to the south side of the Huai or Yangzi rivers to accomplish their goals. Crossing either river without control of it was often simply impossible. The Mongols learned this lesson, and were eventually able to conquer the Song. Nevertheless, the Song–Mongol struggle was remarkably even for decades. Where in other theaters of war the Mongols reached the ecological limits of their mode of warfare as much as anything else, in central China they were fought to a standstill by the Song army for half a century. The contest was very similar to the enervating Song–Jin struggle that began in earnest in 1161.

Prince Hailing and Jurchen failure[7]

The 1141–1142 Shaoxing Treaty had satisfied neither the Song nor the Jurchen, and it was only a matter of time before one side tried to overturn it. Song Gaozong may well have wished he could have retaken the north, or at least renegotiated a less disadvantageous treaty with the Jurchen, but he was not the man to order such an attempt. His reign had already been strenuous enough. Matters were considerably different at the Jurchen court. Emperor Xizong, who had ruled since 1135, was murdered and his throne seized by his cousin. Like Xizong, the man who replaced him, known to us as Prince Hailing despite holding the imperial throne until 1161, was well educated in Chinese literate culture. Hailing was also at least as personally violent and decadent as his cousin, if not more so, and perhaps even more sinified. He determined to transform Jurchen government into Chinese imperial government, and to overcome the political problems that entailed by conquering the Song. In his ambition and method for establishing a Chinese imperial government he was very similar to the founders of the Song, Ming and Qing dynasties, except for one crucial fact: he lost the war.

Hailing openly expressed his intention to conquer the Song on several occasions to Song envoys, but formal planning only began in January 1159, when he ordered warships built, registers made of adult males between the ages of 20 and 50, and weapons manufactured. This put an immense strain on an already overtaxed system, since he was also undertaking the reconstruction of the palaces at Kaifeng and the refurbishment of Yanjing. Prices for goods skyrocketed; some 240,000 Jurchen, Kitan and Xi men were registered, along with a further 270,000 Chinese men. Gaozong, for his part, continued to discount the reports of a Jurchen military build-up.

By April of 1161, Gaozong could no longer deny that invasion was imminent, and finally ordered that defense preparations be made. Jurchen envoys arrived in June seeking the territory along the Huai and Han rivers, an obviously impossible request. Advance Jurchen forces began raiding Song territory on 25 September, and met stiff resistance. Ethnic Chinese in the Central Plains began to respond to Song calls to rebel against Jurchen rule. Prince Hailing launched a four-pronged offensive across the Huai River with an army reportedly one million strong (but probably more like 600,000). Like the Later Zhou, the Jurchen also constructed a pontoon bridge spanning the river. Unlike the Jurchens' previous experience of fighting the Song, they lost more battles than they won, even in direct confrontations. Some cities changed hands, sometimes repeatedly, but the most important contest was taking place on the water. There the contest was decidedly one-sided, with the Song navy winning every battle, usually decisively.

Farther north, disgruntled Jurchen tribesmen, some from the imperial clan, decided to put an end to Prince Hailing's rule, and set up a new emperor. By 15 December the Jurchen commanders in central China had also had enough, and they assassinated Hailing and started peace talks with the Song. Battles and skirmishes continued intermittently as the Jurchen army struggled to disengage and regroup while still maintaining military pressure for the peace talks. This was a losing strategy, however, as they fared no better late in the campaign than they had earlier. The Jurchen army was also needed in the north to put down the various rebellions that Prince Hailing's exactions and ill-considered campaign had produced. The war was not over with the failure of the Jurchens offensive and Hailing's death, however, since thus far the Song had only proved itself capable of a competent defense. For the first time, the strategic initiative lay with the Song.

Gaozong, Xiaozong and the Longxing Treaty

The decisive repulse of the Jurchen offensive, though costly in Song casualties and money, raised the possibility of retaking the north. It was not just the generally good performance of the Song army and navy that fostered these ambitions, but also Jurchen political instability. Gaozong was hopeful, but he was still not the man to take responsibility for such a campaign. Consequently, he stepped down as emperor in favor of his adopted son, posthumously known as Xiaozong, and set his successor to sort out the military situation. This allowed Gaozong to sidestep any responsibility for failure, and to avoid the pressure of another round of campaigns. Xiaozong supported the old, irredentist minister Zhang Jun, brought back to the court by Gaozong, in his bid to shift to an active effort to retake the north.

Opinion at the Song court was still divided in 1162, as indeed it must have been with the return of the radical hawk, Zhang Jun (1096–1164), to a previously peace-at-all-costs court. The Jurchen invasion had started a war that had yet to be resolved, and certainly failed in their military objectives. It was even less clear whether the fluid military situation could or should be exploited militarily, politically, or both. The possibility of improving the Song's position with respect to the Jurchens in any way, even if at the most minor ritual level, created a political imperative to do something. But what? Even assuming that it was militarily possible to retake the north, this would not be easy to do, and would require immense preparation. At the same time, however, the theoretical window of military opportunity might be closing as the Jurchens stabilized their political situation and put down the various rebellions that had broken out.

The concerns of the doves, or at least those skeptical of the possibility of retaking the north, should not be dismissed out of hand. It was probably not possible for the Song army to have prepared and mounted a successful northern campaign in 1162, or even 1163. Much of the strength of the Song defense had been due to the navy, which would be of very limited help once the army crossed the Huai River. The Song army was extremely weak in cavalry, the Jurchen army's strength, which would become a serious problem in the terrain of Central Plains. At root, the Song army was weaker than the Jurchen army, but their difference was small enough that the added strength of fighting defensively had tipped the balance in the Song favor. Even though there had been some Chinese uprisings in response to Song calls during Hailing's invasion, they by no means indicated a truly mass effort by ethnically Chinese people to throw off Jurchen rule and return to the Song. Most Chinese people did not respond to the Song calls, and those who did were in the process of being put down by the Jurchen army.

By 1163, with Jurchen troops gathering for another possible invasion, Xiaozong allowed Zhang Jun to try to retake north China.[8] On 18 June, the Song army crossed the Huai River and quickly defeated a Jurchen force that opposed it. Several other Jurchen armies were defeated in rapid succession, and Xiaozong wrote to Zhang Jun praising him for the greatest victories in ten years. All was not well in the army, however, as an old grudge between the two highest generals compounded a disunified command structure to create internal divisions. When a 100,000-man Jurchen force arrived to retake the city the Song army had captured, the fragmented leadership prevented all of the Song army's units from acting together. Even as Li Xianzhong, the overall commander, saw an opportunity to crush the Jurchen with a concerted attack, his assistant was undermining morale and dissuading the other commanders from facing the Jurchen. With his subordinates already withdrawing, Li had no choice but to retreat himself. His shattered army reached Fuli on 27 June, the entire incident going down in history as "The Rout of the Fuli Expedition."[9]

Zhang Jun's policies were now disgraced, and the peace faction returned to power; Xiaozong was no longer as enthusiastic about trying to recapture the north. Much of the blame for the expedition's failure deservedly fell on Zhang for his poor preparation and choice of generals. Many hawks were extremely frustrated by the failure, seeing it as both a lost opportunity and new ammunition against any future northern campaign. Xiaozong balanced his own irredentist ambitions against the need to shift policies by openly supporting Zhang Jun while entering peace talks. The emperor made it clear that he shared responsibility with Zhang for what happened, and that he would not be severely punished for the failure of those policies. Even though the expedition had failed, however, the Jurchen were not inclined to continue the war.

The Jurchen broached the subject of peace on 19 September, setting territorial claims, continuation of the annual payments, the Song court assuming a subservient position, and the return of northern rebels as the conditions.[10] Zhang Jun saw the matter in terms of power: if the Jurchen were strong, they would attack; it they were weak, then they would stop. A formally established peace had no bearing on the question of whether or not the Jurchen would invade. This was logical, but not actually true; since the Jurchen court directly benefited from the Song's annual payments, the Jurchen leadership was not completely confident that they could win a military contest, and the Jurchens did not share the Song's need to unify "China." It was, after all, the highly sinified ruler Prince Hailing who was so interested in destroying the Song. This was a paradigmatic example of the sinocentric view that imagines that all barbarians always want to conquer and take over the Chinese empire. In political terms, Zhang was trying to salvage the possibility of future northern expeditions.

There were two peace factions, though one did not represent itself as such. The main peace faction continued the same position it had always held: survival with what they had was better than risking everything by starting a war. The second peace faction disguised its position by making peace not the end in itself but a temporary condition. This faction argued for a long-range plan of self-improvement, while awaiting an uprising in the Central Plains. While certainly more palatable, the effect was the same. The Song court was faced with not so much whether or not to make peace, which seemed the best course of action, but under what conditions. As an initial bargaining position, Xiaozong was convinced to reject the Jurchens' conditions.

Negotiations continued until late January 1165, when the Jurchen agreed to forgo any territorial claims, accept a reduction in the annual payment, change the relationship between the two emperors from "ruler–official" to "uncle–nephew," and not require the return of all rebels. The Song court had certainly improved its position after Prince Hailing's invasion and their own failed counter-invasion, winning some significant concessions in the negotiations. Xiaozong had been compelled to accept the conditions by Gaozong, who was extremely pleased by the change in ritual status between the two courts. Jurchen concessions presumably indicate a change in their confidence and priorities with respect to the Song. The new Jurchen emperor had more important things to do with his resources than to make war on the Song.

Han Tuozhou's campaign

While culture was enjoying a brief resurgence in north China, politics in Song China took a turn for the worse after Xiaozong's death in 1194. Both Gaozong and Xiaozong had been actively concerned with the running of the government, despite the immense power of Qin Gui (1090–1155) at Gaozong's court. Xiaozong was careful not to allow any grand councilor the same kind of power or length of tenure in office. His successors were much less capable or concerned, which allowed for considerable political turmoil. An imperial relation, Han Tuozhou (?–1207), managed to achieve the same kind of power toward the end of the twelfth century that Qin Gui had held in the middle of the century. Han defeated many of his political opponents by convincing the emperor that their philosophical school was "false learning," and the means through which they deceived the emperor and controlled the government. By 1205, Han was in full control of the government.

Like Prince Hailing, Han Tuozhou believed that a grand military success would make him politically invincible. He was undoubtedly correct politically, but his military plans were utterly impractical. As early as 1204, Han had begun discussing a campaign against the Jurchen, seeing that the Jurchen army had recently suffered repeated disasters and the government's coffers were empty. Han was correct in his belief that the Jurchens were no longer as formidable militarily as they had been, but he overestimated the extent of that decline, as well as the Song army's ability to project power.[11] He initially encouraged Han people along the Song–Jurchen border to rebel, to destabilize the area, occupy the Jurchen army, and to gather intelligence on conditions. With the emperor's sanction, he began a military build-up. Han also had Yue Fei posthumously promoted, and later had Qin Gui posthumously demoted.

Despite Han's preparations, and his control of the court, a military academy student protested against the coming campaign, and suggested that Han be beheaded. At the same time, the Jurchen court heard that a Song invasion was in the offing and, while many ministers dismissed the possibility, others suggested making military preparations. It was, after all, almost impossible to hope for strategic or tactical surprise in a major military undertaking. Nevertheless, the campaign seemed to start well with some minor territorial gains in May of 1206. These victories convinced Han to have an official edict announce the campaign against the Jurchen in June. Events in the field almost immediately began to go wrong, as Song attacks failed, and Song armies were defeated by Jurchen counter-attacks.

The Song offensive had failed completely by July, and the Jurchen army actually began shifting over to its own offensive in August. This was by no means an active invasion; Jurchen goals were entirely defensive at this point. As the Song army cracked under the counter-offensive, however, the Song court began to worry that the Jurchen army might not just cross the Huai River but the Yangzi as well. Neither side had been well prepared for an extended campaign, so military action bogged down, with the Jurchen forces generally the winners. Failing to obtain the quick and relatively easy victory he expected, the Song emperor readily shifted to peace negotiations. The eventual settlement, reached in 1208, restored what the Jurchen had given up in 1165, and included a demand for Han Tuozhou's head. This was duly produced, and peace was again restored.

Chinggis Khan and the rise of the Mongols[12]

Just as the Han Tuozhou was beginning his ill-advised war against the Jurchen, a man by the name of Temüjin, from the Mongol tribe, was recognized as Universal Ruler or Chinggis Khan by the confederation of steppe tribes he had managed to unite under his leadership in 1206. Temüjin would soon come closer to living up to that title than any man in history. Yet Chinggis Khan, the great conqueror, was not a particularly brilliant general or accomplished warrior, nor was he physically very brave. His abilities in all three areas were respectable, he could not have become a steppe leader otherwise, but he most distinguished himself as a politician, both strategically and charismatically. Chinggis's armies overran most of Asia because he had managed to unite disparate and often warring steppe tribes and turn their preexisting military capabilities outward. His tactics were not innovative, and it seems the only substantive change he imposed upon the steppe armies was to spread a decimal organization system throughout his entire forces. These minor military matters had no real effect on his successes.

Chinggis defies simple description, and not just because the records on his life are so limited. He is the paradigmatic example of a ruthless power-seeker, who used political and military means to elevate himself to unprecedented heights of power, never since equaled, for no other reason than power itself. He was ruthless to his enemies and magnanimous to his followers. Mongol warfare destroyed existing political structures by defeating a state's army, and by reducing its legitimacy and financial base by devastating the countryside. Like the Jurchen before them, the Mongols concentrated their campaigns on the enemy leadership, rather than on gradually taking and holding territory. Once the leadership had capitulated, their state, its territory and resources could be politically incorporated into the Mongol empire. Secondarily, looting and living off the enemy's lands cheaply supplied and rewarded the Mongol armies.

Yet Chinggis's role in all this remains central. The Mongols were unable to remain unified after his death, though they remained a potent military force. The lure of sedentary wealth in different and distant lands certainly contributed to their loss of a common cultural and political orientation, but that change occurred after Chinggis's death. Somehow he managed to choose great generals, balance their ambitions against their loyalty to him, and maintain the precarious political structure of his empire. He was a master politician, and he understood that only an outward military project could satisfy the martial inclinations of his steppe followers and prevent them from turning all of their attentions to each other. Still he was unable to provide for a stable succession, and Mongol culture did not contain the imperial framework that so many of the states within its new empire did.

Chinggis did not immediately attack the Jurchen empire, preferring to pry loose several surrounding steppe tribes and buffer warlords. The Uigher state, based at Gaochang, surrendered to Chinggis in April of 1209 without being threatened. Given the choice between attacking the Tanguts and attacking the Jurchen, Chinggis, like the Song dynasty in the eleventh century, chose to attack the Tanguts first. Chinggis personally led the Mongol invasion in the spring of 1209, which succeeded in surrounding the Tangut capital at Yinchuan in October. An attempt to flood the city, escalade having failed, went awry, inundating besieged and besieger alike. It was nonetheless clear to the Tanguts that they might, at best, temporarily put off subjugation, but that the Mongols were capable of destroying them sooner or later. The Tangut ruler acknowledged Chinggis's overlordship, promised to provide soldiers for future Mongol campaigns, and married a Tangut princess to Chinggis. The Mongol army then withdrew having accomplished its goal.

In early 1211, Mongol forces began raiding across the Jurchen's northwest border, Chinggis having broken relations with the Jurchen court the previous year. By May of 1211, having noted that other neighboring polities like the Tanguts had already accommodated themselves to the looming threat, the Jurchen court sought peace with the Mongols. Chinggis rejected the Jurchen overture, no doubt accurately reading it as a sign of weakness. Jurchen efforts to bolster their northwestern defenses were incomplete when Chinggis overran them, and sent a separate army under his son to attack Datong, the Jurchen Western Capital. His son captured the city in only seven days, after chasing down and defeating its commander, who had fled the city. Mongol armies now fanned out to raid Jurchen territory, accepting the surrenders of local Jurchen officials and subject peoples along the way.

The Jurchen court, after rejecting a fast attack on the Mongol force regrouping in Fuzhou, under Chinggis, advanced its reputedly 400,000 strong army slowly toward them. Chinggis obtained detailed intelligence of the advancing army, and proceeded to deal it a series of devastating defeats, inflicting tremendous casualties, much aided by major Jurchen commanders attempting to flee rather than fight. Mongol armies chased down these commanders and routed their armies individually, opening the way to Juyong Pass. When advance Mongol forces reached the pass, the Jurchen commander fled, allowing them to seize it. The way was now open to the Jurchen Central Capital, at modern Beijing. Mongol scouts were soon beneath the city's walls, prompting the Jurchen emperor to consider fleeing to Kaifeng. The Mongol siege itself was fairly brief, about a month, but it demonstrated the utter ineptitude of the Jurchen leadership to formulate a reasonable, effective response to the crisis. Few Jurchen commanders seemed ready to fight for their dynasty.

The 1211 campaign may well have been aimed at gathering loot and intelligence, but that seems a rationalization for an incursion which overreached itself and made the following year's progress more difficult. Chinggis had probably not expected to penetrate so far into Jurchen territory, or to capture Datong and Juyong Pass. Once in the Yan plain around the Jurchen Central Capital, he was wholly unprepared to conduct a serious siege or to exploit his advance more fully. He withdrew beyond Juyong Pass, but still apparently within what had previously been the Jurchen outer defense line, allowing the critical pass to be reoccupied. It seems most likely that the 1211 campaign had originally aimed to penetrate the outermost line of Jurchen defenses in preparation for a follow-on effort aimed at the Jurchen Central Capital.

When Chinggis returned to the field in late 1212 he was unable to force his way through Juyong Pass, and another, less well defended, pass had to be found in order to outflank this defense line. The Mongol army then drove into the Central Plains, extending their looting and destruction through Shanxi, Hebei and Shandong. These raiding forces generally avoided fortified positions in order to preserve their own strength, while wreaking destruction as broadly as possible. This was warfare at its most ruthless, done to weaken an opponent and politically pressure him without regard for civilian suffering. The Mongol army roamed throughout the Central Plains for most of 1213, before turning north to blockade the Jurchen Central Capital later in the year. Although Chinggis was unable to capture the city, early in 1214 the Jurchen emperor bought him off with gold, silk and horses, and also by recognizing Chinggis as his overlord. The Jurchen emperor was newly installed on the throne, the previous emperor having been assassinated by one of the failed Jurchen generals in September of 1213. Chinggis had succeeded in his goal of subjugating the Jurchen.

It is tempting, in retrospect, to see the Mongol destruction of the Jurchen empire as inevitable at this point, but that end would only be accomplished after another two decades of hard fighting. Chinggis was usually content to obtain a ruler's submission, and did not make total destruction of a kingdom his main goal. Having clearly demonstrated his superior military capabilities, capitulation was the only reasonable, or at least survivable, political course. The Jurchen could well have continued as a subordinate state within the Mongol empire, had the emperor not tried to put some distance between himself and his Mongol overlord. Within months of the Mongol army's departure, the Jurchen court moved to Kaifeng, which became its new capital. Chinggis found out about the move in the fall of the same year, and sent an army to capture the Jurchen's former Central Capital. The Mongols were once again unable to surmount or otherwise overcome the city's walls, but they were able to block any Jurchen relief forces from saving the city. When it became clear to the defenders that there was no hope of rescue, they surrendered in May of 1215. At about the same time, another Mongol army had destroyed Jurchen power in their old homeland of Manchuria, and freed many Kitan from Jurchen rule. These Kitan duly incorporated themselves into the Mongolian empire. It is unclear whether Chinggis was set upon destroying the Jurchen empire at that point; it was certainly within his power, but he was distracted just then by pressing events to his west. Further campaigning against the Jin was left to his extremely capable general Mukhali, who established a semblance of Mongol rule, mostly preventing anti-Mongol action, in Shanxi, Hebei and Shandong.

Li Quan and the contest for Shandong[13]

Chinggis's raids into Shandong, Hebei and Shanxi badly destabilized Jurchen rule, giving rise to a plethora of bandits, local strongmen and "loyalist" armies burning for the return of Song dynasty rule. The Song court could not ignore the possibilities of Jurchen weakness, but it was reluctant openly to support anti-Jurchen armies. It was not clear in the early thirteenth century whether or not the Jurchen empire would survive, or in what form, nor was it certain that the Jurchen army's failure against the Mongols made it any less dangerous to the Song. A sort of covert war was therefore pursued, where some of the more successful warlords who claimed to be Song loyalists were secretly supplied with food and money. These resources were particularly crucial after the Mongols had devastated great swathes of the Central Plains and Shandong. In pursuit of local power and economic resources, a man by the name of Li Quan emerged in eastern Shandong to lead a massive bandit-cum-Song "loyalist" army against the Jurchen.

Song reticence about an open break with the Jurchen court was overcome when the Jurchens attacked them in 1217. It was true that the Song had taken advantage of the Jurchen court's crisis to stop their annual payments in 1214, and that the Jurchens were desperately in need of funds, but the attack was extremely ill advised. The Jurchens, like the Kitan before them, had never established peaceful relations with the Song, in the sense of a mutually satisfactory co-existence valued by both sides. They could not ask the Song for help against the Mongols, nor could they try to convince them that even a temporary alliance of convenience was in their interests. Their only recourse then was either to move themselves south at the Song's expense or to force the Song court to remit the annual payments. So, while Mukhali was capturing the strategic cities of Shanxi (Taiyuan, 1218), Hebei (Daming, 1220) and Shandong (Ji'nan, 1220), the Jurchen court was devoting considerable resources to an inconclusive war with the Song.

Li Quan's Red Coat Army became very important to the Song in weakening Jurchen offensives. By 1220, Li had become so much of a problem that the Jurchen mustered a force to destroy him at his base in eastern Shandong. Li was saved from possible defeat when Mukhali attacked and destroyed this new Jurchen army in order to secure control of western Shandong. But Li was not the only local strongman in Shandong, and all three sides – the Song, Mongols and Jurchen – actively began to recruit local leaders and troops. Shandong became the cockpit of the struggle between the three empires for control of north China. Li Quan, like most of the Shandong strongmen, was not truly loyal to any particular government, despite the titles he received from the Song court and his theatric pronouncements of fealty. To be fair to Li, however, the Song was similarly uncommitted to any particular strongman, as they tried to balance their need to find effective forces against their need to control them. As Li became stronger, the Song court became more anxious about his loyalties. His eventual break with the Song was thus almost inevitable.

Song efforts to diminish Li Quan's power by breaking up his army were only partially successful. When the Song court tried to take advantage of the Mongols besieging Li in Qingzhou in 1226 to get his subordinates to break with him, the attempt badly miscarried. Li was now even prepared to consider switching his allegiance to the Jurchen, as two former subordinates of his had already done. He did not reject a Jurchen offer in 1227 out of hand as he had previously done, which proved to the Song court that he was, in fact, disloyal. Given how much they had done to undermine him, Li must have concluded that he no longer had a future with the Song. Jurchen rule was clearly failing, or, in any case, too distant to relieve his siege, leaving only the Mongols as a practical option. After a year under siege, Li duly surrendered to the Mongols and was placed in charge of Shandong.

Li's loyalties were still uncertain, however, and he continued to exploit the power struggle among the three powers to further his own position. He began actively to recruit northerners in southern China, and build ships for his own navy, while allying himself with the Jurchen and requiring the Song to send him provisions to keep the border safe. It was clear to some that he was planning to invade the Song even before he openly admitted it, but with an army of about 100,000 crack troops, the Song court was reluctant to antagonize him. Li's need for food and money from the Song delayed taking revenge on the Song for killing his older brother, son and concubine. The unstable relationship continued until Li formally rebelled at the end of 1230, and the Song emperor was convinced that he should send an army to suppress him.

Li was then occupied with besieging Yangzhou, where he had settled in to starve the city. He was killed in battle near the city in February of 1231. At his commanders' request, his wife, Yang Miaozhen, then took over command of the army. Yang led the army back to Shandong, knowing that, as she did so, the Song army would recapture the territory her husband had just taken. She was most concerned at that time to consolidate control over her late husband's territory for their adopted son, Tan. After an audience with her Mongol superiors in 1233, she was confirmed in power, which she held briefly before handing control to Tan. Hereditary control of lands was a standard Mongol practice, so this posed no customary problems. The Mongols were certainly willing to keep a nominally loyal local ruler in power in Shandong while they destroyed the final remnants of the Jurchen.

The end of the Tanguts and Chinggis's death[14]

When Chinggis had been pulled away from the destruction of the Jurchen empire in 1218, the Tanguts had refused to honor their earlier promises to supply him with troops. They did send troops to aid Mukhali a few years later, and then withdrew them in 1223. The Tangut court's behavior was extremely odd, for they then proceeded not only to not respond to a final Mongol offer of peace but also to sign a treaty with the Jurchens in 1225. Chinggis attacked the following year, this time determined to destroy the Tangut state, rather than merely put pressure on its court. By the end of the summer he had overrun several cities and was approaching the Tangut capital, Zhongxing. Late in 1226, Chinggis crushed a large Tangut army trying to relieve Lingzhou, south of Zhongxing. He invested the Tangut capital itself early the next year.

While the siege of Zhongxing dragged on through 1227, Chinggis sent forces to attack the western border of the Jurchen empire. These incursions might have developed into a full-scale invasion after the Tangut issue was settled, but the Universal Ruler became ill and died in August. His death was kept secret until after the Tangut capital was captured and sacked in September. Mongol operations slowed considerably as Chinggis's body was interred and the matter of his succession settled. There was no question that Chinggis had designated his third son, Ögödei, to succeed him, and that other dispensations of territory would be made to his other sons as per his orders. Ögödei was, in theory, supreme among the sons, though distance and sibling rivalry mitigated this in practice. He became Khaghan (khan of khans) in 1229, to distinguish him from his brothers who were all now khans, in 1229, and began operations against the Jurchen empire in 1231. Other Mongol armies also renewed their campaigns across Asia.

The end of the Jurchens[15]

A massive three-pronged attack aimed at Kaifeng commenced in 1231, with the westernmost column actually passing through Song territory in northern Sichuan to avoid Jurchen defenses. The Song had refused the Mongol request for passage, leaving Tolui, the commanding general, to ignore their refusal and pass through their territory anyway. This was an early sign of how poorly the Song court understood the Mongols and the threat they posed. Ögödei returned to Mongolia after Kaifeng was surrounded in the summer of 1232, leaving the protracted siege as it dragged on into the next year. The garrison surrendered several weeks after the last Jurchen emperor managed to flee the city in February of 1233, with the Mongols actually entering the city in May. The Jurchen emperor finally committed suicide in Caizhou in early 1234, besieged by a Song–Mongol army.

The Song court's attempt to establish a more productive relationship with the Mongols fell foul of its own irredentist ambitions and serious underestimation of Mongol military power. Although the Song army participated in the Mongol *coup d'grâce* of the Jurchen regime, it was by no means an equal partner. A less emotionally driven court might have been able to accept that the Mongols would not simply yield north China to the Song, that the Mongol army was the superior force, and that a wiser course would have been to subordinate itself to the new dominant power. This was obviously beyond the emotional and intellectual capabilities of the Song court, and it chose, instead, to launch a badly organized campaign to seize three of their former capitals after the Mongol armies withdrew. The campaign was also fueled by a political struggle at court, with one side, once again, attempting to bolster its position by a great military success. On the military side, it was pressed by the generals who had just defeated Li Quan, and wanted to make sure a rival did not receive sole glory for retaking the capitals.

What became known as the "Duanping reign Luoyang campaign" never even made it to Luoyang.[16] A 10,000-strong force reached Kaifeng in July of 1234, followed by the main army of 50,000 men. The army was ambushed by the Mongols on its way to Luoyang, however, and destroyed. In a single ill-considered stroke, the Song court needlessly poisoned its relations with the Mongols, and threw itself into a political struggle that distracted it at a critical time. The Mongols had carefully fulfilled the terms of their agreement with the Song in their joint campaign against the Jurchen, despite the Song army's less-than-required performance (a repeat of the Song–Jurchen alliance against the Kitan). The Song court could not claim the high moral ground for its actions, nor even the practical basis of military opportunity. Bad policy decisions had endangered the empire.

Möngke's campaign against the Song

The Song court did not pay an immediate price for bungling its relations with the Mongols. Ögödei was occupied with consolidating and exploiting his hold over the former Jurchen empire, and the Song army was obviously no threat to that, so a serious attack was not urgent. The Khaghan was beginning to face the administrative problems his father had ignored. At root was the choice between a Mongolian style of rule, wherein individual princes and aristocrats were given mostly independent appanages to rule and exploit as they would, and a more centralized system, where the Khaghan's government bureaucrats directly controlled the subject populations and their resources. No final solution was ever really reached on this issue by Ögödei or any of his successors, since each one's political and military situation demanded greater or lesser concessions to the other Mongol aristocrats. Neither a fully Mongol nor a fully centralized system, nor even a split, Kitan-style administration, was instituted, but a variety of messy compromises somewhere in between. Even apart from the kind of administration, there was also the issue of how best to exploit the subject population, which was ultimately the rulers' interest. Thus, under Ögödei, while one minister could suggest a centralized financial system of taxation, another suggested depopulating north China and turning it into pasture land. Although the former won the day by arguing that more could be gained by taxation, it could have gone the other way.

Ögödei spent most of his years following the Jurchen conquest in dissolute alcoholism, dying on a hunting trip on 11 December 1241. A brief regency followed, before the contested elevation of Güyüg in 1246. The circumstances of his enthronement, combined with personal inclinations and failings, caused government administration under Güyüg to swing back toward decentralization. Güyüg was also a prodigious drinker, and often in poor health, which exacerbated the uncertainties of the already unstable Mongolian political milieu. In a surprising act of vigor, in 1247 Güyüg set in motion a plan to face down and destroy one of his major political rivals, Batu. The confrontation never took place, however, as Güyüg died en route in the spring of 1248.

Another regency followed Güyüg's death, with the intense competition between the rival descendant lines of Chinggis's sons concluding with Möngke's elevation to Khaghan in 1250, and then again, somewhat more convincingly, in 1251. The new Khaghan's enthronement by no means ended the violent rivalries within the Mongolian ruling line. This continuous rivalry was the most significant weakness of Mongol rule. For the moment, however, Möngke proved to be an effective ruler. He instituted a wide-ranging centralization of financial and political power in his own hands, and restarted the campaigns of conquest that the regencies and succession struggles had delayed.

Although Möngke ordered campaigns in western Asia and Korea, he only personally participated in the campaign to conquer Song China. His younger brother Khubilai, whose appanage was in north China, was ordered to conquer

Dali, a kingdom in Yunnan to the southwest of Song territory, as a prelude to the larger effort to conquer the Song. The campaign was risky, as well as logistically challenging, because of the mountainous jungle terrain, but Khubilai acquitted himself reasonably well. It began in 1253, and Khubilai was soon able to defeat the main Dali army after some initial difficulties, but the Dali ruler resisted stubbornly, and it was not until 1255 that the kingdom was subjugated.[17]

Möngke began open discussions of plans to conquer the Song in 1256, though he did not actually take the field until the fall of 1258. Unhindered by a major river-crossing, the Mongol campaign into Sichuan was initially successful, and Möngke stormed or compelled the surrender of numerous Song towns and cities. His efforts began to founder in early 1259, however, at the city of Hezhou. He was forced to abandon the siege in July, just as Khubilai and another Mongol army were about to commence their invasions of the Song in central China, and a third Mongol army was marching northeast from con-quered Dali. Möngke's plan was completely aborted when he died in August, once again throwing the Mongol leadership into a bitter political struggle.[18]

Khubilai initially resisted abandoning his attack on the Song city of Ezhou, only relenting in early 1260 when his wife informed him that his own lands were threatened. Song troops soon dislodged the small Mongol force he had left behind, much to the inflated military glory of the Song chief councilor, Jia Sidao (1213–1275). Perhaps even more significantly, Khubilai's withdrawal after failing to take the city inclined Jia to reject Khubilai's subsequent offers of peace terms. These terms were similar to what the Song had accepted from the Kitan and then Jurchen, but Jia had staked his political position on belligerent oppos-ition, and rejected repeated overtures. His intransigence would soon destroy the Song.

Khubilai's victory and Li Tan's rebellion[19]

Khubilai's struggle for dominance with his younger brother Arigh Böke lasted until 1263, giving him tenuous claim to the title of Khaghan. The struggle had pitted a Mongol controlling the resources of a sedentary, agricultural society against a Mongol isolated in the steppe. Arigh Böke might have been able to survive living a traditional steppe lifestyle, but he could not supply armies, win and maintain political allies or even construct a large polity without access to extensive resources. Once he was cut off from those resources, his position became untenable. Khubilai benefited from years of cultivating the productivity of his sedentary territories, and drew closer to those lands as he harnessed their resources for his war. He would have been on his way to further commitments to Chinese institutions had Li Tan and a number of other Chinese regional strongmen previously loyal to the Mongols not rebelled in early 1262.

Li Tan, like his father Quan before him, was mostly interested in his own economic self-interest. He managed an extensive trade in all manner of licit and illicit goods between Mongol and Song territories, took as little part in Mongol attacks on the Song as possible, and generally worked to preserve his own power. He kept in touch with other Chinese regional strongmen in north China who had also been given hereditary control of their own territory by the Mongols, and patronized literati. Li even worked to undermine Mongol–Song peace talks, since much of the basis of his power was his critical position on the border. Khubilai was aware of these actions, as well as Li's disobedience to his court in matters of taxes, trade and law. Like the disobedient Mongol princes, the hereditary Chinese strongmen had to be brought under control.

In 1260, Khubilai set up a system of government officials to supervise these hereditary nobles, with the intention of applying Han law on Han officials. The following year, he replaced one of these nobles, Yan Zhongji, with his younger brother, Yan Zhongfan, thus maintaining that family's hereditary rights while also asserting the Khaghan's right to choose who was in charge. It was clear to Li Tan that his own days were numbered, so he decided to rebel while Khubilai was occupied fighting Arigh Böke. He surrendered to the Song, who accepted him after some initial suspicions, and tried to link up with the other Chinese hereditary nobles in north China. Neither of these strategies proved very helpful, and he was soon surrounded in Ji'nan and captured after a failed suicide attempt. Li was then executed Mongolian-style by being tied in a sack and trampled to death by horses.

Li Tan's rebellion made Khubilai much more suspicious of his Chinese subjects, despite his growing use of Chinese-style imperial institutions. He had already instituted a reign period for his rule as Khaghan over China in 1260, and was edging toward more sinified imperial ceremonies just as he was also moving to conquer the Song. The Dali staging area Khubilai had worked so hard to capture was no longer useful, and Sichuan itself had become even more formidably fortified in depth since Möngke's aborted invasion. This time the Mongols headed directly into one of the strongest points on the Song defense line, the city of Xiangyang. The struggle for Xiangyang, which lasted from 1268 to 1273, was a struggle not just for a city but also for the allegiance of the Lu family, who controlled most of the Song defense line in central China. That struggle is part of the final destruction of the Song empire, and will be dealt with in the next chapter.

As Khubilai invaded the Song, he also established a Chinese covering for his rule. In 1272 he proclaimed the founding of a new dynasty, the Yuan, fully in keeping with the appearance of Chinese rule. Khubilai was now a Chinese emperor, with Chinggis and his successors all given appropriate posthumous Chinese imperial titles. Perhaps more importantly, Khubilai would soon demonstrate that he had the military power to match his new title.

Notes

1 Quoted in Huang K'uan-ch'ung, "Geju shili, jingji liyi yu zhengzhi jueze," *Nansong Difang Wuli*, Taibei: Dongda tushu gongsi, 2002, p. 275.

2 This discussion follows Huang K'uan-chung, "Cong Hezhan dao Nanbeiren" in *Zhongguo Lishishang de Fenyu He Xueshu Yantao hui Lunwen Ji*, Taibei: Lianhe baixi wenhua jijinhui, 1995.

3 Richard L. Davis, *Wind Against the Mountain*, Cambridge, Mass.: Harvard University Press, 1996, is a broad-ranging discussion of loyalty and the motivations behind sacrifice for a dynasty.

4 Herbert Franke, "The Chin Dynasty," in Herbert Franke and Denis Twitchett (eds), *The Cambridge History of China*, Volume 6: *Alien Regimes and Border States*, Cambridge: Cambridge University Press, 1994, pp. 235–257.

5 Ibid., pp. 250–254, pp. 259–265.

6 Huang K'uan-ch'ung, "Songting dui minjian ziwei wuli de liyong he kongzhi," in Huang K'uan-ch'ung, *Nansong Difang Wuli*, pp. 145–202, and "Lianghuai shanshu- izhai – difang ziwei wuli de fazhan," in Huang K'uan-ch'ung, *Nansong Difang Wuli*, Taibei: Dongda tushu gongsi, 2002, pp. 203–238.

7 Herbert Franke, "The Chin Dynasty," pp. 239–243.

8 Lin Ruihan, *Songdai Zhengzhishi*, Taibei: Da xue lian he chu ban wei yuan hui, 1989, pp. 348–349.

9 Ibid., p. 349.

10 Ibid., pp. 349–350.

11 Ibid., pp. 358–361.

12 On the rise of Chinggis Khan and the creation of the Mongol empire, see. H. Md. Desmond Martin, *The Rise of Chingis Khan and his Conquest of North China*, Baltimore: Johns Hopkins University Press, 1950; Thomas Allsen, "The Rise of the Mongolian Empire and Mongolian Rule in North, China," in Herbert Franke and Denis Twitchett (eds), *The Cambridge History of China*, Volume 6: *Alien Regimes and Border States*, Cambridge: Cambridge University Press, 1994, pp. 333–365.

13 On Li Quan and his son Li Tan, see Huang K'uan-ch'ung, "Geju shili, jingji liyi yu zhengzhi jueze," pp. 275–306.

14 Thomas Allsen, "The Rise of the Mongolian Empire," pp. 364–365; Desmond Martin, *The Rise of Chingis Khan*, pp. 283–308.

15 Herbert Franke, "The Chin Dynasty," pp. 259–264; Thomas Allsen, "The Rise of the Mongolian Empire," pp. 370–372.

16 Li Tianming, *Song–Yuan Zhanshi*, Taibei: Shihuo chubanshe, 1988, pp. 181–188.

17 John E. Herman, "The Mongol Conquest of Dali: The Failed Second Front," in Nicola Di Cosmo (ed.), *Warfare in Inner Asian History*, Leiden: E.J. Brill, 2001, pp. 295–334.

18 Huang K'uan-ch'ung, "Shancheng yu shuizhai de fangyu gongneng," in Huang K'uan-ch'ung, *Nansong Difang Wuli*, pp. 307–328.

19 Huang K'uan-ch'ung, "Geju shili, jingji liyi yu zhengzhi jueze," pp. 275–306.

CHAPTER FOUR

A Chinese empire, 1272–1355?

> Great Yuan shall be the title of the dynasty . . . We alone have brought peace to the myriad lands. This is particularly in accord with the essential importance of embodying benevolence. In our endeavors there are continuities and discontinuities, but our Way connects Heaven and humanity.
>
> Edict of 1272 by the order of Khubilai Khan (1215–1294),
> Emperor of China[1]

Khubilai Khan formally established a Chinese-style dynasty, the Yuan, in 1272, as a practical measure designed to make the exploitation of Chinese resources easier and to reinforce his own position as khan. The Mongol empire itself had already fragmented during Khubilai's struggle with his younger brother Arigh Böke, and Khubilai needed to strengthen his control over the subject populace of his domain. Khubilai was nominally Khaghan, but he would have had to have embarked on a long, costly, and risky war against his Mongol relatives if he wanted to make that title carry real weight. He did not choose that course, though it is intriguing to speculate what would have happened had he succeeded in reuniting the Mongol empire and resuming Chinggis's goal of world conquest. A rich economic prize was close at hand, however, and though it also entailed enormous military difficulties, the conquest of the Southern Song was a much less risky endeavor. Perhaps the Khaghan believed that he could exploit the enormous resources of southern China to support a later campaign for greater Mongol political power.

Li Tan's rebellion had made Khubilai justifiably wary of his Chinese officials, which, added to his concerns about Mongols and Central Asians being overwhelmingly outnumbered in China, convinced him to build an imperial system which limited Han Chinese influence in the government. There were three official classes of people in Yuan China: Mongols, Semu (various Central Asians) and Han, in descending order of rank. Most *darugachi*, or overseers, usually the lowest level of central-government-appointed official, were Semu or Mongol, rather than Han. Khubilai did not institute a civil service exam system, though it should be pointed out that both Song Taizu and Zhu Yuanzhang, the founder of the Ming dynasty, were at best ambivalent about the exams as a means of recruiting. The Yuan government went to great lengths to check on the loyalty, effectiveness and ethics of its officials. These efforts were never wholly effective, however, even during Khubilai's reign.

In matters of religion, Khubilai was all-inclusive. He patronized, or at least sanctioned, every religious group in his realm, from Daoists and Buddhists to Christians and Muslims. This was a practical matter for winning the allegiance of the populace, rather than a matter of spiritual belief. He added imperial Chinese ceremonies to his government's practice, and built the most ritually correct Chinese city ever constructed for his capital at Dadu (modern Beijing).[2] Yet even while he provided a formal Chinese education (which necessarily centered on Confucian texts) for his heir, Khubilai did not officially patronize Confucianism in the same way as previous, or subsequent dynasties. His heir's education was strongly supplemented with Buddhist and Daoist teaching as well. For some reason, Khubilai chose to keep the literate culture of the Chinese elite at arm's length. And while his successors embraced this tradition more closely, only in 1315 did the Yuan government itself try to connect to the local Chinese elites through that culture and the exam system that was associated with it.

Their attempts to reassert control and tie the local elites more tightly to the central government proved to be too little, too late, and the Yuan dynasty shattered along the fractures within the Mongol leadership and Chinese society. Mongol rule had further reinforced the separation between the imperial government, local power-holders and the general populace that had begun in the Song. The Yuan system had structural weaknesses within the Mongol elite, and in its relationship with the local Chinese elites. Yuan dynasty government had all the political problems of both Mongol society and Chinese society. Had the Mongol elite maintained unity and the ability to lead, the government's loose connection to Chinese elites would not have been fatal. As it was, collapse was almost avoided in 1355. Military success could still make up for institutional mistakes.

The Southern Song government faced a similar problem in the thirteenth century as the Mongol onslaught began in earnest in the 1270s. Many literati and their families, not all of them serving officials, committed suicide rather than face Mongol rule; most, though, easily accommodated themselves to the new dynasty.[3] This was true despite Khubilai's decision not to institute the exam system, and the new category for the former Song subjects, *nanren* (southerners), whose political power was even more circumscribed within the Yuan government. More than anything, this makes clear how peripheral office holding had become for local elites, now perhaps appropriately called "gentry."[4] The Southern Song gentry already knew the importance of local power strategies, and the volatility and danger of a career in the government.[5] A promising career could be easily derailed by factional politics, or by offending a powerful man. Government service was also coming to be seen as morally fraught, rather than the realization of Confucian service that every educated man aspired to.

The moral absolutism of the many *Daoxue* (Neo-Confucian) adherents, coupled with the government's impotence externally and internally, further distanced many gentry from the dynasty.

Gentry ambivalence contributed very little to the Song's defeat, though many Chinese historians found their easy accommodation of Yuan rule unseemly and immoral.[6] By the time Khubilai undertook the destruction of the Song in earnest, the Song military establishment on the northern border was almost entirely disassociated from the rest of Song society, and only tenuously connected to the Song court. Civil officials entirely dominated the Southern Song court, preventing serving military officers from obtaining political power and influence. On the northern border, however, military commanders were given extraordinary power to control civil and military affairs. Their local achievements could not lead to real power at court, so their field of political operation remained sharply circumscribed. The court effectively cut the army off from the government.[7]

The political separation of the army from the court was a serious flaw in the Southern Song system, but one that was incipient in the original Song administration. Increasing civil dominance over the course of the eleventh century was mitigated by several factors. First, many senior civil officials spent time in command of border armies (e.g. Han Qi, Fan Zhongyan), creating a connection between the armies in the field and the central court. And while many historians have seen this phenomenon solely in terms of the increasing dominance of civil officials and their values during the militarily weak Song dynasty, it can also be seen as a militarization of civil officials. Second, the imperial clan was heavily intermarried with a group of families descended from the generals who founded the dynasty.[8] These families also continued to produce field generals, providing a familial link between the army and the ruling house. Third, fully half of the imperial army was posted to Kaifeng. Fourth and finally, policy issues of war and peace were not closely associated with the regional origins of officials.

These circumstances changed dramatically with the loss of the north and the court's move to Hangzhou. Senior civil officials no longer commanded border armies (with a few notable irredentist exceptions like Zhang Jun); generals no longer intermarried with the imperial clan; most of the imperial army was posted on the northern border; and regional origins, northern versus southern, became closely associated with military policy.[9] A military buffer zone was created between the Jurchen and then Mongols, and the civil society of the Southern Song. Local military forces were developed to suppress bandits and keep the peace, but many of these units, the most effective ones, were drawn off to the northern border.[10] Imperial armies were seldom seen outside of the border region, and local armies were closely identified with the place they were raised. Similarly, southerners valued military efforts to retake north China much less than northerners (with the exception of *Daoxue* adherents who saw it as a moral issue).

Military officers were further isolated from the rest of officials by the nature of their skills. Song efforts to improve and regularize the officer corps through a military academy and exam system similar to the civil system were a total failure. As late as 1253, the Song emperor complained that the military exam system had not produced any talented generals.[11] In the absence of a formal education-based system, the court had to rely upon hereditary military families and the incidental appearance of talented men rising from the ranks. The Song's bureaucratic machinery was ill-suited to accepting hereditary military men or to incorporating talented newcomers. Worse still, the most effective officers were frequently linked to one another through family connections that undermined government control. Up until 1142, the court had been forced to accept a larger amount of decentralized military power than it was comfortable with. Much of the impetus for peace with the Jurchen came from a desire to reassert control over the army.

The Song court was forced to reverse course again and cede more power to the border generals even before the Jurchen empire was destroyed by the Mongols. After 1234, greater defensive preparations required even more troops and more independent power on the border. The "Three Borders," the three strategic and administrative districts along the northern border (Sichuan, Jinghu and Huainan), were established where permanent garrisons were placed under the command of military commissioners who controlled civil and military affairs.[12] It was in this milieu that the general Lü Wende emerged in 1237, and made a name for himself fighting successfully against the Mongols.[13]

General Lü, as well as his younger brother and his cousin, became prominent because of his military skills. Lü fought in all three of the Three Borders, and was entrusted with greater and greater authority by the Song court. When Möngke invaded Sichuan in 1259 and besieged Hezhou, Lü led a fleet up the Yangzi River, first driving off a Mongol army before Fuzhou, and then relieving Chongqing. Möngke died shortly afterward before Hezhou, but Khubilai followed the deceased Khaghan's orders and crossed the Yangzi to besiege Ezhou (modern Wuchang). Jia Sidao took personal command of the Ezhou's defense, while Lü Wende's son defended the sister city of Hanyang. Lü Wende returned back down the Yangzi to break through the Mongol lines around Ezhou and reinforce the city.[14] It was about this time that Khubilai received word from his wife that his own territory was threatened by a Mongol army, and he was forced to lift the siege and attend to his struggle with Arigh Böke. Jia Sidao drove off the token force Khubilai left behind and reported it as a great victory to the court.[15] As a reward, Jia was promoted to prime minister.

The emperor was also suitably impressed with Lü Wende, and this led to his promotion to military commissioner of Jinghu. Lü's high rank was due not only to his military achievements but to his political wiles as well. Although he apparently despised the abilities of civil officials and literati, he concealed his feelings and cultivated good relations with them. This was wisdom born of knowledge, as two brave contemporary generals had been executed for showing arrogance to civil officials. The government was wholly run by civil officials and, regardless of a general's achievements, he was subject to their evaluation. Lü, unlike some of the other generals, had treated Jia Sidao with respect during the defense of Ezhou. Jia's elevation to prime minister was a political windfall for Lü, though Lü had assiduously cultivated an earlier prime minister as well.[16]

Jia Sidao was a civil official who became prime minister through military accomplishment, and his continued hold on power depended upon his handling of the Mongol military threat. By 1260, of course, the Song dynasty's own survival hinged on somehow preventing or dissuading the Mongols from invading. Jia failed to work out a diplomatic solution while Khubilai was occupied with Arigh Böke, however, which left the dynasty's fate in the hands of its army and navy. Even at the time many officials understood the seriousness of this failure, and not many were confident that the Song empire could survive a military confrontation with the Mongols. These practical considerations were often drowned out by irredentist, or at least rashly belligerent, posturing on the part of students in the capital. Government officials were rightfully afraid of the students, since they were frequently violent and had a surprisingly strong influence over the weak court.[17] Mongol policy was politically paralyzed, which in turn froze strategic military planning, leaving the initiative in both spheres to the Mongol court, and devolved operational command to the border generals.

Lü Wende thrived under these circumstances. He held the military commissionership of Jinghu until he died in 1270, as well as de facto control over military affairs in Sichuan. Jia Sidao was happy to support Lü and other military men on the border because they, unlike other civil officials, could not threaten his own position through military accomplishment. A general was effectively disqualified for the position of prime minister in the Southern Song, so generals were not a political threat to Jia. Jia's position was based upon the need for his military acumen in the face of the looming Mongol invasion, something that surely diminished any desire on his part for a diplomatic solution. When a new Song emperor was enthroned in 1264, Jia asked Lü Wende to falsely report an impending invasion just after Jia had resigned all of his posts. Once Lü's report was received, the new emperor anxiously brought Jia back with even higher titles.

Given his importance and reliability, Lü was well favored by the Jia Sidao dominated court. His control extended beyond his military titles, through a broad network of family members, former subordinates and friends scattered throughout the army, bureaucracy and central court. Lü even patronized literati, some quite famous, and recommended them for office. Civil officials and literati alike were pleased by what they took as the appropriate attitude of a military man, successful on the battlefield, yet humble and respectful of men of letters. Lü cynically and effectively played upon the literati's desire to have their values demonstrated by a man of action, all the while despising them for their inadequacies. A few officials complained about Lü's demands, but the government as a whole continued to support him and to undermine his rivals. Clearly, by the 1260s, the Song government had ceased to be able to process military information objectively, let alone to formulate rational policies based upon that data.

Liu Zheng, an accomplished general groundlessly accused of misusing government funds by Lü Wende, surrendered to the Mongols with his army in 1261. Liu became the key strategic adviser to Khubilai in the next phase of his invasion of the Song. Mongol tactics had changed over the course of their conquest of the Jurchen empire, most obviously with Mukhali's shift away from devastating broad swathes of territory. But they still conceived of campaigns in terms of fast-moving cavalry armies, living off the land and their herds, and striking in coordinated armies, even when their armies were no longer predominantly cavalry or even Mongol. This helps explain why they fared so poorly against fortifications, particularly when organized as defenses in depth, as in Song Sichuan. Möngke's invasion of the Song bogged down in Sichuan, while Khubilai's army foundered against Ezhou. Mongol strategy had thus far proved ineffective against the Song's defenses.

General Liu proposed a much different approach. Rather than launch several widely separated armies against the Song defense line as Möngke had done, Khubilai should concentrate his attack on a strategic city, which would both break the defense line and provide a jumping-off point for further campaigns. A single, concentrated attack would also be easier logistically (something which had hobbled previous Mongol invasions), more sustainable, and help overcome the Mongols' naval weakness. Liu's targets were Xiangyang and neighboring Fancheng, which protected the Middle Yangzi area. Attacking such important and heavily defended cities would obviously take a long time, and draw in Song and Mongol resources. In effect, Liu was proposing to wage a war of attrition in circumstances extremely favorable to the Mongols. Since the Mongols retained the strategic and tactical initiative during the entire Song–Mongol conflict, due largely to the Song army's inability to project power effectively and the court's defensive mindedness, Khubilai could choose where and when to fight, while the Song had to be prepared to defend everywhere. This allowed the Mongols to concentrate their army, and particularly their navy, thus overcoming the Song's greater material resources.

Khubilai saw the advantages of Liu's plan and adopted it, though it represented an enormous change in Mongol strategic practice. In late 1267, the Mongol army began to ring Xiangyang and Fancheng with forts and contest the Song navy for control of the river. By 1269, Lü Wende realized that not only were the Mongols settling in for an extended siege but also that the contest for Xiangyang and Fancheng was a mortal threat to Song defenses. His intended attack on the Mongol army to dislodge it was aborted when he died at the beginning of 1270.[18] Lü Wende's death was a terrible loss for the Song since he was one of the only generals who had successfully attacked and defeated Mongol armies in the past. Moreover, he unified command of Song defenses through his leadership of his family network. His younger brother, Lü

Wenhuan, was in charge of Xiangyang, which gave the Lü family network a continued interest in supporting its defense, but this personalized system was less amenable to outside participation. Jia Sidao was similarly worried about new players on the military scene who could threaten him politically.

Xiangyang and Fancheng were still in danger, so Jia was forced to appoint a new military commissioner for Jinghu whose first task was to raise the Mongol siege. Jia was prevented from taking personal command of the operation by the emperor. Here Jia's political needs clashed with the dynasty's military needs. The obvious power of the Lü family made the court nervous and argued for appointing an outsider as military commissioner. Furthermore, although Lü Wende's extraordinary personal achievements had allowed him as a military man to be appointed to such a high position, no other general inside or outside the Lü network was qualified for that post. Jia was forced to appoint a civil official, though one who had served on his own staff, to the position. Li Tingzhi was a direct threat to Jia, and resented by the Lü network. Jia therefore allowed members of the Lü network to defy Li, compromising operations to rescue Xiangyang and Fancheng. Worse still, Li's appointment made clear the court's mistrust of the Lü family.[19] Perhaps the wisest course would have been to have allowed Jia to take personal command of the mission.

Li Tingzhi's appointment would have disastrous consequences for the dynasty. The Mongols had already suggested surrender to Lü Wenhuan as early as 1269, pointing out that the Lü family's loyalty could be called into question because it was so powerful. Li's appointment confirmed these suggestions, beginning the alienation of the Lü family from the Song court. Undermined by a divided command, Li Tingzhi was unable to raise the siege of the two cities, only managing on several occasions briefly to penetrate the blockade and partially re-supply them.

The Mongol blockade tightened in response to Song relief efforts, though as late as the summer of 1272 Song naval militiamen still made it through with large amounts of supplies. These successes came at a high cost in lives, however, and could not be sustained. Khubilai's offers of high post and great reward still did not convince Lü Wenhuan to surrender. The Mongol blockade had greatly weakened the defenders of both cities, despite the occasional influx of supplies, and limited the Mongol army's casualties by its less aggressive siege tactics. Khubilai aimed not only to capture the two cities but also to convince Lü Wenhuan to switch sides. After five years of pressure and entreaties, it was finally time to force a decision.

The fall of Fancheng and the surrender of Xiangyang[20]

By the end of 1272 Khubilai agreed with his advisers, Liu Zheng among them, that Xiangyang and Fancheng were completely interdependent, and that if Fancheng were captured, Xiangyang would have to surrender. The first step was to isolate Fancheng by destroying the pontoon bridge that connected the two cities across the Han River. The bridge was above a line of wooden piles driven into the river bed connected by iron chains protected by a Song naval squadron. While one force launched an attack on the city from the land, a second force used saws to cut the piles, axes to break the chains and incendiaries to burn the bridge. The attack on the piles and bridge was successful, but this was only possible because the Mongol navy won the fleet action on the river. Many Song warships were burnt and some 30 captured. The first stage of the strategy was successful.

With Fancheng isolated, the Mongol army launched an all-out assault on the city from all sides. Liu Zheng assaulted the south side, from the river. Liu's troops broke through and burned the palisade wall along the river and constructed platforms for the new "Muslim" (*huihui*) trebuchets before the *fausse-braye* – a second rampart, exterior to the main one and below its level – in front of the moat in the face of a withering Song arrow and stone barrage, and repeated sallies. When the Song navy attempted to dislodge the Mongol troops, the Mongols took advantage of the winds to launch a fire attack that destroyed over a hundred Song vessels. The Mongol foothold was firmly established after two days of fierce fighting, part of it during a great snowfall, with high casualties on the Mongol side. A second assault army then took over the position, and completely uprooted the wooden river palisade wall and filled in the moat. Its first attempt to capture the *fausse-braye* at the foot of the wall was repulsed by a heavy barrage of missiles from the city wall. A second attempt at dawn the following day carried the *fausse-braye*; they then scaled the wall and captured its top.

Other Mongol armies were similarly successful, filling in the moats and scaling the walls. The costs in casualties were extremely high for the Mongol army, with most of the commanders personally sustaining many wounds themselves. Desperate street fighting by some of the Song defenders proved futile, and several of the commanders committed suicide by throwing themselves into burning buildings. By 2 February 1273, Fancheng was completely under Mongol control. The Mongol army was utterly ruthless, putting the entire population to the sword and stacking the bodies up, about 10,000 of them, outside the wall in view of Xiangyang. The mound rose higher than Fancheng's wall.

Lü Wenhuan's position in Xiangyang was no longer sustainable. After six years of siege, with no hope of rescue and clear signs that the Song court suspected his loyalty, his capitulation to the Mongols was entirely understandable. Fancheng's capture clearly demonstrated that the Mongol army could overcome Xiangyang's defenses as well, and that, should they do so, the city's inhabitants would be massacred. Khubilai transferred Liu Zheng away from Xiangyang to Huaixi, since his presence might anger Lü Wenhuan, and waited for Lü to submit. Lü's surrender was still the greater political and military goal of the Xiangyang–Fancheng campaign. And, given the high casualties the capture of Fancheng had cost, Khubilai was not eager to repeat that sort of action again. Any realistic hope of continued resistance in Xiangyang was undermined both by the enormous pile of corpses rotting across the river and by the trebuchet stone thrown by the new machine set up southeast of the city which struck a turret on the wall with a thunderous crash. Lü finally surrendered on 14 March 1273.

Xiangyang's surrender stunned the Song court. It was not just a military loss that threatened the Middle Yangzi, but also a political failure which undermined the credibility of Jia Sidao and the Song emperor. Under these circumstances, the court felt it better not to try and dismantle the Lü family network, and rejected the resignations of two Lü family members. To do so would have admitted the emperor and Jia Sidao's mistakes, and disrupted the entire defense system. The court never seemed to accept that Lü Wenhuan's surrender and subsequent service to the Mongols demonstrated he was no longer loyal to the Song. The Song court continued to communicate with Lü, asking him to intercede with his Mongol superiors, up until the Song emperor's submission to the Mongols in 1276.

Given Lü's situation after the fall of Fancheng, and his staunch defense for so many years, it is easy to see why the Song court did not condemn him for his defection. Certainly the appointment of Li Tingzhi, and the undermining of his command, had much more to do with placing Lü in an impossible situation. From a purely military perspective, fighting to the death in Xiangyang would have been pointless; the city would still have fallen. Lü could have surrendered the city and then committed suicide, dying as a martyr for his dynasty, or even gone into retirement rather than serve the Mongols. That he did neither of these things, and actively participated in the conquest of the Song, shows a break between Lü and the Song court specifically, and the army and the civil administration more generally.

Lü Wenhuan and his family's estrangement from the Song court goes directly to the question of why the Song fell to the Mongols when it did. Although the Lü family network developed outside of the official administrative structure of the government, it created an effective defense against the Mongols for a decade. Mongol success was not inevitable, nor was the destruction of the Song a given just because so many other states had fallen. Under different political circumstances, the Song could have worked out a tributary relationship with the Mongol state. And even with Liu Zheng's new strategy, Lü Wende might have been able to withstand the siege of Fancheng and Xiangyang. Indeed, a better coordinated response, one not undermined by *de facto* divided command under Li Tingzhi, might also have raised the siege. At root, however, was the problem that Lü Wende's death and the court's suspicions about Lü family power broke the preexisting defense system. In exchange for trust and local power, the Lü family's network defended the Song loyally and effectively against the Mongols. When the Song court showed that it no longer fully trusted the Lü family, and sent an outsider to rein in their power, they no longer owed the court their service.

Many civil officials did not understand the implicit agreement that the court, partly in the person of Jia Sidao, had made with the Lü family. In the civil officials' view, generals served the dynasty in the same way as civil officials, and owed the dynasty loyalty in the same way. Just because the military situation seemed futile was no reason to give up or defect to the enemy. They should fight to the death because that was the most honorable course. Members of the military reacted differently to the Mongol invasion than the gentry and official class, not simply because they believed that resistance was futile – many officials felt the same way – but because their own culture was different than the civil elite class. Officers fought to the death in battle, and committed suicide rather than be captured (as one member of the Lü family did when Fancheng fell), but outside of a battle could surrender when the situation was clearly hopeless. Many of those who identified themselves as members of the civil elite class, by contrast, might be captured during a war but could not serve a new dynasty, and some even felt they had to commit suicide when their own dynasty fell.[21]

When the Mongols continued their invasion the following year, Lü Wenhuan led the way, convincing his family network to defect. These defections ramified into even more defections as each surrender helped convince other commanders and prefects to surrender. Jia Sidao had finally taken command of a large Song army to block this invasion, but he was too late to prevent the defenses from unraveling. He was then relieved of command and sent into exile, where he would be assassinated six months later. The damage had already been done, however, and the Song capital at Hangzhou was now vulnerable. In 1275 the Song court desperately tried to establish a truce with the Mongols, asking Lü Wenhuan to act as interlocutor. It was Jia Sidao, the court claimed, who had caused the problems. Even if this belated recognition of the court's betrayal of its relationship with the Lü family had convinced Lü Wenhuan, his Mongol masters were now fixed on the destruction of the dynasty. Having suborned the Lü network, compromise was no longer necessary. The Song emperor formally surrendered on 4 February 1276.[22]

Wen Tianxiang and the continuing struggle

The third patriotic figure to emerge from Song history after Kou Zhun and Yue Fei was a civil official by the name of Wen Tianxiang. Unlike the first two, Wen had the distinct advantage of writing his own account of his actions in the final years of the Song. This historiographical caveat has not tempered the universally positive evaluation of his life among Chinese historians both modern and premodern.[23] Wen Tianxiang came in first in the civil service examination of 1256, and rose rapidly in the chaotic conditions at court after Xiangyang's surrender to temporarily become chief councilor in 1276, just in time to negotiate the dynasty's surrender to the Mongols. The new chief councilor was far too militant for the task, and, in a famous scene described by Wen himself, he denounced the Mongol generals at a face-to-face meeting in the Mongol camp and expressed his willingness to die for his dynasty. Although Wen related that this elicited a respectful response from the Mongols, it was beside the point. Most of the Song court's officials had deserted it, the Song army had melted away from Hangzhou, and the Mongol army was approaching in overwhelming force. Since the chief councilor was clearly not prepared to discuss practical matters, his posturing was either irrational or a ploy to win more time for something. Wen was imprisoned and sent north.

Hangzhou's surrender was carefully worked out and Bayan, the supreme Mongol commander, entered the city on 28 March. All of the dynasty's appurtenances were secured, from buildings and people to works of art, and the city itself carefully preserved. As Bayan had pledged, there was no looting or indiscriminate slaughter. The Song court fulfilled its promises with less fidelity, having secretly sent two of the emperor's brothers to the south. Hangzhou in 1276 was one of, if not the, greatest city in the world. It was far wealthier than China's northern cities, conquered by the Mongols after decades of war had impoverished them. The Jiangnan region of China Bayan was now taking control of had avoided devastation in the Song–Jurchen wars, and would escape widespread destruction now. It would only suffer the effects of war in the fourteenth century, and even that only briefly disrupted its economic development.[24] Even today, the Jiangnan region is one of the most prosperous areas of China. Bayan had captured one of the greatest prizes ever taken by a Mongol army, easily on par with Baghdad.

Song resistance, however, had not entirely ceased with the formal surrender of the emperor. The imperial party was briefly intercepted and prevented from proceeding on its way into northern captivity by none other than Li Tingzhi, now commanding a ruthless defense of Yangzhou. Li had simply rejected the imperial surrender, inflicting immense suffering on the city's inhabitants in what was either a pointless gesture of loyalty or an egotistical attempt to secure his honor (or both).[25] An assistant engineered the city's surrender in August of 1276, and Li was captured and executed after a failed suicide attempt. In his brief period as a loyalist without a cause, Li had also unsuccessfully attempted to have Wen Tianxiang, who had escaped his Mongol jailers, assassinated. Wen fled to the south in search of the two imperial sons, finding them at Fuzhou on 9 July, where the elder of them, aged seven, was now "officially" emperor.

Wen Tianxiang was not welcome at the new court, which was controlled by men who had actually fled Hangzhou when the Mongol army was approaching. He took up arms in the southern interior instead, and preserved some measure of nominally Song power there by raising armies, and trying to assert or reassert government authority. It was a losing battle, and Fuzhou fell early in 1277, the Song court fleeing further south. On 9 May 1278, the Song emperor died, and was succeeded by his 6-year-old younger brother. The court now moved to Yaishan, an island 100 kilometers south of Guangzhou. Wen himself was captured on 2 February 1279, and would be a prisoner aboard a ship in the Mongol navy when it finally brought an end to the last Song court.

The Battle of Yaishan

The final battle in the bay of Yaishan saw 1,000 Song warships awaiting attack by a smaller Yuan navy of somewhere between 300 to 700 ships. Although the outcome of the battle was uncertain, the Song court was certainly doomed. It was isolated without hope of rescue or resurgence, a spent political force playing out the final act of a tragedy.

The Mongol navy's commanders, Zhang Hongfan (1238–1280), a northern Chinese, and Li Heng (1236–1285), a Tangut, had been ordered to annihilate this last Song remnant, and they acted with great deliberation. A plan to bombard the Song fleet using catapults was rejected on the grounds that it would scatter the Song fleet. They chose to wait instead, and let the Song navy's supplies of water and food run down. A bolder Song court or commander might have made a break for the high seas and a new base, but without such a base already established the leadership was resigned to a final battle. The Song fleet itself was roped together in a solid mass that pre-empted the possibility of it attacking or even maneuvering.

Some Song ships defected on 12 March. The following night a Song squadron attacked the Mongol's northern patrol boats, perhaps in an attempt to break out, but the Mongol navy responded quickly and defeated the Song squadron with heavy loss of life. By 17 March, Li Heng and Zhang Hongfan decided it was time for a decisive battle. They called in their ship commanders the following night, and ordered them to position themselves for an attack the next day. The Mongol navy was divided into four fleets: Li Heng would attack from the north and northwest; Zhang Hongfan would attack from the southwest; the remaining two fleets would attack from the west and south.

A dark cloud arose from west of the island mountain and heavy rains filled the sky, which Zhang Hongfan recognized as an extremely lucky accident. Li Heng opened the attack at daybreak, taking advantage of the tide and the south-flowing current to descend rapidly upon the Song fleet from the north. Li ordered his ships to enter the Song fleet stern first in order to use the Mongol ships' higher sterncastles, where they had set up archery platforms, to dominate the Song ships. He took care to place seven or eight expert archers there to enhance the effects of this missile fire. Li's first wave also cut through the ropes holding the Song ships in place, and closed to hand-to-hand fighting distance. The Song navy fought back with its own barrage of arrow and missile fire, and though by eleven in the morning Li had taken three of the Song warships, casualties were high on both sides. By noon, Li Heng had broken through the outer line of the Song fleet, along with two other Mongol squadrons, shattering the northwest corner of the Song formation.

The tides shifted at noon, and the current now reversed and flowed north. This carried Li Heng's fleet back out of the Song formation. The Song sailors heard the sounds of military signaling coming from the south and erroneously assumed that the Mongol fleet was breaking off for a meal. They relaxed a bit just as Zhang Hongfan's fleet rode the north current into their clustered ships. Zhang's target was the flagship of the Song admiral Zuo Tai, and he specially prepared his ship with shields and matting to absorb Song missile fire. By the time he approached Zuo Tai's ship, Zhang's warship looked like a porcupine. In a heated battle of arrow, missile and incendiary fire, Zhang carried the day and captured Zuo Tai's ship.

Li Heng reentered the battle with his fleet, and by the late afternoon the Song navy began to strike their colors and surrender. Tens of thousands of Song officials, and women, threw themselves into the sea and drowned. The last Song emperor went to the bottom with his entourage, held in the arms of his councilor. With his death, the final remnants of the Song dynasty were eliminated. Khubilai's Mongol Yuan dynasty completed the conquest of China with a naval campaign and a climactic battle at sea more than 2,000 miles south of the Mongolian homeland.[26]

Most Song loyalists outlived their dynasty, though thousands chose to kill themselves instead. Even Wen Tianxiang's brother, Wen Bi (1237–1298), who had also served as a Song official, surrendered himself and his prefecture to the Mongols after Yaishan, and accepted office under the Yuan government. The Wen brothers represent the two poles of Song officials' responses to the military defeat of their dynasty, resistance until eventual execution at one end, and acceptance of the new political reality at the other. In between them were former officials who chose not to serve, and retreated to private lives. Literati who had not served the Song were in a more ambiguous position, since their loyalty to the late dynasty was more notional than required. Many of these men also chose to stay clear of the Yuan government, joining the ranks of the loyalists who made fidelity to the old dynasty a fetish and an identity. Wen Tianxiang himself was executed in Beijing in January 1283.

Khubilai's Chinese empire

Khubilai balanced his rule of China as a Chinese emperor against his image as a Mongolian khan. His vast Chinese domain supplied most of his wealth and contained most of his subjects, but he did not conform to Chinese culture because of this. Khubilai selected what he liked or what served his interests, rejected what did not, and ignored the rest. Mongol rule itself had a profound impact on Chinese society and culture, though one of the most lasting of these effects, the Confucianization of laws regarding women's rights, was unintentional.[27] Where earlier dynasties taxed land, the Yuan dynasty originally taxed adult males and households, before reverting to the earlier system of land tax. People rather than land was the priority in steppe governance.

Households were categorized as military or civilian, and the latter designation also included a large number of other professional sub-designations. Military households were supposed to be the mainstay of the army, each producing and maintaining a fully equipped soldier in perpetuity. This also reflected the steppe practice of militia armies, rather than standing professional armies. Both the Ming and Qing dynasties that succeeded the Yuan would follow the practice of creating designated military families to supply their armies with soldiers. This was consistent in some ways with the growing separation of the army from the rest of society during the Song, though now within an explicit legal and institutional framework. The Song government had never recognized military households as a legal category. And as the direct instrument of government power, the growing distance of the imperial army from society was a further sign of the government's retreat from the grass-roots level.

Yuan rule was always loose, and only partly followed the imperial Chinese model, but its authority ultimately crumbled because of internal political struggles. The central weakness of the Yuan system was the lack of an orderly imperial succession. Khubilai's designated successor had predeceased him, undermining any precedent to counter the Mongol custom of electing a khan. The Mongol aristocracy was also at odds with the government's bureaucrats, who tried to influence succession in favor of candidates who supported the Chinese imperial system. The unresolved question was whether the ruler was the Mongol Khaghan or the Yuan emperor. It remained unresolved until the end of the dynasty. There were nine Yuan emperors in the 39 years from Khubilai's death in 1294 until the enthronement of the last emperor in 1333, with no consistency in their policies or procedures for ruling. Khubilai alone had ruled for 34 years, from 1260 to 1294, creating stability by his long tenure. His military adventures had been mostly successful, with the important exception of his wars with the other Mongol powers, and the considerably less-significant failed attempts to bring the Japanese to heel in 1274 and 1281, as well as his Southeast Asian campaigns.[28] None of his successors had his military credibility.

Yuan rule after Khubilai

Peace proved difficult for the Yuan dynasty, since it retained the military orientation of Khubilai and the Mongol war machine. Chinggis created the Mongol polity and found that it needed the goal of conquering the world, and both Möngke and Khubilai had perpetuated a nearly continual state of war. The Yuan government was built on the assumption that it would continually need to extract resources from its subject population for the next campaign. This explains Khubilai's desultory campaigns late in his reign, which drained financial resources and accomplished very little. Furthermore, the imperial family was a constant and uncontrollable drain on the imperial treasury. In many respects, the Yuan state primarily served the interests of the Mongol aristocracy. That aristocracy fought jealously over the control of Yuan state through the imperial family.

Khubilai's grandson Temür (1265–1307) succeeded to the throne and tried to maintain his grandfather's policies as best he could. The main exception to this policy was in the realm of war.[29] Temür cancelled a planned campaign against Vietnam (Annam) and chose not to invade Japan a third time. Most importantly, he was fortunate in his conflict with Khaidu (c. 1235–1301) and Du'a (1282–1307), khans, respectively, of the Ögödei and Chaghadai khanates. Both men had opposed Khubilai's claim to be Khaghan since the late 1260s, and had not only resisted his attempts to destroy them but even expanded their realms.

Temür continued to commit China's resources to this Mongol political and military struggle, initially without much success. Du'a destroyed the main Yuan army in Mongolia in a surprise attack in 1298, necessitating a change of command and the dispatch of new Mongol and Chinese troops from China the following year. Although the Yuan army managed to defeat Khaidu that fall, the decisive battle occurred in September of 1301. The clash of the armies was not decisive, but, as was so often the case in the steppe environment, where wars were often fought based upon personal politics rather than the interests of a coherent polity, it was the fate of the political leaders, who were also the commanding generals, which made the battle important. Khaidu died shortly after the battle and Du'a was wounded, prompting Du'a to initiate peace talks with Temür.

Temür was acknowledged as Khaghan over all the Mongol khanates in 1304, something Khubilai had never been able to achieve.[30] Mongol unity was still notional, however, and did not lead to a reinvigorated project to conquer the world. Even within Yuan territory, Temür failed to address the problems of the imperial treasury, or the bloated and ineffective bureaucracy. His attempt to set up a smooth succession foundered when his designated heir suddenly died in 1306. Temür himself died the following year without having established a new heir. The succession broke down into bloodshed, with one of the contenders for the throne, Ayurbarwada (1285–1320), actually storming the palace to displace the empress's regency. Ayurbarwada deferred to his older brother, Khaishan, in return for being made heir apparent.[31]

Khaishan was not a Chinese emperor in manner or attitude. He was an outstanding military commander who'd spent most of his life leading armies in the steppes. Khaishan's rule was financially disastrous, mitigated only by its brevity; he died in 1311. Ayurbarwada succeeded peacefully to the throne, reversed his older brother's policies and sacked (and executed) many of his officials. The new emperor was highly Confucianized, and strove as much as possible to bring the Yuan government into line with the Chinese imperial system. For the first time, the Yuan really tried to become something like a Chinese dynasty. Ayurbarwada announced civil service exams based upon the *Daoxue* Confucianism of Zhu Xi in 1313, and greatly increased the status of Confucian officials in his court.[32]

The Yuan was still a Mongol dynasty, however, and Ayurbarwada could not abolish the privileges of the Mongol aristocracy, or fundamentally rework society. His efforts to revise the tax system and take into account the size of landholdings, particularly in what had formerly been the Southern Song empire, not only failed because of administrative incompetence and corruption but also incited a brief rebellion. Yuan finances remained a disaster. The Khaghan was unable to resolve the tension between Mongol and Chinese government practices, and died in 1320, having changed the Yuan system only slightly. His eldest son, Shidebala, succeeded him at the age of 18.

Shidebala was as well educated in Chinese and Chinese culture as his father, and so continued his father's efforts to make the Yuan dynasty follow the Chinese imperial system. He initially succeeded where his father had failed largely because he was able to overcome his grandmother's power, as his father had failed to do. She died in 1322, Shidebala having already made great progress in undermining her. He purged her faction more fully the following year. But Ayurbarwada had been wise to avoid opposing the Mongol aristocracy too directly; Shidebala was assassinated in 1323 by a conspiracy of Mongol princes, aristocrats, and officials, many of them the remains of his grandmother's faction. Shidebala had cut back on funds to the princes, and it seemed likely that he would attempt to root out the rest of his grandmother's faction.[33]

Yesün Temür took the Yuan throne in Mongolia once he received the imperial seals from what were probably his co-conspirators. He executed all of the officials involved in the coup a month later, and exiled the princes. The new emperor was a steppe Mongol, untempered by a Chinese education. Although he did not make much real use of Chinese officials in his administration, he did try to gain their support by giving them prominent positions. He made similar conciliatory efforts with the Mongolian princes. This placated both sides of the Yuan dynasty power struggle, with the usual dire consequences for the imperial treasury. Yesün Temür patronized everyone without even attempting to solve any of the underlying conflicts. No one was really satisfied, and when the emperor fell ill and died in August of 1328, the contest for the throne became extremely violent.[34]

An attempted *coup d'état* was partly foiled in September when the conspirators in Shangdu were discovered and executed before they could act. The conspirators succeeded in storming the palace in Dadu, however, thus dividing control of the two political centers. Yesün Temür's son and designated heir was made emperor in Shangdu in October, while Tugh Temür, one of Khaishan's sons, was made emperor in Dadu the same month. Tugh Temür supposedly held the throne for his older brother Khoshila, who would take over once he returned from his exile in Central Asia. The loyalist forces fought with some success, but were entirely undone by a surprise attack on Shangdu in mid-November while their army was occupied campaigning around against the Great Wall defenses. With most of the army away, the Shangdu court surrendered. Loyalist forces held out in the far southwest for four years until 1332, however, virtually the entire tenure of Tugh Temür's reign.[35]

Tugh Temür duly offered Khoshila the throne, and Khoshila unwisely accepted it. He made himself emperor on 27 February 1329, on the way to

China, and designated Tugh Temür his heir. Khoshila met his younger brother on 26 August, at Zhongdu, and died four days later. Tugh Temür resumed the throne at Shangdu the next week. A bloody purge of Yesün Temür's and Khoshila's officials and supporters followed; it seemed a fact of Yuan dynasty politics that the new emperor had to slaughter some of his predecessor's supporters. Tugh Temür himself was mostly a figurehead, with real power held in the hands of his top two officials, the men who had been instrumental in putting him on the throne.

Chinese officials were once again excluded from the highest ranks of power, and the state once again bankrupted in providing largesse to win over Mongol aristocrats and officials. The other khanates were also convinced to accept Tugh Temür's nominal rule. But despite this, there were repeated plots against the emperor, demonstrating deep fractures within the Mongol aristocracy. By comparison, the Yuan's Chinese subjects were relatively quiescent. There were very few rebellions among the Chinese; rather, it was the steppe tribesmen and the southern tribesmen who kept rising up against Mongol rule. With all of these demands on the government, not to mention the natural disasters and the cost of the war of succession, it is surprising that the imperial finances were stabilized during Tugh Temür's reign. The emperor himself had little to do with this feat, and generally occupied himself with Chinese poetry, painting and calligraphy.

With Tugh Temür's death in 1332, the last Yuan emperor, Toghon Temür, took the throne at the age of 13. The young emperor may have been the son of Khoshila; his paternity is uncertain. He was not the first choice to succeed Tugh Temür, but the 6-year-old son of Khoshila first put on the throne in 1332 died after two months as emperor. Toghon Temür was actually the third choice, since the son of Tugh Temür was determined by his own mother to be too young to succeed, and was made Toghon Temür's heir instead. The new emperor was enthroned in 1333, wholly untrained and unprepared to rule. As was so often the case, a bloody purge followed his succession, though it waited until the summer of 1335. His chancellor, Bayan, dominated the early years of his reign.[36]

Toghto and the end of the Yuan

Bayan attempted to separate the respective ethnic groups that had become so intertwined, particularly at the highest levels. He even abolished the exam system in 1335, which had actually come to benefit Mongol and Semu as much as, if not more than, Chinese. His measures to improve imperial finances by cutting expenditures, and efforts to improve famine relief, were desperately needed, but his ethnic program aroused tremendous opposition. He was soon overthrown by his nephew Toghto. Toghto was an able and active chancellor, and his successes in rerouting the Yellow River and suppressing rebellion dramatize the importance of individual political figures at the head of a dynasty. A point driven home by the collapse of the dynasty after Toghto's dismissal.

The Yuan army may not have been ready to handle all the rebellions that broke out in the early 1350s, but under Toghto's leadership it nonetheless came together and responded effectively to the challenge. Like most military organizations, particularly pre-modern ones, the Yuan army could not maintain a high level of training and proficiency while waiting for action. Moreover, the Yuan army had never fully evolved into an army of occupation; it simply became one, without much attention to the changes in operational requirements that shift entailed. Armies of conquest and armies of occupation confront different challenges and function differently. The early Mongol forays into Jurchen China had destroyed both military and civilian targets in their efforts to conquer the Jurchen empire. Those tactics changed as the Mongol leadership wanted to exploit the civilian population on a more long-term basis. Toghto overcame these military limitations and almost saved the dynasty.

Just as Toghto was about to complete the destruction of one of the main concentrations of rebels in 1355, Toghton Temür sacked him. The chancellor was personally commanding the siege of Gaoyou at the time, and his generals and advisers begged him to either ignore the emperor or complete the subjugation of the rebels beforehand. Toghto obeyed his sovereign, the siege failed, and the dynasty fell apart. The emperor may have been motivated by Toghto's slowness in carrying out the ceremonies officially to designate his son as heir. Toghto's effectiveness had certainly made him many political enemies, so there was a large opposition faction. Yet the question of why the emperor made the disastrous decision he did is less important than what its effects show about the nature of the Yuan dynasty.

The central tension in the Yuan dynasty between a centralized, bureaucratized Chinese-style imperial government and a dispersed, personal and consensual, feudal Mongol system was never fully resolved, but Toghto's successes and the results of his recall suggest that by 1355 the power and importance of the central government was considerable. Indeed, there appear to have been no other significant sources of military or political power capable of suppressing even local rebellions, or addressing large-scale economic problems. Despite ample support for the dynasty from Mongols and Chinese, the government rapidly lost control of its territory. A government without effective military resources could not capitalize on the support of local power-holders. Toghto showed that the Yuan dynasty had sufficient military resources to deal with its problems, and that it was healthy enough in 1355 to continue ruling. Yet it was Toghto himself who was the key to the dynasty's survival, a strong and effective chancellor acting for the emperor at the pinnacle of a centralized imperial system. Like the Song, Kitan, Jurchen, and Southern Song regimes, poor decisions by the emperor or his court undermined the dynasty at a critical time and brought it to ruin. The Yuan dynasty fell because, having centralized power in the emperor's hands, his mistakes ramified throughout the government. Thus the Yuan collapsed, not because it was Mongol ruled but because it was a Chinese dynasty.

Notes

1 Edict promulgated on 18 January 1272 by Khubilai Khan's order naming the Mongol dynast the Yuan. Translated in John D. Langlois, "Introduction," in John D. Langlois (ed.), *China Under Mongol Rule*, Princeton: Princeton University Press, 1981, p. 4.

2 Nancy Shatzman Steinhardt, *Chinese Imperial City Planning*, Honolulu: University of Hawai'i Press, 1990, pp. 147–160.

3 Richard L. Davis, *Wind Against the Mountains*, Cambridge, Mass.: Harvard University Press, 1996, for the suicides, and Jennifer Jay, *A Change in Dynasties: Loyalism in Thirteenth-Century China*, Bellingham, Washington: Western Washington University, Center for East Asian Studies, 1991, for the loyalists who refused to serve the Yuan dynasty.

4 My extension of the term "gentry" to the Southern Song local elites is consistent with Paul Jakov Smith's discussion in Paul Jakov Smith and Richard von Glahn (eds), "Problematizing the Song–Yuan–Ming Transition," *The Song–Yuan–Ming Transition*, Cambridge, Mass.: Harvard University Press, 2003, p. 20, where he describes the Southern Song local elites as "emerging gentry." This view contrasts with Shigeta Atsushi and the Marxist Japanese historians who follow him in confining the "gentry" to the Ming–Qing period. I do agree with Shigeta's emphasis on the gentry's local economic and political control.

5 Robert Hartwell, "Demographic, Political and Social Transformation of China, 750–1550," *Harvard Journal of Asiatic Studies*, 42 (1982), no. 2, pp. 365–442.

6 Paul Jakov Smith, "Problematizing the Song–Yuan–Ming transition," p. 21, points out that, "nothing captures the incompetence – and irrelevance – of the late Song state more than the ease with which its elites accommodated themselves to Mongol rule."

7 Huang K'uan-ch'ung, "Cong Hezhan dao Nanbeiren," in *Zhangguo Lishishang de Fenyu He Xueshu Yantao hui Lunwen Ji*, Taibei: Lianhe baixi wenhua jijinhui, 1995.

8 Peter Lorge, "The Entrance and Exit of the Song Founders," *Journal of Sung–Yuan Studies*, 30 (1999), pp. 43–62; and "Northern Song Military Aristocracy and the Royal Family," *War and Society*, vol. 18, no. 2 (October 2000), pp. 37–47. John Chaffee, *Branches of Heaven*, Cambridge, Mass.: Harvard University Press, 1999.

9 Huang K'uan-ch'ung, "Cong Hezhan dao Nanbeiren."

10 Huan K'uan-ch'ung, "Guangdong Cuifengjun," in Huang K'uan-ch'ung, *Nansong Difang Wuli*, Taibei: Dangda tushu gongsi, 2002, pp. 9–50; "Fujian Zuoyijun," in Huang K'uan-ch'ung, *Nansong Difang Wuli*, pp. 51–108; and "Hunan Feihujun," in Huang K'uan-ch'ung, *Nansong Difang Wuli*, pp. 109–142.

11 Yao Mian, *Xuepo Ji*, 7.23, cited in Cheng-Hua Fang, "Military Families and the Southern Song Court," *Journal of Sung–Yuan Studies*, 33 (2003), p. 51. Professor Fang also provides a brief overview of military education in the Song in the same article, pp. 50–53.

12 Li Tianming, *Song–Yuan Zhanshi*, Taibei: Shihuo chubanshe, 1988, p. 219.

13 Cheng-Hua Fang, "Military Families," pp. 53–56.

14 Morris Rossabi, *Khubila Khan – His Life and Times*, Berkeley and Los Angeles: University of California Press, 1988, pp. 49–50.

15 Li Tianming, *Song–Yuan Zhanshi*, pp. 770–773.

16 Cheng-Hua Fang, "Military Families," pp. 56–61.

17 Richard L. Davis, *Wind Against the Mountains*, pp. 64–69.

18 Cheng-Hua Fang, "Military Families," p. 62; Li Tianming, *Song–Yuan Zhanshi*, pp. 970–971.

19 Cheng-Hua Fang, "Military Families.," pp. 62–63.

20 Li Tianming, *Song–Yuan Zhanshi*, pp. 954–1055; Richard L. Davis, *Wind Against the Mountains*, pp. 52–59; Morris Rossabi, *Khubilai Khan*, pp. 82–86; and Cheng-Hua Fang, "Jia Sidao yu Xiang Fan zhizhan," *Dalu Zashi*, 90.4 (1995), pp. 32–33.

21 Richard L. Davis, *Wind Against the Mountain*, pp. 133–199.

22 Toghto (ed.), *Songshi*, Beijing: Zhonghna shuju, 1995, 47.937–938.

23 Richard Davis is the sole exception to the relentlessly positive view of Wen (see *Wind Against the Mountains*, pp. 133–141, and passim). For a note on the self-created legend of Wen Tianxiang, see Peter Lorge, review of *Wind Against the Mountains*, *Journal of Sung–Yuan Studies*, 29(1999), pp. 195–201.

24 Paul Jakov Smith, "Problematizing the Song–Yuan–Ming Transition", pp. 11–19, for the development, economic, cultural, and political importance of Jiangnan.

25 Richard L. Davis, *Wind Against the Mountains*, pp. 119, 122–123.

26 Ibid., pp. 1–5; Li Tianming, *Song–Yuan Zhanshi*, pp. 1477–1482.

27 Bettine Birge, "Women and Confucianism from Song to Ming: the Institutionalization of Patrilineality," in Paul Jakov Smith and Richard von Glahn (eds), *The Song–Yuan–Ming Transition*, Cambridge, Mass.: Harvard University Press, 2003, pp. 212–240.

28 The Mongol attempts to invade Japan were extremely significant in Japanese history, giving rise to the idea of the "divine wind" or *kamikaze* so familiar to readers of WWII history that saved them from being overrun.

29 Hsiao Ch'i-Ch'ing, "Mid-Yuan Politics," in Herbert Franke and Denis Twitchett (eds), *The Cambridge History of China*, Volume 6: *Alien Regimes and Border States*, Cambridge: Cambridge University Press, 1994, pp. 496–505.

30 Ibid., "Mid-Yuan Politics," p. 503. An official *kuriltai* was not held, but peace was agreed to by all the warring parties, functionally sanctioning Temür as Khaghan.

31 Ibid., "Mid-Yuan Politics," pp. 505–507.

32 Ibid., "Mid-Yuan Politics," pp. 513–527, for Ayurbarwada's reign.

33 Ibid., "Mid-Yuan Politics," pp. 527–532, for Shidebala's reign.

34 Ibid., "Mid-Yuan Politics," pp. 535–541, for Yesün Temür's reign.

35 Ibid., "Mid-Yuan Politics," pp. 541–556, for Tugh Temür's reign.

36 This section follows John Dardess, "Shun-ti and the End of Yüan Rule in China," in Herbert Franke and Denis Twitchett (eds), *The Cambridge History of China*, Volume 6: *Alien Regimes and Border States*, Cambridge: Cambridge University Press 1994, pp. 561–586, for Toghon Temür's reign and the fall of the Yuan dynasty.

CHAPTER FIVE

The Chinese conquest dynasty, 1355–1435

> Today's officials ... obscure the ruler's brilliance, extend the
> ruler's mistakes, and treacherously conspire in factions almost
> without cease.
>
> Zhu Yuanzhang (1328–1398), Emperor of China[1]

The decades of war among regional powers following the collapse of Yuan
central control demonstrated the underlying geographic and social fault lines
intrinsic to the Chinese ecumene. While the regime that unified the Chinese
empire, the Ming, was run by Chinese, this did little to reverse the social,
political and military developments of the Yuan. The Ming proved as interested
in territorial expansion as the Yuan, though not as effective, and as concerned to
keep domestic local power-holders weak, scattered and disorganized. Unlike the
Yuan emperors, however, the first Ming emperor, Zhu Yuanzhang, was keenly
interested in making society all the way down to the local level conform to his
vision. Zhu explicitly set out to create a stable social order in which farmers
remained in their villages, the hereditary military was self-sustaining on its own
lands, and the government bureaucracy was efficient and uncorrupt. He even
interceded in the details of religious worship. Although he was not fully successful in these efforts (the government bureaucracy, for example, proved frustrat-
ingly slow and corrupt even during Zhu's own rule), they nonetheless had a
lasting effect on Chinese culture and society.

Ming rule was dominated by the military until 1435, when power decisively
shifted to civil officials. This was perhaps the final act in the shift of the Ming
government's priorities from near continuous fighting, first for survival and
then for expansion, to ruling a pacified realm. In this respect, early Ming rule
was not a continuation of Yuan practice but rather the natural development of
an emerging empire. What would become the Ming regime emerged from the
religion-inspired rebellions of the 1350s to become a regional power in the
Yangzi River valley, and then a force capable of expelling the Mongols from
north China. War was paramount in building both Zhu Yuanzhang's own
power and that of his empire. Zhu attended to civil administration to support
his armed forces.

Unlike any previous or succeeding dynasty the Ming created its Chinese empire starting in the south, and then moving north to conquer the Central Plains. Even more uniquely, the decisive campaign in the rise of the Ming and its ability to conquer the rest of China was a naval encounter in and around Lake Poyang. Although it is tempting to see this change as the result of the south's increase in wealth and population compared to the north, the subsequent conquest of China in the more usual north to south sequence by the Manchus in the seventeenth century belies this interpretation. In that sense, the long-term changes in China's population and economy did not change the political and military center of gravity of the empire. Rather, what allowed Zhu Yuanzhang to conquer north China starting from south China was the political chaos on the Central Plains.

The Red Turbans[2]

Internal political problems within the Yuan dynasty were compounded by the rise of a large-scale religious movement, the Red Turbans, in the 1330s. The Red Turbans were a Buddhist sect that focused its worship on Maitreya, defined in China as the Future Buddha, who would descend upon the earth and make it a heavenly paradise. Such a Messianic vision was particularly compelling to large numbers of impoverished people, and was part of the general religious ferment of the fourteenth century. What troubled the authorities and existing elites was the connection of the arrival of Maitreya with the end of the dynasty, and the overturning of the current order. By the 1340s many popular movements were arming themselves in response to the government's attempts at suppression, and also going underground to become secret societies.

The religious history of these popular movements is quite complex, but it is the emergence of two Red Turban groups, one in the North China Plain under Han Shantong, and the other in the central Yangzi River area under Chen Youliang, which directly affected the future political and military development of the Ming dynasty. In order to gain some shred of legitimacy, Han Shantong claimed to be descended from Song emperor Huizong, in addition to his religious titles. Although Han himself was caught and killed before his planned uprising in 1351 really took off, in 1355 Liu Futong, Han's successor as leader of the movement, set up Han's son, Liner, as Song emperor and a manifestation of the King of Light who would prepare the way for Maitreya's arrival. Liu's organization was loose, but widespread, with little or no central control. It nevertheless won some important victories, with one army destroying the palaces at Shangdu, the Mongol's summer capital, and the main force, under Liu Futong, capturing Kaifeng and installing Han Liner there to rule the revived Song dynasty in 1359.[3]

In the central Yangzi region, the southern Red Turbans were more successful in 1351, setting up their own emperor and taking control of large swathes of territory on both sides of the Yangzi River. Their fortunes declined significantly during Toghto's campaigns, and then revived following his dismissal. Chen Youliang took control of the southern Red Turbans in 1357; in 1360 he had his emperor beaten to death, and was able to establish himself as emperor of a new Han dynasty. Chen's Han dynasty mustered a formidable army and navy, but loyalty within the military was tenuous. In this respect, at least, the Red Turban forces, both north and south, resembled the crumbling Yuan armies.

Although Yuan control was slipping, the Yuan emperor could not tolerate a Song emperor occupying Kaifeng. By 1359, regional Yuan forces in north China had grown strong enough to beat back the Red Turbans, and a strong army dislodged Liu Futong from Kaifeng late in 1359 after a three-month siege. Liu, however, escaped with Han Liner. Yuan concern with north China between 1355 and 1359, however, had allowed the regional warlords in the south to consolidate their own power.[4] Although the dynasty was not faced with as formidable and unified an opponent as the Southern Song in 1359, the Yuan itself was not the unified military machine it had once been.

Not all of the newly risen regional powers were religiously inspired or Yuan splinters, however, the lower Yangzi being controlled by Zhang Shicheng, a former salt merchant and smuggler. Zhang and his brothers began their military careers by leading a rebellion of the salt-working population in Jiangsu, near the Grand Canal, in 1353. He seized control of several cities on the Grand Canal, including Gaoyou, which allowed him to interdict the transport of grain from the south to the capital in the north. Toghto's work on the Grand Canal, which had been undertaken in order to free the court from the blackmail of a pirate who controlled the transportation of grain by the coastal route, was now undone. The chancellor quickly retook some areas and restored order while preparing to crush Zhang Shicheng in Gaoyou. It was at Gaoyou that Toghto was recalled just before eliminating Zhang Shicheng. When Toghto departed, Zhang quickly dispersed the now demoralized Yuan army and soon created a firm power base on the lower Yangzi.[5]

Zhu Yuanzhang and the beginning of Ming power

The founder of the Ming dynasty, Zhu Yuanzhang, came from a desperately poor farming family in northern Jiangsu. Much of his immediate family died from starvation, and he spent some time as a novice in a Buddhist temple, three years as a mendicant monk, and then three more years back in his original temple. He was, by all accounts, a fascinatingly ugly man, so much so that his looks marked him as extraordinary, rather than simply repulsive.[6] Zhu joined a group of local rebels associated with the northern Red Turbans in Anhui in 1352. He quickly distinguished himself as a military leader, building his own units from a core of 24 men from his hometown area. The 21 who survived the next decade and a half of war were all ennobled when Zhu officially founded the Ming dynasty in 1368.

Zhu expanded south of the Yangzi River, building up the forces under his control and increasing his resources. His army soon exceeded that of his immediate superiors; after some internecine struggles, he superseded them. He still nominally owed allegiance to Han Liner, though the connection was tenuous. Zhu's forces were held together by ties of loyalty extending from him through individual commanders and so on to each soldier. Loyalty was personal, not institutional, but many of the ordinary soldiers and officers also believed strongly in the religious doctrines of the Red Turban movement. Zhu could not simply abandon the religious ideology under which he fought, and this limited his ability to connect with local Confucianized gentry, for whom those beliefs were anathema. For practical reasons of control, he put considerable effort into winning over those gentry, though he remained extremely suspicious of them to the end of his life.[7]

Outright warfare between Zhu and his former patron in 1355 was only averted by the latter's death. The same year Zhu took two important steps: attempting to capture Nanjing, and forming an alliance with some of the commanders of the fleet on Lake Chao. His first effort to capture Nanjing failed, but, rather than discouraging him, it probably convinced him of its desirability. He withdrew a short distance and prepared for a second attempt the following year. Most of the Lake Chao fleet had sailed west to join Chen Youliang, but with the remainder added to his forces Zhu was able to defeat the Yuan Yangzi fleet at Caishi on 27 March. Zhu's second attempt on Nanjing was strengthened not only by his recent naval victory but also by the surrender of 36,000 Yuan troops to him on the eve of the assault. This time the city was carried in a day of brutal fighting, falling on 10 April.[8]

Zhang Shicheng had also moved south of the Yangzi, and soon clashed with Zhu's forces. Zhu's subordinates repeatedly defeated Zhang in 1356 and 1357, prompting Zhang to offer Zhu annual tribute in payment for autonomy. Zhu turned Zhang down, though in retrospect he must have realized that he had made a serious error. Faced with the growing power of Zhu Yuanzhang's regime to his west, upriver on the Yangzi, Zhang Shicheng had no alternative but to offer his annual tribute and nominal loyalty to the Yuan court. This was immediately accepted, bolstering Zhang's position centered on Suzhou and Hangzhou, and creating a constant threat to Zhu Yuanzhang. Zhu's power base was now caught between Zhang Shicheng to his east and Chen Youliang upriver to his west. This extremely bad strategic situation was only ameliorated by Zhang Shicheng's general indolence. Had Zhang been more active and effective, Zhu Yuanzhang's regime might have been crushed in its infancy.

The contest along the Yangzi and its tributaries was fought on land and water. As the three regimes – Chen Youliang's farthest upstream, Zhu Yuanzhang's in the middle, and Zhang Shicheng's farthest downstream – struggled with each other they repaired and expanded the city walls which had been purposely allowed to crumble under the Yuan. By 1359, the renewed fortification of the cities in the Yangzi valley and the expansion of the three regimes had solidified their borders. It was difficult to capture cities by direct assault, though the loyalty of the commanders of the cities was less certain. To make matters more indecisive, all three regimes were now large enough that a single setback, or even a series of setbacks, would not destroy them. But the nature of the regimes' political structures prevented the formation of a peaceful interstate system.

In 1360, Chen Youliang sent an army to prevent Zhu's re-conquest of Chizhou. Chen's army was ambushed, and most of the 3,000 prisoners taken executed. In response, Chen launched a major attack with 100,000 men on the city of Taiping in mid-June, capturing it after a few days because of his innovative exploitation of his ships' high sterncastles to overtop the walls.[9] The capture of Taiping started an escalating series of battles between Chen's and Zhu's regimes that culminated in the Lake Poyang campaign in 1363. This clash was probably inevitable. The Yangzi valley regimes could not have reached a stable balance of power because each leader's control over his subordinate city commanders depended more upon continued military victory than real loyalty. Since cities dominated their surrounding territory, it was control over the cities that mattered. Thus losing a major city, while not fatal, required an immediate response to shore up support. But it was only capturing major cities that satisfied the need for military victories required by the political situation.

A direct clash with Chen would be unwise, since Chen's navy was ten times the size of Zhu's, but something had to be done to regain military credibility. Zhu lured Chen, now overconfident after capturing Taiping, into an ambush near Nanjing, Zhu's capital, in June. Chen's force was ambushed after it disembarked, losing 20,000 soldiers killed in battle, 100 large warships, a few hundred smaller ships, and 7,000 prisoners, the majority of whom were from the contingent of Lake Chao sailors that joined Chen several years before. This changed the naval balance considerably, making the contest on the Yangzi much more even. Zhang Shicheng, for his part, remained inactive until later in the year, when, seeing that Chen and Zhu had not destroyed each other, he launched a few failed attacks on Zhu's territory.

Chen returned to the offensive in 1361 to reconsolidate his political position. Zhu's successes were equaled by Chen's and it became clear that Chen, rather than Zhang Shicheng, was Zhu's most pressing problem. In September Zhu took personal command of the fleet and sailed upstream to confront Chen directly. Zhu's fleet badly defeated Chen's, and Chen withdrew, falling back to Wuchang. While Chen and his fleet were kept bottled up at Wuchang, Zhu's forces captured several important cities, or convinced them to surrender. Zhu could not sustain the pressure, however, and rebellion and Zhang Shicheng stirring to the weakened rear of Zhu, forced him to return to Nanjing.

Zhu spent 1362 consolidating the previous year's gains as best he could, but disloyalty and limited forces constrained those efforts. In April, he was forced to shift the forces containing Chen Youliang at Wuchang in order to recapture the city of Nanchang. Once recaptured, Nanchang's walls were shifted back from the river bank to prevent someone using Chen's technique of ship-borne assault. Chen, of course, escaped from Wuchang and set about building a new fleet. Zhu himself narrowly avoided assassination in August, demonstrating just how tenuous his position was. His life depended upon the loyalty of his generals. Early the following year, Zhu was forced to rescue Han Liner, his erstwhile sovereign and religious leader, from one of Zhang Shicheng's generals. It was an odd distraction before the decisive campaign of the Ming dynasty founding.

The Lake Poyang campaign, 1363[10]

Chen Youliang's formidable fleet sailed downstream in the spring of 1363. The core of the fleet was massive three-deckers, with iron-armored castles, holding as many as 2,000 or 3,000 men each. Including the personnel on the many smaller vessels, Chen had nearly 300,000 men. His first target was Nanchang, which was the key to controlling the entire Jiangxi region. The city walls no longer stood directly on the river bank, however, and Chen was forced to conduct a conventional siege. Fighting was fierce, often involving the extensive use of firearms, and continued for 85 days before the defenders offered a truce, with a set surrender date, as a ruse to buy more time. Chen's immediate campaign goals had already been undercut by Nanchang's determined resistance, but Zhu Yuanzhang had not come to the city's rescue sooner because of his own military commitments, a failed siege and a rebellion, and concerns over the obedience of his generals.

Zhu could not afford to allow Nanchang to fall, nor could he ignore Chen's challenge. He was forced to stake all his political capital and take the risky military course of another direct naval confrontation with Chen. Although Zhu would win the contest, it was extremely close. Chen's fleet was much stronger than Zhu's, in both the number and the size of ships, and Chen had the strategic advantage of only needing to not lose, where Zhu really needed an outright, decisive victory. This explains Zhu's extremely aggressive tactics and operations; the high political stakes went beyond the military need to break the siege of Nanchang.

Zhu set sail on 15 August with a reported 1,000 ships and 100,000 men; nine days later he established forts at the mouth of Lake Poyang to bottle up Chen's fleet if it outmaneuvered him. Zhu's fleet entered the lake on 28 August. Chen raised the siege and brought his ships and men into the lake to confront Zhu. Beginning on 29 August, the two fleets began a bloody four-day battle resulting in heavy casualties on both sides. Zhu's fleet fared poorly on the first day, though it attacked aggressively and did some damage. Chen's triple-deckers were nearly invincible, particularly as the backbone of a fleet sailing in close formation. He was content to allow Zhu Yuanzhang's fleet to grind itself down attacking him. The second day Zhu attacked with fireships, packed with gunpowder, when the wind was favorable. This destroyed several hundred warships and inflicted some 60,000 casualties, without actually crippling Chen's fleet.

Zhu still took 7,000 casualties in the day's fighting, and both sides spent the next day regrouping and repairing their ships.

While the naval battle was raging, one of Zhu's armies reached Nanchang overland, sweeping away whatever forces Chen had left to maintain the siege. Zhu's and Chen's fleets clashed again on 1 September, and while Zhu's ships did somewhat better against Chen's more open formation, he could afford the losses much less than Chen. By noon Zhu disengaged, falling back to blockade the lake mouth on the night of 2 September. The situation that Chen faced at this point seems to have baffled him, since he waited a month with dwindling food to act. It was pointless to try to resume the siege of Nanchang now that it had been reinforced and Zhu's fleet threatened his ships. He had no choice but to break out, which he finally undertook on 3 October. Chen's fleet had successfully broken out to the Yangzi and was headed upstream when Zhu's fleet attacked, spearheaded once again by fireships. Combat broke down into individual contests floating downstream, and might well have proved as inconclusive as the previous encounters, had Chen Youliang not been struck by an arrow and killed. This was more decisive than the fleet battle, handing Zhu the outright victory he needed. Some of Chen's fleet did escape, but 50,000 men and hundreds of ships surrendered.

The conquest of Zhang Shicheng

Zhu's victory elevated him above his generals politically, creating the kind of authority necessary for establishing a more stable and legitimate regime. What was important was that he had taken a great military risk, prosecuted it aggressively and won decisively. The closeness of the fighting during the campaign was unimportant when compared to the completeness of victory when Chen Youliang was killed. Zhang Shicheng understood that he was next on Zhu Yuanzhang's list, but rather than attempt to surrender to him he adopted a belligerent position. Zhang's loyalty to the Yuan dynasty brought him little direct military benefit, though it allowed him to keep the loyalty of the gentry. The wealthy families of Jiangnan would pay a heavy price for their loyalty to Zhang and intense antipathy for Zhu, when Zhu ultimately won out.

Zhang was not immediately attacked, however, as Chen Youliang's death did not result in the immediate surrender of all of his former territories. Chen's control had been loose, and so it took Zhu and his armies until 1365 to reduce or force to surrender all of the cities of his former co-religionist. Also important was Zhu's reorganization of his armies in 1364. His new prestige enabled him to gain greater control over the army as well as the new cities, though this was functionally the same thing, and to elevate himself further above his generals. Zhu's forces were placed under bureaucratic control for the first time, with units of regular size commanded by officers of specific, appropriate rank.[11] Zhang Shicheng was not inactive during this time, but his two attempts to attack Zhu's territory were both beaten off decisively. Since the remains of the

Yuan regime in north China was occupied with its own problems, Zhang was left to face Zhu alone.

Zhu struck Zhang's northern territory first to cut him off from any possibility of Yuan aid, taking control of Gaoyou on the Grand Canal on 24 April 1366. After a summer spent farming and integrating the captured troops into his army, Zhu sent a strong invasion force of 200,000 men to capture Hangzhou in September. This was a bold strategy, aimed directly at Zhang's center of political gravity. One of Zhu's best generals, Chang Yuchun, had argued for a concentric strategy of capturing Zhang's outlying territory before attacking his capital. Zhu overrode Chang, though it is unclear why he opted for the faster but more risky strategy. Perhaps the immense political and military payoffs from his recent, similarly bold, gambles convinced him that fortune was on his side.

Hangzhou fell surprisingly quickly, and the army continued on to surround Suzhou, Zhang Shicheng's capital, in late December. Although Suzhou was not a notably strong city, Zhang held out for ten months. Zhu's army hammered at the city from a continuous circumvallation, complete with firing platforms for its siege artillery. Zhang personally led repeated sorties to break the siege, but to no avail. On 1 October 1367 Zhu's artillery breached the walls, and Zhang Shicheng made a fighting retreat into the city's interior. With no hope of escape or rescue, Zhang attempted to hang himself in his palace. He was discovered while still alive and made a prisoner, but succeeded in a second attempt while incarcerated in Nanjing. The end of his regime added another 250,000 troops to Zhu Yuanzhang's army.[12]

The end of the Yuan

With the entire Yangzi valley outside of Sichuan under his control, it was time for Zhu Yuanzhang to confront the remnants of the Yuan dynasty in north China directly. The Yuan court's authority had already collapsed as regional strongmen arose to put down the rebellions the government's regular army could not, and it was this struggle within the forces nominally loyal to the Yuan which had kept the Mongol government from interfering with events along the Yangzi River. Strongest of these regional warlords was Kökö Temür, based in Shanxi and Shaanxi, who had just recently defeated a combined effort of the other warlords, instigated by the Yuan court, to destroy him.[13] Zhu Yuanzhang called a council of war to discuss the strategy for eliminating the Yuan dynasty.

In a striking reverse of their previous positions, Chang Yuchun argued for a direct drive to capture Dadu (modern Beijing), the Yuan capital, but Zhu Yuanzhang overrode him and insisted on a four-step plan to conquer separate regions of the remaining Yuan territory. First they would conquer Shandong, then Henan to the Tongguan Pass in the west, followed by Dadu and its surrounding area, and finally Shanxi and Shaanxi. Even though Zhu's army was almost certain of ultimate victory, the choice was difficult nonetheless. Although the Yuan court no longer had any real authority, the political significance of capturing its capital might have induced many regional warlords to surrender to Zhu. Conversely, a drive on Dadu might have netted a worthless symbol, overextended Zhu's army, and made consolidation more difficult as the last vestiges of nominal Yuan government collapsed. Zhu Yuanzhang's choice of strategies seems to indicate that he felt that directly seizing territory would both further weaken the Yuan court and make the imposition of real control much easier. Zhu's plan would first isolate the Yuan capital from outside aid. Moreover, Shandong was much more accessible by sea and thus a good place to start for a naval power like Zhu's.

While the 250,000-man northern expeditionary army under Xu Da and Chang Yuchun began preparing on 13 November 1367, a southern expedition was also put under way. The southern force rapidly conquered Fujian, Guangdong and Guangxi over the course of the winter and into the spring. Xu and Chang meanwhile overran Shandong, beginning at the end of December 1367 and finishing at the start of March the following year. With Shandong under their control, Xu and Chang turned east into Henan, while a second army attacked from the south. Kaifeng, the old Song capital, surrendered on 16 April, and Luoyang nine days later after a Yuan army was defeated. Tongguan was captured on 13 May.

Back in Nanjing, Zhu Yuanzhang founded the Ming dynasty and assumed its throne as emperor on 23 January 1368. With his victorious armies just then conquering the north and south, he took the reign title "Overflowing Martiality" (Hongwu). Unlike previous emperors in Chinese history, Zhu would use only one reign title during his rule, a practice which would continue throughout the Ming dynasty, and even to the end of the Qing as well. The new emperor conferred with his generals at Kaifeng and reconfirmed his original plan. The Ming army attacked Dadu in August, after harvesting their summer crops, capturing the city on 14 September. Both the Yuan emperor and the crown prince escaped to Inner Mongolia just ahead of Xu Da's army.[14]

As was always the case, the official founding of a new dynasty marked a political milepost rather than the end of the military actions. The Yuan court was still in existence, and Sichuan, Yunnan, Manchuria, Mongolia, Shanxi and Shaanxi remained unconquered. These were important caveats to the Ming founding, but the Ming army in 1368 was still recording victory after victory in the field. Furthermore, no other regime could seriously threaten the Ming's existence. Over the next four years, Zhu Yuanzhang discovered the limits of his military power, which in turn affected the nature of Ming rule.

The march on Dadu, now renamed Beiping ("the north is conquered"), had bypassed many cities and other fortified positions, all of which needed to be secured before launching an attack on Shanxi. It was only on 9 January 1369 that Xu Da was able to capture Taiyuan, the central city of Shanxi. The remaining local warlords in Shanxi and Shaanxi were still unable to unite in opposition to the Ming armies, making it easier to pick them off individually but also forcing Xu Da and Chang Yuchun to defeat many small opponents. The greatest warlord, Kökö Temür, was forced to fall back to the west into Gansu to avoid being destroyed. On 3 March Chang Yuchun captured Datong, the major northern city of Shanxi, which would also serve as a jumping-off point or defensive position for campaigns into the steppe. After further Ming campaigns in April through Shaanxi, Kökö Temür was the only Yuan "loyalist" left.

Chang Yuchun passed away on campaign in August after capturing Kaiping, in the north, a significant loss for the Ming cause, and Xu Da closed out the Ming season by conquering Qingyang on 22 September. Kökö Temür launched several attacks on Ming positions in the west that fall and winter, making it clear that the remnants of the Yuan regime were not entirely prostrate. Continuing Mongol power was now a significant threat to the ability of the Ming to complete its conquest of the former Yuan territory, or to at least reach a stable resting point. Accordingly, two expeditions were sent out in 1370, one to pursue and hopefully destroy the Yuan emperor and his court, and one to eliminate Kökö Temür. It was also possible that if the Mongols could success-fully be brought to heel, the still independent regime in Sichuan would surrender.

The first expedition, under Li Wenzhong, was extremely successful. The Yuan emperor died in May at Yingchang, but his successor was barely on the throne before Li's army stormed the city on 10 June. Some 53,000 Mongol troops surrendered, and the new emperor's son fell into Li's hands. Although the Yuan emperor escaped across the Gobi, Li had secured the Shanxi and Beiping from the Mongols. Xu Da was similarly successful in Gansu, shattering Kökö Temür's army on 4 May. Xu had been forced to take direct command the previous day to shore up his army after a subordinate commander nearly lost the battle in the face of a Mongol assault. Xu's counterattack broke the Mongol army, forcing Kökö Temür to flee across the Gobi and capturing 86,000 men.[15]

Despite these victories, and the obvious power of the Ming empire, the regime in Sichuan still refused to surrender. This was yet another example of how regional powers throughout Chinese history defied a new dynasty claim-ing to hold the Mandate of Heaven until military force compelled them to do so. In 1371 two Ming forces invaded Sichuan, one over the northern route through precipitous mountain roads, and one sailing up the Yangzi River. The Yangzi force was initially repulsed, unable to break through the heavily fortified Qutang gorge, but the northern force fared much better, overrunning Jiezhou by the early summer. The northern force continued its march through Hanzhou, despite the Sichuan regime transferring reinforcements up from the Yangzi. A second Ming commander blasted his way through the fortifications of the Qutang gorge with cannon and trebuchet[16] and captured Kuizhou, thus opening the way into Sichuan. Chongqing then fell, and the regime's leader capitulated; even so, it took another month for the northern force to capture Chengdu.[17]

The victories of 1371 did not, however, convince either Kökö Temür or the Yuan emperor to give up, despite the Hongwu emperor's good treatment of the

Yuan emperor's captured son. Most of the Ming army's striking force was now freed up to concentrate on the continuing Mongol problem. Kökö Temür still reportedly controlled an army of 100,000 men, so in 1372 three Ming forces totaling 250,000 troops were sent to destroy the recalcitrant Mongol warlord. The main force, under Xu Da, some 150,000 strong, was initially successful, but ultimately forced to withdraw after losing tens of thousands of troops in a battle on 7 June. A second Ming army of 50,000 men was drawn deeply into Mongolia and barely managed to extricate itself after a three-day defensive battle. The third Ming army was entirely successful in the Gansu corridor, but this did little to recompense the other losses.[18]

Mongol resistance became intractable after the losses of 1372, and the Hongwu emperor shifted to a defensive stance with respect to the steppe. Overall, the Ming military posture became that of an established empire trying to hold on to what it had, rather than an expanding empire attempting to acquire new territory. There were now internal rebellions of aboriginal peoples to put down, and even threats to the coast by "Japanese" pirates. Diplomatic efforts to establish some sort of *modus vivendi* with the Yuan emperor failed, despite returning his son to him. Ming expansion ended with serious border issues unresolved, on the one hand leaving the Mongols the initiative in military matters, while on the other having established an empire whose existence was not really threatened by even large-scale Mongol raids. The Ming did not reach the territorial extent of the Yuan, nor was it able to convince the Yuan emperor explicitly to accept the passing of the Mandate of Heaven. Nevertheless, Yuan power was effectively over within the Chinese ecumene.

Ming government

Zhu Yuanzhang had begun moving away from his religious ideology consider-ably before he founded the Ming dynasty. Although many of his followers were motivated by that ideology, it was an obstacle to winning over the local, Confu-cianized elite. Zhu began to employ Confucian-educated scholars in his nascent bureaucracy in order to gain credibility with similarly inclined elites, and to exploit their literate skills in administering a vast territory. The bureaucratic demands of efficient rulership forced Zhu to use a class of men that he sus-pected and despised. Zhu's hostility to the Confucian elite shaped many of the choices he made in setting up the Ming government.

No other founding emperor in Chinese history had come from as desper-ately poor a background as Zhu Yuanzhang. Most of his family died of starva-tion when he was young, and he became a Buddhist novice at the age of 16 in large part to get enough to eat. It was there that he learned to read, though he was not very well educated. His weak education, combined with his famously unattractive appearance, fueled a deep insecurity when dealing with his highly educated officials and their refined manners. As a practical matter, Zhu recog-nized that the Confucianized local elites were so deeply entrenched that they could not be done away with and so had to be co-opted.[19] This was a further example of the development of local power separate from whatever governing imperial political regime wielded nominal authority over an area. Zhu's challenge was to make them feel a part of his regime without actually giving them any power in it. This was impossible, and the tension between what the Hongwu emperor wanted to do and what he was able to accomplish, with respect to the Confucianized elite, explains both his experiments in government and his brutal responses when some of those experiments failed.

Ming government initially followed Mongol precedent, itself a development of Jurchen, rather than Song, institutions. General administration was under the Secretariat, the Chief Military Commission handled military affairs, and censorial functions were carried out by the Chief Surveillance Office. Standing atop this bureaucratic structure were the two most senior heads of the Secretariat, who were effectively grand counselors. This concentrated immense powers in the hands of the heads of the Secretariat, a situation that the Hongwu emperor could not tolerate. In 1380, Chancellor Hu Weiyong was accused of treason and executed. The purge that followed resulted in some 30,000 executions, as civil and military officials with any connection to Hu, along with his family members and relatives, were eliminated. Ming government was then reorganized.[20]

All of the top positions of the Secretariat were abolished, the Chief Military Commission was split into five regional military commissions and the positions of censor-in-chief and vice censor-in-chief were similarly done away with. The emperor had beheaded his own government, preventing any individual apart from himself from holding significant power. Zhu Yuanzhang now had to control his government directly, engaging in much more day-to-day business than he could reasonably expect to manage. Without its top ranks, the heads of the Secretariat's six boards reported to the emperor personally. The dispersal of military power was quite strange and would grow stranger still over the next decades. Since the Board of War (*Bingbu*) handled most of the peacetime concerns of keeping the army supplied, the five equal military commissions seem to have mostly provided posts for officers waiting for assignment to expeditionary armies. At the same time, various frontier commands were being placed under the control of Zhu's sons. These imperial princes were gradually put in place as the original generals who created the empire died, or were purged, by Zhu.

The Hongwu emperor also experimented with the exam system, evincing the same skepticism about the system's value as Song Taizu. More faith was put in recommendations and a national school system leading up to a national university; the Hongwu emperor repeatedly used university graduates on large-scale projects, like the cadastral surveys of the Yangzi delta prefectures in 1387. The first civil service exams were held at the lowest level (of three) in 1368, leading up to the metropolitan exam (the highest level) in 1371. They were suspended two years later by a disgusted emperor, who found the graduates literary but impractical. Further recruitment by recommendations stressed virtue over book learning, but the exams were revived again in 1384 and remained in place from then on. Serious problems remained, however, as the metropolitan exam of 1397 did not pass a single northern scholar. Given that the emperor was a northerner, and that he was particularly suspicious of the southeastern elites who dominated the exams, it is not surprising that he reacted strongly to the situation. A new evaluation added 61 names; the original examiners were punished, and the precedent of quotas of regional graduates was established. The purely meritocratic aspect of the exam system was thus overridden by the need to create a fully empire-wide bureaucracy, or at least one in which the particular advantages of a few regions in the south did not dominate the government.[21]

The Hongwu emperor remained an extremely violent man, however, and the attractions of government service were strongly mitigated by the real danger of that occupation. Officials were often beaten in court before the emperor if they offended him, sometimes fatally. Several purges, in addition to the Hu Weiyong episode, resulted in thousands or tens of thousands of executions, along with widespread torture and frequent exile. Zhu's personal bodyguard, the Embroidered Uniform Guard, functioned as a secret police force acting outside of the established legal system. All of this was part of the emperor's reconfiguration of the relationship between ruler and official.

Economic and social policy was similarly heavy-handed, with mass relocations of thousands, tens of thousands, and, on at least one occasion, 140,000 families into less-populated regions to reinvigorate agriculture. Artisan families were officially registered in their occupations, as were farmers, merchants and soldiers. Zhu Yuanzhang's vision appears to have been a static one in which the society and government he would dictate would continue in perpetuity. Religion was strictly regulated, with heterodox sects like the Red Turbans prohibited.

The entire population was divided into communities of 110 adjacent households as the basic unit of self-government and state control. Each year one of the heads of the ten wealthiest households held the position of community chief, who served as representative to the local magistrate and the local tax collector. The other 100 households were grouped into ten groups of ten, with each family head acting as representative for his group to the community chief on an annual rotation. Everyone in each group was responsible for the actions of the other members, creating a vast mutual surveillance system. It was much easier for the government to control these larger units, to draw taxes and labor from them, and to subject them to the ideological exhortations the Hongwu emperor was so fond of.

Although it is impossible to judge the real effects of the ideological program on local society, the emperor's attempt to reach so far down into the community to control society was impressively ambitious. On a practical level, however, this system institutionalized the dominance of local power-holders. Problems within a given community were supposed to be solved internally by the community chief, and only brought to the magistrate for adjudication if that process failed. Thus, those in power at the local level were explicitly charged with deciding local issues, and anyone who was not satisfied with that process and moved to the next level was actively discouraged by the magistrate from doing so. The Hongwu emperor's prescriptions, read out loud at the monthly community assemblies, specifically admonished members to respect their superiors, be content with their position and be harmonious with their neighbors.

The Ming military

The Hongwu emperor tried to create a military system that would not be a burden on society. In practice, this meant separating the army from the rest of society and making it as self-sufficient as possible. Members of the army and their families were registered as military households, with an obligation to provide an adult male for service in return for reduced tax and labor requirements. This status was permanent. These families were themselves organized along the lines of the military system, rather than the community system.

When Zhu Yuanzhang regularized his army, he formed it into units derived from Yuan practice. The *weisuo* system established Guards (*wei*) of 5,600 hereditary soldiers, named after its garrison location. The five battalions (*qianhusuo*) of 1,120 men were further divided into ten companies (*bohusuo*) of 112 men.[22] These smaller units were often detached from their Guard unit for service outside of the larger formation's theater of operations. In 1392 there were 1,198,442 regulars in this system – at least on paper. The regional military commissions directly controlled some battalions that did not belong to Guard units. Local militia units performed many low-level military tasks, but under the control of the civil authorities.

Troops trained within their Guard units as well as rotating through the training divisions at the capital. These training divisions served to raise the level of training and homogenize it so that units scattered across the empire could be integrated into larger armies as needed, and functioned as the source of most expeditionary armies. This made great sense since the training division troops were putatively the best trained. The importance of firearms in the Ming army was explicit insofar as one of the training divisions was specifically tasked with firearms training. Thus all Ming troops would have been either trained in firearms use or, at least, familiar with their operation. It does not appear as if any major Ming expeditionary army took the field without a significant firearms capability.

A massive military establishment guarded the capital, which shifted from Nanjing to Beijing in 1420. Thirty-three Imperial Guards responsible for the security of the palace were bolstered by a further 41 Capital Guards posted in and around the capital. The emperor himself personally controlled 15 of the Capital Guards, and none of the total of 74 Guards around the capital were controlled by the military commissions. Even after the capital was moved, 32 Capital Guards and 17 Imperial Guards remained posted in Nanjing. The provisioning of these enormous concentrations of troops in Beijing, as well as the large numbers of government officials, spurred considerable spending to improve the canal system that transported the agricultural surpluses of the south to the poorer north.

One of Zhu Yuanzhang's experiments in structuring the military proved to be more politically significant immediately after his death than any other. By enfeoffing his sons in important defense commands along the northern border, he created a highly militarized generation of imperial princes. Theoretically, these princes would bolster the dynasty by controlling the military for the Zhu family, replacing the founding generals whose loyalty Zhu Yuanzhang had come to suspect. These princes were tutored in war, and several managed to acquit themselves well in their responsibilities. The problem was what to do when Zhu's eldest son, the heir-apparent, died in 1392. Rather than appoint his next oldest surviving son to succeed him, the emperor upheld the principle of primogeniture and appointed the late heir-apparent's son as his heir-apparent. This decision created a direct military threat to the succeeding emperor, a situation that the Hongwu emperor did almost nothing to address in his remaining years on the throne.[23]

Civil war[24]

When the Hongwu emperor passed away on 24 June 1398, his grandson inherited a powerful empire with several structural political problems. The Jianwen (Establishing Civil Accomplishment) emperor had a completely legitimate succession, but knew that he faced internal threats to his rule from his powerful uncles. The Jianwen emperor's grandfather had stipulated that the imperial princes were not to leave their fiefs to attend his funeral, an act that seems to have provoked some justified anger. The new emperor and his advisers took it as a given that the imperial uncles were in conspiracy against the throne. Zhu Di, the Prince of Yan, was now the oldest surviving uncle. The fourth son of Zhu Yuanzhang, based at Beiping, was an able military leader as well as extremely ambitious.[25] Many of the criticisms that have been made of the Jianwen emperor and his advisers in how they attempted to de-fang the imperial princes may be true inasmuch as they failed disastrously, but it seems highly unlikely that they could have somehow convinced the Prince of Yan not to rebel.

Rather than attempt to dispose of Zhu Di immediately, the Jianwen emperor decided to first whittle away his power by removing the other princes in their fiefs. The utility of this approach depended upon the other princes actually being in league with or ready to make common cause with Zhu Di. Certainly once their brothers began to be dispossessed of their fiefs this became a self-fulfilling prophecy. Surprise was not lost by this indirect strategy since Zhu Di intended to rebel and expected to either attack or be attacked by the court. A direct attack by the court on Zhu Di when he had not as yet done anything wrong might undermine elite opinion of the new emperor. Conversely, if Zhu Di were induced to rebel, elite support would accrue to the court.

Five princes were found guilty of unrelated crimes and dispossessed of their fiefs, and administrators loyal to the court began to encroach upon Beiping. Zhu Di feigned madness and bided his time, building up a personal bodyguard and remaining in touch with the commanders of the Guards units nearby. The court finally accused Zhu Di of treason in 1399, but the men sent to Beiping to arrest him on 6 August were killed outside the gates of the city. Zhu Di was now officially in rebellion.

Nineteen Guards and one detached battalion based in and around Beiping came over to the Prince of Yan's banner less than three weeks after he rebelled. By 17 August the last member of the Beiping area military command loyal to the court was dead. A major military campaign would now have to be mounted to put down the Prince of Yan. Herein lies the major mistake made by the court in its indirect strategy: when it finally turned to dispossessing Zhu Di it should have expected and been prepared for a direct military challenge. Perhaps the court became overconfident that its strategy had been so effective up until that point, and believed that its "soft" political means would have sufficed by then to induce a peaceful surrender, but that was no excuse for not having already mobilized an army to prevent an armed rebellion. The court lost precious time while it concentrated forces to put down the Prince of Yan.

By 1399 few effective generals were available to the court. Most of Zhu Yuanzhang's original generals had died or been killed, along with many of their subordinate commanders. Geng Bingwen, one of the last remaining generals of that earlier generation, was placed in command, and by early September had mobilized an army of 130,000 men at Zhending. The Prince of Yan struck first, however, attacking Geng's army where it was camped outside of Zhending on 24 September. Geng's three main subordinates were captured and some 30,000 heads taken, but the rebel army failed to overwhelm the city even after surrounding it for two days. Geng had lost the initiative, though his defense of Zhending contained the Prince of Yan's southern expansion. Meanwhile, other loyal Ming armies marched on the rebel strongholds, putting further pressure on the rebellion.

Geng Bingwen was replaced with Li Jinglong, son of Li Wenzhong, another of Zhu Yuanzhang's great generals. Unfortunately for the court, the younger Li proved no more competent than Geng Bingwen. The Prince of Yan first beat back the smaller Ming armies threatening his territory and then dealt Li's main army a severe setback as it besieged Beiping. Yan cavalry took advantage of a frozen river to get behind the Ming army, surprising it in camp on 2 December. The siege was lifted as Li and his dispersed army fell back in confusion to the south. Yan retained the initiative, and had dealt the Ming army two serious defeats within barely four months. To keep Li completely off balance, the Prince of Yan feinted at Datong during the winter, forcing Li to exhaust his army on a long march over difficult terrain during the coldest weather. With the Yan army already gone when Li arrived in March, the Ming army could do nothing accept return to its base.

The Jianwen emperor took various steps to enhance his image as a legitimate monarch in the civil sphere, though this had no discernible effect on his fortunes. More importantly, Li Jinglong began his offensive in May, marching again toward Beiping. The Prince of Yan continued to exploit his advantage in cavalry and unified command to fall on one column of Li's force on 18 May. This column was defeated and forced back, but when the Yan army then shifted to another part of Li's army it was itself beaten. Nightfall allowed the Prince to reassemble his army, and then cross a river separating Li's army. The Yan rearguard was defeated during this operation, but the Prince continued his plan, sending part of his army against the Ming center while personally overseeing the attack on the Ming left. Li's army initially withstood these attacks, its mass now proving a great help on the defensive, but late in the day the Ming army pulled back to its pre-prepared defensive positions. The Yan army was demoralized and tired after a day of mostly ineffective assaults, and the Prince was forced to rally them for another attempt. Luck was very much on his side this time, as a wind gust broke Li Jinglong's standard, giving the impression that he was no longer on the field, and the shift in wind allowed the Yan forces to set fire to the Ming positions. The Ming army collapsed and Li fled, with tens of thousands dead on the field and a reported 100,000 drowned in the river. Despite this impressive victory, the Prince failed to capture the city of Ji'nan in June, and withdrew to Beiping at the beginning of September 1400. The Ming army then reoccupied much of the territory it had lost, finishing the campaign season where it started.

The Prince of Yan launched yet another surprise attack in October, capturing a Ming general, and then rode further down the Grand Canal to threaten Ming communications. On 9 January 1401, however, he was badly defeated at Dezhou, taking extremely heavy casualties from Ming crossbow and cannon fire. He was then attacked in the rear, leaving tens of thousands of his soldiers captured in Ming hands. Two more battles were fought as he retreated to Beiping, having suffered his most serious losses so far. But he refused to give up the initiative, and returned to the field at the end of February. This was not just a display of good generalship, it was also a clear demonstration that the Prince understood that if he lost the initiative he would have likely lost the war.

The area around Dezhou was once again the battlefield as the two armies clashed from 5 April to 6 April. Although Yan fared poorly the first day, the balance shifted the second day, and the Ming army fell back into Dezhou. The Prince once again proved incapable of capturing a city, and marched off when a relief army appeared. Ming forces also showed their inability to coordinate disparate commands and support each other in a timely way, thus undermining much of their advantage in numbers. A similar story repeated itself on 27 April, when the Prince defeated a Ming army at Gaocheng, which then retreated into Zhending, where he could not dislodge it. After winning most of his battles, though, he seemed no closer to overthrowing his nephew.

In tactics reminiscent of those of the Mongols, Zhu Di sent raiding parties into Ming territory to disrupt the supply system and maintain the tactical initiative. These efforts were partly successful, with the supply barges sent to Dezhou burned in July, but the Prince was forced back to Beiping when the Ming army marched on his capital. By the end of 1401 Zhu Di was depressed, considering that he held no more territory than when he had started. He did not see the fragility of the Ming army that the July interdiction of supplies had caused. Perhaps it was the idea that his tactics up to that point had failed, despite many battlefield victories, that drove him to a new and desperate plan for 1402. He would now strike at the political center of gravity of the Ming dynasty, rather than attempt to expand his own territory methodically.

The Ming army was concentrated around the Prince of Yan's territory, so when he rode south in January of 1402 and bypassed those positions few loyalist troops stood between him and Nanjing. After ignoring Dezhou and crossing the Yellow River, a series of towns and cities fell to him, temporarily making up for his non-existent supply lines. Zhu Di headed for Suzhou just as Xu Huizu, son of the great Xu Da, was sent to bolster Ming forces with a newly mobilized army. A major victory by Ming forces on 16 May convinced the Jianwen emperor to make the critical mistake of the campaign and recall Xu Huizu, just as his army arrived to support the now successful Ming field force. Xu's recall left the Ming field army vulnerable, and it was destroyed on 29 May. The Prince then marched directly on Yangzhou, where the surrender of the river fleet gave him the means to cross the Yangzi.

Once the Prince of Yan was able to cross the Yangzi, military and political logic convinced most Ming officials that the Jianwen emperor was finished. Li Jinglong, along with Prince Gu, actually betrayed the emperor and opened the gates to Nanjing when the Yan army arrived on 13 July. In the confusion, a fire broke out in the imperial palace and the Jianwen emperor and his empress were reportedly killed. The civil war was over.

Eternal happiness

Zhu Di, the Prince of Yan, assumed the throne of the Ming dynasty and proclaimed his reign name: Yongle, "Eternal Happiness." Although he killed the Jianwen emperor's closest officials (some committed suicide), often with great brutality, he did not attempt to reorder or restructure the government bureaucracy. Indeed, the new emperor sponsored literary projects and sanctioned the civil dominance of the government, while also reinstating the imperial princes' titles, though not their fiefs or control of troops. Unlike his father, the Yongle emperor left the Confucian-educated officials in charge of the bureaucracy; he focused his energies on the army and military campaigns. In even sharper contrast to his father, the new emperor was not resolutely hostile to the Mongols, many of whom had served him in his war with the court. The Uriyangqad Mongols were rewarded with the withdrawal of the Ming garrison from Daning, leaving the surrounding territory to them.

Although the Yongle emperor had good relations with many foreign powers, two external military problems occupied him during his reign: The Mongols still required considerable efforts to keep them in line, and the Ming interceded directly in Vietnam. During all of these campaigns the emperor was building up Beiping, now renamed Beijing ("Northern Capital"), and preparing to transfer the capital there from Nanjing. Initially, the Oyirods (Western Mongols) had good relations with the Ming, and their leaders accepted Ming titles. The Eastern Mongols were a different story, and when a Ming army sent to punish them for executing a Ming envoy was annihilated at the Kerülen River on 23 September 1409, the emperor decided to take the field personally.[26]

The Yongle emperor's army left Beijing on 15 March 1410 and campaigned successfully through the summer, defeating and driving off several Mongol armies. None of the victories was decisive or even particularly impressive, but they did bring the Eastern Mongols to heel. By 1414 the emperor had to campaign against the Oyirods, this time with an army 500,000 men strong. This vast host crossed the Gobi and was attacked by the Oyirods on 23 June at Qulan Qushwan. The Ming defeated the Oyirods, but did not pursue them after they disengaged for fear of ambush. Once again, although the battle had not been decisive, it was enough to convince the Oyirods' leadership to submit.

The Mongols were quiet until 1421, when conflict with the Eastern Mongols erupted again. The Yongle emperor began preparations late in the year for a campaign the following spring over the strenuous objections of several of his senior officials. Grain was transported by some 235,000 porters, and the army left Beijing on 17 April 1422. The two-month march to Kaiping was used to put the army in shape, and it marched into the steppe in a massive square formation. Unfortunately, the Uriyangqad Mongols, who had been so important to the previous campaigns, had joined the Eastern Mongols, but a Ming detachment of 20,000 men battered them into submission by early July. The main Ming army burned the Eastern Mongols' camp and captured their livestock, but the Mongols themselves withdrew into the steppe. Rather than be drawn into a probably fruitless chase, the emperor returned to Beijing. Another campaign in 1423 also accomplished nothing. The Yongle emperor's final campaign in 1424 repeated this process, and he died on 12 August while the army was returning home.[27]

Ming relations with Vietnam were also inconclusive inasmuch as the Ming army, while often victorious in battle, could not create the political situation the emperor required. In 1388, Le Qui Ly, a general and minister, assassinated the ruling king and took real power over the Tran government recognized by the Ming. By 1400, Le Qui Ly had enough of ruling through Tran puppets, and proclaimed himself king, before retiring and placing his son on the throne. The

Ming court initially sanctioned this change, but reversed itself when a man purporting to be a Tran prince reached the court and claimed the Vietnamese throne. A Ming escort sent to return him to power in 1406 was ambushed, forcing the emperor to launch a punitive invasion.

The Ming army invaded in the winter of 1406, capturing both Vietnamese capitals in eight days. Over the next six months the Ming army defeated the Vietnamese in three ferocious battles, capturing Le Qui Ly and his son in the third. The Yongle emperor annexed Vietnam the following year. Although much of the ruling class in Vietnam was somewhat sinicized, they did not welcome Ming control of their country. A rebellion in 1408 was finally crushed only in 1413. Two more rebellions were put down in 1417, but another two broke out in 1418, and despite several defeats remained active past the end of the Yongle reign.[28]

Civil government

With the death of the Yongle emperor, the Ming dynasty was no longer controlled by a military-focused ruler, and a more regular, civil-dominated government emerged. The Hongxi emperor took the throne and proceeded to reverse almost all of his father's policies. He was in the process of shifting the capital back to Nanjing when he died at the end of May 1425, after less than a year on the throne. His son, the Xuande emperor, ruled until 1435, and it was during his reign that the government became dominated by civil officials exclusively selected through the exam system. The war in Vietnam was abandoned, Beijing remained the capital, and eunuch power continued to grow. Had the Hongxi emperor lived longer, the course of Ming history might well have been different, but the growing power of the civil bureaucracy was an inevitable development of peaceful times. Military activities died down and the government shifted its attention quite naturally to administering a stable empire.

Notes

1 Translated by Edward L. Farmer in *Zhu Yuanzhang and Early Ming Legislation: The Reordering of Chinese Society Following the Era of Mongol Rule*, Leiden: E. J. Brill, 1995, p. 55.
2 For the origins of the Red Turbans see Frederick Mote, *Imperial China, 900–1800*, Cambridge, Mass.: Harvard University Press, 2003, pp. 530–533.
3 Edward L. Dreyer, *Early Ming China*, Stanford: Stanford University, 1982, pp. 17–19.
4 Ibid., p. 33.
5 Ibid., pp. 20–21, 25–28.
6 For Zhu Yuanzhang's early life, see Mote, *Imperial China*, pp. 541–548.
7 Ibid., pp. 550–552.
8 Edward L. Dreyer, *Early Ming China*, pp. 34–35.
9 Ibid., pp. 39–40; and pp. 40–52 for the events leading up to the Lake Poyang campaign.

10 For this account of the Late Poyang campaign, see Edward L. Dreyer, "The Poyang Campaign, 1363: Inland Naval Warfare in the Founding of the Ming Dynasty," in Frank A. Kierman and John K. Fairbank (eds), *Chinese Ways in Warfare*, Cambridge, Mass.: Harvard University Press, 1974, pp. 202–242.

11 Edward L. Dreyer, *Early Ming China*, pp. 55–57.

12 Ibid., pp. 58–59.

13 Ibid., p. 61.

14 Ibid., pp. 62–64.

15 Ibid., pp. 71–74.

16 Dreyer believes that many of the *pao* were still trebuchets and not cannon. Personal communication with the author.

17 Edward L. Dreyer, *Early Ming China*, pp. 73–74.

18 Ibid., pp. 74–76.

19 Ibid., pp. 66–69.

20 Ibid., pp. 87–106.

21 Ibid., pp. 131–140.

22 Romeyn Taylor, "The Yüan Origins of the Wei-so System," in Charles Hucker (ed.), *Chinese Government in Ming Times*, New York: Columbia University Press, 1969, pp. 23–40.

23 Edward L. Dreyer, *Early Ming China*, pp. 76–87.

24 Ibid., pp. 157–172, for the following discussion of the civil war; and Shih-Shan Henry Tsai, *Perpetual Happiness*, Seattle: University of Washington Press, 2001, pp. 57–76.

25 For Zhu Di's pre-imperial life, see Shih-Shan Henry Tsai, *Perpetual Happiness*, pp. 20–56.

26 Ibid., p. 167; Edward L. Dreyer, *Early Ming China*, pp. 177–178.

27 Shih-Shan Henry Tsai, *Perpetual Happiness*, pp. 169–176; Edward L. Dreyer, *Early Ming China*, pp. 179–182.

28 Shih-Shan Henry Tsai, *Perpetual Happiness*, pp. 178–186; Edward L. Dreyer, *Early Ming China*, pp. 206–212.

CHAPTER SIX

The politics of imperial collapse, 1435–1610

> When discussing the fall of the Ming, in actuality its demise
> started with Shenzong [the Wanli emperor]; certainly he cannot
> be excused from blame.
>
> *Mingshi*, the Veritable Records of the Ming dynasty[1]

The Ming dynasty's retreat from Vietnam brought Ming territorial expansion to a close. Ming power generally declined until 1565, before briefly reviving from 1570 until 1610. This period exposed the problems of the Ming's military system, while at the same time making it clear that decline was not inevitable and that effective reform was possible. The erratic and only occasionally effective Ming response to the empire's many military problems highlights the political flaws in the system. Ultimately, Ming failures were more the result of the regime's inability to make practical decisions because of political problems than of any kind of fundamental, irreconcilable military conditions.

Most scholars of the Ming dynasty have, until very recently, asserted that the army went into a prolonged decline after the vigorous military activity of Hongwu and Yongle. Edward Dreyer, whose classic account of the early Ming provided so much of he background for the previous chapter, saw precursors to that decline in Yongle's indecisive later campaigns. Ray Huang, following a long tradition, entirely dismissed the mid- and late-Ming military as weak and ineffective, despite ample evidence that this was not entirely the case. Recent work by Kenneth Swope, however, has convincingly argued that the Ming military in the Wanli reign (1573–1620) was quite effective during the Three Great Campaigns. Swope does not dispute the general trend of decline, or the late Ming army's problems, but he makes it quite clear that a vigorous emperor was able to invigorate the army when he so chose. That Wanli was a vigorous emperor in the military sphere is a similarly revisionist position, since he has been almost universally scorned as an indolent, inattentive ruler.

Hongwu built a structural flaw into the Ming government by truncating the apex of the bureaucracy. The system required a strong, active ruler to tie together the sedulously separated parts of the government. Moreover, a single man, no matter how active, could not personally handle the vast amount of

119

paperwork generated by the bureaucracy, and some kind of secretarial organ had to be created to keep track of it. Hongwu established the roots of the Grand Secretariat when he employed members of the Hanlin Academy to help him with the workload he was saddled with after he abolished the executive posts in the Secretariat. Under Xuande the system became more regular with a complement of three or four grand secretaries drawn from the Hanlin Academy as assistants to the emperor. Still, the grand secretaries were not formally connected to the bureaucracy in a chain of command, and could not, therefore, provide any kind of unifying leadership for the government.

Even with the Grand Secretariat's assistance, it was difficult for an emperor to rule the dynasty, and most simply retreated from the tedious job into their personal pursuits. Headless, the government was incapable of reacting quickly or rationally to crises requiring decision-making at the highest level. Accustomed to interacting mostly with his *camarilla*, the emperor became less inclined to trust or seek advice from the regular apparatus of government. This not only separated the emperor further from his officials, but also increased the influence of eunuchs, the castrated men who were his personal body servants and beholden entirely to the imperial will for their social and political standing.

Not surprisingly, the regular bureaucracy drawn from the ranks of the Confucianized local elites who had passed the exams regularly railed against eunuch influence. Not only was eunuch influence a direct challenge to the officials' presumed right of exclusive advice to the throne, it also further expanded the influence of palace women over the emperor. Such a presumption or assertion of the right of advice had great literary support, but had never completely existed in practice. Emperors throughout Chinese history listened to palace women, eunuchs, generals, monks, priests and even their own relatives in addition to the Confucianized officials. After 1435, however, it often seemed that imperial reliance on groups other than the official bureaucracy had badly isolated the emperor from the mechanisms of his own government, and placed the ruler almost in competition with that institution.

Local society continued to develop along the trajectory it began in the Song, where local elites, now clearly deserving the term "gentry," mostly concerned themselves with local power and status. More and more educated men found that passing the exams was so statistically unlikely that it seemed pointless to try, while at the same time using their education as a marker of their class. A member of the gentry had to be educated and demonstrate the appropriate manners and values as a means of identification. These values placed a moral fig leaf over the real economic and social power wielded by the gentry. But government service was no longer a requirement. Thus on the top and bottom, the government bureaucracy was cut off from its leader and its roots.

Hongwu had already separated the military from the rest of society; civil officials now dominated it within the government. Yet this is not to say that universal peace reigned throughout the Ming empire. The Mongols remained a threat, Japanese–Chinese pirates raided the southeast coast, and the Japanese invaded Korea. These external threats, along with a few internal ones, did not destroy the dynasty or overwhelm its military resources. By itself this is prima-facie evidence that the Ming was less weak than most previous interpretations would have us believe. Very few of these military problems were completely "solved" in the sense that an unequivocal and crushing victory by the Ming army decided the issue. The Mongols remained a problem, the pirates were eventually driven off but also placated, and a military draw in Korea obtained the Ming's political goal of rescuing Korea without the satisfaction of completely destroying the Japanese.

Given enough time, the apparatus of government could be set into motion by an active emperor, and great military power brought to bear on a problem. But in all of the military problems faced by the mid-Ming dynasty, its goals were defensive: to keep out the Mongols, to stop the pirates, to drive the Japanese out of Korea. These negative objectives were inherently unsatisfying to many officials and historians. As a reactive power, it is easy to see the mid-Ming dynasty as passive, and the string of external threats dealt with in so unsatisfying a way as part and parcel of the threats that eventually destroyed the dynasty. Yet these threats were dealt with effectively enough in the mid-Ming, and much less well, by definition, in the late Ming. Clearly then, the Ming dynasty was capable of military feats through most of its reign, even with increasingly indifferent gentry and a flawed government.

The Tumu Incident[2]

In 1449, for only the second time in Chinese history, a reigning emperor was captured on the battlefield.[3] But the dynasty did not fall, and the event was surprisingly unimportant in military and political terms. The Tumu Incident encapsulated the strengths and limitations of the Ming dynasty, as well as the unresolved problem of the dynasty's relationship to the Mongols. The confusion was not one-sided, however, as the Mongols also struggled to understand what they had accomplished and how to exploit their unexpected prize.

The Zhengtong emperor was eight when he took the throne on 31 January 1435. His grandmother, Senior Empress Dowager Zhang, effectively controlled his rule until her death in 1442. Zhengtong then came under the influence of the chief of palace eunuchs, Wang Zhen. The elderly officials who had run the government under Empress Dowager Zhang for so many years would not or could not intervene, a further example of their abject failure to reform the Ming imperial system substantially during their tenures in office. Whatever their personal merits as officials, they were impotent in the face of the institutions built by Hongwu, and could not even control the personnel within those structures well enough to have a positive legacy beyond their own careers.

In 1443, Esen succeeded his father as head of the Oyirod, and soon became ruler of most of Mongolia in all but name.[4] Esen's abilities enabled him to break through all of the compartments the Ming government had set up to keep the different Mongol groups separate and weak, a process the Ming court was aware of but could not prevent. As the 1440s progressed, Esen used raids upon Ming territory to bolster his political activities. Like all steppe leaders before him, Esen needed to obtain the manufactured goods of a sedentary society to prove that he was qualified to rule. The Ming in turn attempted to use trade in goods to control the steppe, thus limiting the ability of any one leader to create broader political structures. A further factor in this developing clash of interests was corruption. Frederick Mote asserts that eunuch corruption under Wang Zhen exacerbated these frictions in Ming–Mongol relations by cheating the Mongols in their annual tribute exchanges with the court;[5] the more important issue was probably Ming refusal to establish regular border trading posts, something unconnected to eunuch control of the government.

Wang Zhen understood that in the Ming imperial system the emperor was the only constituency that really mattered. Were it not for the Tumu Incident, it seems entirely likely that the eunuch would have remained in power to the end of his or Zhengtong's days. In 1449, Wang decided that the escalating border problems with the Mongols provided him with the opportunity to cover himself in military glory. He convinced the emperor personally to accompany an army of 500,000 men under Wang's command into the steppe from Datong to punish the Mongols. The army would pass through Wang Zhen's hometown on the return march, where the emperor would meet Wang's relatives and other local power-holders.

Official objections were acknowledged, but not accepted, and the emperor set out on 4 August. Only the day before it was reported that the Mongols had cut off an outpost near the border, and that another unit had been annihilated. As the army marched north and then west Wang Zhen became increasingly intransigent as not only civil, but also military, officials repeatedly requested delays and more caution. The haste with which the campaign had been organized and the heavy rains undermined troop morale, and Wang's insistence on all officials approaching him on their knees angered the leadership. Reports of Mongol activity raised tensions further, but did not dissuade Wang from his plan. Several officials discussed assassinating Wang, but no one had the leadership to actually decide that it should be done.

The army passed the field where the Ming unit had recently been destroyed, with the remains of several thousand two-week-old Chinese corpses still there. It was only when Wang Zhen reached Datong, and the eunuch commander he had placed there (who was responsible for the lost unit, though he managed to escape) told him that it would be folly to strike out into the steppe, that he began to rethink his plan. All of the omens indicating that the campaign was ill-starred that he had previously dismissed, as well as the continuous unseasonable heavy rains, finally convinced him to return to the capital. But the low morale of the troops dissuaded him from taking the route through his hometown, where they might damage his estates, and the army marched back the way it came.

On 30 August the rearguard, two days' march behind, was attacked and destroyed. A new rearguard some 30,000 to 50,000 strong was created and sent to block the Mongols, but it rode into an ambush and was also annihilated. The emperor reached Tumu on 31 August and was urged to ride ahead to get out of danger. Wang Zhen rejected this proposal, reportedly because he did not want to abandon his personal baggage train of some 1,000 wagons to Esen. Wang had the minister of war physically removed by guards. He may well have feared for his valuables, but he probably feared for his life and his influence more. As the official commander of the army it would have been difficult for Wang to have left it while the emperor rode away. Yet Wang could not risk the emperor getting out from his immediate control, lest Zhengtong hear things or order actions the eunuch did not want him to.

The army camped in a place with no water, and the advance forces of Esen's army prevented anyone from reaching a nearby river. At this point, after several days without water, there was a complete leadership breakdown. Wang Zhen disregarded the emperor's order to treat with the surrounding Mongols and ordered an advance; the army advanced in poor order, and then collapsed when the Mongols attacked. The emperor was unable to break out, and all of his entourage, including Wang Zhen, were killed. Zhengtong himself somehow survived unscathed through the hails of arrows, and was recognized as someone important by a Mongol officer. Esen was stunned to find out that he had actually captured the emperor.

It was by no means clear that Esen's political and military objectives were advanced by Zhengtong's capture. In some sense, it might have been more to Esen's advantage had the emperor been forced to flee while his army was destroyed behind him, leaving a cowed ruler on the throne of China. Esen had not been trying to destroy the Ming empire but to establish his fitness to rule Mongolia through military success and increased trade with the Ming. While he considered what to do, ministers in Beijing placed a new emperor on the throne, Jingtai, and firmed up the capital's defenses. When Esen arrived beneath the capital's walls on 27 October, he found that his captive's value had considerably diminished, and that his army was unable to make an impression on the city's defenses. The truth was that Esen's ambitions had to be limited to the steppe because, for all of its problems, the Ming still disposed of more military resources than the Mongol leader could match. Esen returned Zhengtong unconditionally in September of 1450, having gained almost nothing.

The Great Wall

As the Ming dynasty's shift to a defensive stance with respect to the steppe went from a temporary policy to a permanent one, the military establishment on the border had to transform itself structurally to carry out that change. Under Hongwu the eight outer garrisons in the steppe were the front line of a defense in depth that also included fortified passes and other strong points, particularly around Beijing. Although Yongle led several campaigns into the steppe he also oversaw the withdrawal of that outer line of Ming garrisons, thus shrinking the defense system to a shallower zone. For both cultural and military reasons the Ming presence in the steppe was never as strong as that of the Yuan, but ultimately the major difference was that the Yuan court, being Mongol, did not balk at the cost of maintaining garrisons in the steppe (though these costs would have been considerably lower for the Yuan) and the Ming court did. Unfortunately for the Ming court, however, a less militarily engaged relationship with the steppe was not necessarily any cheaper or safer.

Yongle ordered improvements to the fortifications guarding the passes from the steppe, though these were not linked by continuous walls. What would later come to be known as the Great Wall formed as a response to increased Mongol raiding after Esen was killed in 1455. Having failed to capitalize on the capture of Zhengtong, Esen lost the political momentum that had held the disparate Mongol groups together. The ensuing civil war spread into Chinese territory as warring factions sought economic resources to support their military efforts. One faction moved into the Ordos region, now no longer supervised by a Ming garrison, placing the Mongols squarely against Ming territory. The Mongols still wanted to present tribute, and receive gifts in return, and to trade with the Ming; failing that, they raided. Meanwhile, the Ming court was itself distracted by Zhengtong's return to power in a *coup d'état* in 1457.[6] Jingtai died of illness or was poisoned, and Zhengtong resumed as emperor with a new reign period: Tianshun.

It was difficult to establish a consistent policy toward the Mongols given their ongoing civil wars, a situation further exacerbated by Tianshun's weak leadership. A proposal to launch a campaign to retake the Ordos and establish garrisons, fortified positions, and agriculture, and so maintain control of the area, was approved, but nothing came of it. Further proposals for offensive action were sanctioned and left unfulfilled. In the interim, some commanders suggested pulling back to more hilly areas to the south that were easier to defend. This too was rejected. In 1471, Yu Zijun submitted a plan to build a wall between Yansui and Qingyang to aid in defense.[7]

A wall-based defense was expensive to construct and of questionable effectiveness. Yet the court did not have the will to devote the economic and military resources necessary to launch its desired offensive. Wall building won out because it was cheaper than any offensive; the first two long walls were finished in 1474, one 129 miles long and the other 566 miles long.[8] Over the next century more and more walls were built; in many places there were actually two lines, with forts and watchtowers, evolving into what we now know of as the Great Wall. Although the walls were useful, they were never intended as a complete solution to the Mongol problem. The difficulty was that the same economic, political and military problems continued to obtain, leading successive generations through the same debate that put additional resources into wall building. The short-term question was how to make the wall system more effective, since the long-term problem of the Mongols could not, apparently, be solved. It is important to keep in mind before leaving this topic that the walls were effective in many instances, even if they did not completely resolve the Ming dynasty's northern border problem.

Guns

The Ming dynasty was the first Chinese dynasty systematically to produce and deploy firearms throughout its military. Some guns were used during the Ming conquest, along with gunpowder-fueled incendiaries, and new cannon and hand-held guns were introduced starting in Yongle's reign. Yongle began the process of placing cannon in forts along the northern border, thus connecting the use of guns to the collapsing and hardening of the border with fortifications. Wall building, cannon and guns were used together to enhance the garrison troops' ability to fend off Mongol incursions. Indeed, one of the most characteristic aspects of Ming military development was the intense interest in the use of firearms as a force-multiplier. Generally speaking, the Ming emphasized cannon over hand-held guns, though both were understood to be much more effective against steppe cavalry when deployed behind fixed fortifications.[9]

Portuguese arquebuses[10] were introduced in 1529, and "Red Barbarian Cannon" came in during the Wanli reign (1573–1620). These new weapons were more powerful and more reliable than contemporary Chinese arms. Contrary to many people's impression of the Chinese, they were extremely interested in new military technology, and deployed it widely. In 1536, for example, 2,500 arquebuses were supplied to the soldiers in Shanxi, and the following year they received another 3,800 arquebuses and 3,000 brass cannon.[11] The Ming army developed a much greater facility with cannon than with arquebuses, in contradistinction to the Japanese army, which became extremely skilled with arquebuses but was entirely lacking in cannon, at least in Korea. This may have been due to the way firearms were deployed in China – in fixed defensive positions rather than in offensive arrays.

Chinese warfare was, in fact, transformed during the Ming dynasty by improvements in firearms technology and its more widespread use by the army. The government spent considerable sums of money on the manufacture of arquebuses and cannon, and sought the best technology available. When the court found out that the Portuguese at Macao had better weapons than the current Chinese models, they acquired examples and obtained the technical assistance to learn how to manufacture them.[12] It may well have been the widespread adoption of the newest firearms that preserved the Ming in its contest with the Mongols; cannon were unquestionably key to the Ming army's ability to defeat the Japanese invasion of Korea. The Ming was a time of eager advances in military technology, much of it obtained from foreigners, not stagnation or xenophobic denial.

The *wokou*

Japanese pirates, *wokou* (literally "dwarf bandits"), had raided up and down the Chinese and Korean coasts since perhaps the thirteenth century, but they became a serious problem during the Ming. They were not, however, exclusively or even predominantly Japanese in the sixteenth century. The vast majority of the *wokou* were Chinese from the southeast coast engaged in foreign trade. As international traders, these Chinese seafarers were well acquainted with Japan and did make use of some number of Japanese fighters when they turned to raiding China. Other *wokou* at the beginning of the Ming may well have been exclusively Japanese, but these faded into insignificance when compared with the mid-sixteenth-century phenomenon manned and led by Chinese.

The *wokou* flourished in the sixteenth century for several related reasons. Population pressure had pushed more and more people out of farming and into trade and manufacturing. These non-agricultural activities were also more profitable than farming. This increased economic dependence upon making and selling goods, and upon foreign seaborne trade, meant that the Ming court's prohibition of foreign trade at Ningbo after fighting broke out between two rival Japanese traders in 1523 undermined the livelihood of many people. But illicit trade certainly predated the end of government-sanctioned trade, since the prohibitions on Chinese emigration and sailing to foreign countries to trade were decreed at the beginning of the dynasty. Taking iron products, copper coins and silk abroad was specifically banned, precisely the staple items of much of the Chinese trade with the Japanese. Only tribute trade by a strictly limited number of Japanese ships and men was still allowed, but this was disrupted by political turmoil in Japan.

Chinese traders, some from locally powerful families, could not afford to cut off foreign trade because they were in debt to their foreign counterparts. Their only means to repay them was to suggest that they raid the coast, and support them in those activities. Thus not only were many of the pirates Chinese, but all of the pirates, whether Chinese or foreign, had local help to plan and execute their raids. They knew exactly where to go, who to rob, and what the state of the police and military were beforehand. So intertwined were local families with the *wokou* that local power-holders were able to dissuade some government officials from acting against the illicit trade and the pirates, and to convince the central government to sack the rest. This was another example of the separation between local society and the government, and the difficulty the court had in actually exercising power at the local level against the interests of the residents.[13]

Quite apart from the indifference or collusion of government officials, the military establishment along the coast was undermanned and run down. Units were at a fraction of their paper strength, training was non-existent, and equipment, including ships, was often lacking. The escalating problem forced the court to react, however, and to reverse these problems. Once the *wokou* began to attack market towns, small forts and some local cities successfully, military and official incompetence could no longer be tolerated. The regular military establishment seemed incapable of responding effectively, and the civilian leadership was equally compromised, either through incompetence, corruption or sheer cowardice. A change in leadership and system was therefore required.

New governors who supported the new military commanders and their methods were the first step in making an effective response possible. Without the support of the civilian leadership, money, provisions and rewards were impossible. The main military commanders were Yu Dayou (1503–1579) and Qi Jiguang (1528–1587). Qi has the more unalloyed reputation, boosted in no small measure by the training manual that he wrote. Although successful on land as well as sea, Yu advocated shifting more resources to the navy in order to build more and bigger ships with larger cannon. As he saw it, a powerful navy would take care of the threat much more effectively. Yu's proposals were not sanctioned, however, and it was Qi's approach that was followed.

Qi Jiguang's force was never very large, starting with 3,000 men in 1559 and growing to first 6,000 and then 10,000 men, mostly recruited from Yiwu county in Zhejiang. He carefully selected his men from the farming population, explicitly rejecting city-dwellers because he wanted solid, reliable soldiers accustomed to hardship. Discipline was harsh and punishments collective, creating strong unit cohesion. Men were trained to act as a unit with a combination of long weapons, spears and bamboo branches (sometime replaced with metal-branched pole-arms), and shields and close-range weapons. Very few firearms were used, and missile weapons in general do not appear to have been very important. Qi's men closed with the enemy and beat them in hand-to-hand fighting.[14]

The paucity of firearms in Qi's infantry units was an indication of the limited resources he was given by the central government. All of the armaments used were simple, and readily available by requisition from local craftsmen. What firearms he could obtain were frequently dangerous, blowing up when used, and in very small number. With poor ammunition, an understandable reluctance to get too close to a weapon in order to properly aim it, and insufficient numbers to be truly effective, firearms were simply not a realistic infantry weapon to rely upon. And despite reports of the ferocity, discipline and effectiveness of the Japanese pirates, Qi was almost always able to overcome them with his simply armed troops.

The navy made much more use of firearms and cannon. In Qi's system a war junk had 55 troops divided into five units. Two units used arquebuses, two used cannon, flame-throwers and rockets, and one unit used other types of gunpowder weapons. Naval combat required firearms by this point, a marked change in warfare.[15]

Qi Jiguang realized that the *wokou* often won the initial clash of arms, but collapsed during the following round. If he could keep his men together after the first setback, he knew he could defeat the pirates. As their losses mounted, the pirates became less and less active. Confronted on both land and sea by effective troops, the *wokou* were soon brought under control.

Although the Ming military was briefly revived to fight off the *wokou*, Qi Jiguang's changes did not last. They were essentially alien to the Ming military system, constructed outside of it under very particular conditions. What Qi Jiguang proved was that an effective army and navy could be created out of raw recruits if the leaders were good and the civil authorities supportive. If troops were paid decently and regularly, and vigorously led, they could win. Unfortunately, what the subsequent response of the Ming bureaucracy to these victories proved was that its civil government could not tolerate successful generals. All of the military commanders were persecuted afterward, some to death, and even Qi Jiguang died in disgrace.

Wanli's Three Great Campaigns

The hereditary military system was virtually dead by the 1570s, replaced by a paid army. Although some Western scholars have argued that the Ming's military fortunes were the result of economic factors caused by the flows and interruptions of flow of silver bullion, hence the importance of a paid army, others have pointed out that these silver problems either did not exist or had no bearing on the dynasty's military situation.[16] Certainly by the 1570s, the government could afford the massive military expenditures necessary to prosecute the wars that would come to be called the Three Great Campaigns.

The emperor Wanli was nine when he took the throne, and in the early years of his reign policy was dominated by the grand secretary Zhang Juzheng (1525–1582). Zhang was one of those extraordinary men who occasionally managed to get control of the Ming government, enact sound policies and generally revive the dynasty's fortunes. He was particularly interested in reinvigorating the military, and improving administration so as to place more power in the hands of the central government. Zhang was an excellent example of how much could be accomplished by a strong leader willing to overcome the factionalism so rife in the Ming government. But unfortunately that leadership could not be systematically created or ensured a place at the top of the government. Perhaps what really made Zhang powerful, more than just personality, was that he spoke for the emperor. As Wanli would prove in his early years of rule, the Ming bureaucracy could function when the emperor led. Zhang Juzheng had that power in Wanli's minority, and he used it well. Without a strong emperor to lead it, however, the Ming bureaucracy ground to a halt.

Wanli took control of his government after Zhang's death and played an active and aggressive part in the dynasty's military stance. Kenneth Swope has asserted that from 1580 to 1600 the Ming was as powerful as it had been since Yongle's reign,[17] and the course of the Three Great Campaigns bears him out. The first campaign was against a troop mutiny led in some sense by a Mongol named Pubei; the second was a response to a Korean plea for Chinese help in freeing their country from a Japanese invasion; the third was against a tribal rebellion in southeastern Sichuan. Wanli was actively engaged in all of these campaigns, albeit from his capital, and their successful prosecutions owe a great deal to his willingness to override his civil officials and put the most effective generals in charge. The emperor, it might be said, fought his bureaucracy so that his generals could fight the dynasty's enemies.

Pubei[18]

Ming–Mongol relations had been stable for the two decades before Pubei declared himself king of the Mongols in the spring of 1592. Zhang Juzheng negotiated a treaty with the Mongol leader Altan Qan in 1573 that provided for border markets and nominal Mongol recognition of Ming sovereignty. Lack of great Mongol leaders, combined with the mature development of the Great Wall, kept the Ming's northern border mostly quiet. There were occasional raids and punitive expeditions, but nothing that threatened the dynasty.

Ming troops in the northwest were subject to the same sorts of raids, but very difficult conditions in poor areas far from supplies made it very hard for them to mount effective punitive attacks on the Mongols. The best troops for these tasks were Mongols in the employ of the Ming army, and a Mongol by the name of Pubei was one of the best. Pubei had joined the Ming army after a Mongol chief executed his father and older brother for incessant raiding of other Mongols. He proved to be an excellent commander, keeping the area around Ningxia free from raiders. Rewards and promotions followed, with Pubei becoming the regional military commissioner of Huamachi in 1569, and being given command of 1,000 men in 1577. His power and effectiveness were a double-edged sword, however, since as his service became more and more critical to keeping the border peaceful, the consequences of him turning against the Ming also grew. Zhang Juzheng specifically rejected efforts to reduce Pubei's power for fear that he might switch sides.

Pubei's power was of particular concern to Dang Xin, the grand coordinator, who feared that the Mongol leader, who by 1589 had a personal retinue of 2,000 to 3,000 men, was plotting rebellion. Raiding in the Ordos by Mongols under Qulaci in 1591 brought matters to a head. Although Dang Xin did everything in his power to prevent Pubei's success, denying his men horses and supplies, Pubei, along with his sons, was victorious. As a result of this, Pubei concluded that his private retinue, the force which had allowed him to defeat Qulaci despite Dang Xin's efforts and the weakness of the regular Ming troops, was the most capable army in the area.

Whatever his goals, Dang Xin was clearly a fool. He continued to withhold rations, pay and winter clothes from Pubei, flogged his son for taking other men's wives, and investigated Pubei for lying about his grain requirements. Dang felt that his actions would ultimately destroy Pubei's power, and discounted any concern that his denial of pay to Pubei's troops would lead to mutiny. The Mongol leader tried to address his grievances through official channels, but was stonewalled. When Dang did relent, and provided one year's pay out of the three years owed, this actually convinced some Chinese officers to side with the Mongolians. The situation continued to deteriorate as Dang refused any further pay for the soldiers. Two simultaneous investigations actually got under way: one instigated by Pubei and one by Dang Xin. Dang seems to have hoped that the investigation carried out by Shi Jifang, related to him by marriage, would succeed in seizing Pubei, and either exiling or executing him. Dang had apparently convinced other local officials not to fear the Mongolian soldiers. Throughout the entire process Dang does not appear to have understood the very real threat Pubei and his men posed.

On 28 March 1592 an angry mob of soldiers led by Liu Dongyang, a Chinese officer, and accompanied by Pubei, who was now well into his sixties, confronted Dang Xin in Ningxia. Dang not only refused the back pay, but even threatened the soldiers. The mob then stormed the government offices, seizing Dang and Shi Jifang and then executing both men. After a frenzy of destruction, mainly targeting government offices and the homes of officials, the mutineers organized themselves under the command of Liu Dongyang. At least outwardly, Pubei played a supporting role in all this, but was not the main actor.

Other troops in the region threw in their lot with the mutineers, and many forts were quickly captured while the government scrambled to take control of the situation. By late April all of the forts initially captured by the mutineers were retaken, and the uprising prevented from spreading further into the empire. Some Mongols from the steppe, however, were ready to join Pubei's cause, thus raising the possibility of a much larger problem if the situation was not quickly settled. Wanli paid close attention to the unfolding events, carefully deciding on the commanders.

By the middle of May, even before some of the new commanders had reached the field, the Ming army had already taken the fight to the walls of Ningxia. Both sides used cannon extensively, though bows and arrows also played an important role. Without reinforcements, the Ming forces initially could not overcome the mutineers in Ningxia, while the mutineers continued to send valuables and women to the Mongols to buy their loyalty. The campaign developed into a siege of Ningxia, with the Ming army digging in to protect themselves from outside Mongol attempts to raise the siege. Hard fighting continued into June, when Wanli was convinced to appoint a new commander to speed the suppression of the rebellion.

Although Wanli originally appointed Li Chengliang to overall command, this was quickly switched to his son, Rusong, since Li Chengliang was needed elsewhere. While Li Rusong was raising troops and proceeding to Ningxia, the commanders on the scene were doing their best to contain and destroy the rebellion. The city itself was proving too difficult to capture, with solid fortifications and a good number of cannon. A great deal of effort was expended in keeping Mongol forces from linking up. The 50,000 to 60,000 Ming troops available were hard pressed to accomplish these goals.

By the time Li Rusong arrived at Ningxia on 30 July, the court was turning its attention to the Japanese invasion of Korea, discussed in the next section. Even with all of the supplies and troops at hand, it was clear that Ningxia might hold out for some time. Cannon fire proved ineffective against the city's thick walls, and repeated attempts to scale them were turned back with heavy casualties. The siege settled into a contest of provisions.

In late August the besiegers decided to construct a dyke that would flood the city. Conditions became more desperate as the Mongols outside the city tried to break through and raise the siege, and the Ming army repeatedly beat them off. As the dyke expanded and the Mongols did not arrive, many rebels deserted. But the Ming army was also anxious because the siege was taking so long, and they were subject to continual Mongol raids. As the waters rose around Ningxia, the Ming court realized it would have to intervene in Korea. By 6 September there was eight or nine feet of water around the city wall. In late September a determined Mongol relief force was destroyed in a running six-hour battle that finally convinced the Mongols to abandon the rebels.

By mid-October the walls of the city were collapsing and the mutineers were turning on each other. Some rebels surrendered, but others, like Liu Dongyang, were murdered by their comrades. Pubei's compound was surrounded on 21 October, though it held out for some hours, with Pubei immolating himself in his house. The court heard official word of Ningxia's fall on 28 October, with the official declaration of the pacification of Ningxia uprising declared on 10 January 1593, after the execution in Beijing of some of the captured leaders. Li Rusong and some of the victorious generals had little time to rest, as they were immediately assigned to deal with the Japanese invasion of Korea.

Korea[19]

The Japanese invasion of Korea in 1592 was probably the most important event of the sixteenth century in East Asia, and it demonstrated the central role that arquebuses and cannon had come to play in Chinese, Japanese and Korean warfare. This vast conflict was extensively described by participants from all three groups, and then subjected to modern interpretation by historians of all three countries with vastly different agendas. The basic facts are generally agreed upon, however, though not their underlying motivations or significance. Toyotomi Hideyoshi, having just unified Japan, launched an invasion of Korea with the avowed intention of then conquering China. Some have argued that he wanted to take control of trade with China, or that he needed an outlet for the large armies still present after the wars of unification in Japan, or that it was an act of pure megalomania. The Koreans declined to assist Hideyoshi in his attack on the Ming and were therefore invaded; initial Japanese successes were turned back after the Ming intervened, and the war deteriorated into a stalemate, with the Japanese unable to advance but continuing to retain a foothold in Korea. Confused diplomacy followed, and then a second Japanese invasion that also failed. Ultimately, the Japanese withdrew, shortly after Hideyoshi's death.

Hideyoshi obviously failed in his objectives, even the preliminary one of conquering Korea. It is perhaps the very ridiculousness of his goal of conquering Ming China that has led historians to search for hidden agendas. Korean historians have stressed the role of Admiral Yi Sun-sin and his turtle boats in defeating the Japanese navy and cutting their supply lines. Japanese historians, and Westerners relying on Japanese sources, have focused on their initial victories and excused the Japanese withdrawal as the result of Hideyoshi's death. Chinese historians point out that the Ming came to the aid of a vassal state and drove out the Japanese, but argue that the expense involved undermined the Ming state, leading to the dynasty's fall in the seventeenth century.

When the Japanese army landed at Pusan on 23 May 1592, it found a poorly prepared and weakly defended kingdom. The Korean army was, with a few notable exceptions, badly led, disciplined and equipped. In sharp contrast, the Japanese army was a highly disciplined, veteran force with excellent commanders, well provided with arquebuses. Indeed, the Japanese dependence upon arquebuses, combined with their short stature, convinced some Korean commanders that the Japanese could not fight at close range. The only firearms in the Korean arsenal were mounted on ships, though these would be of great significance later. Most of the Korean army was a paper force, and its fortifications were barely garrisoned. The total Japanese invasion army was 168,000 men, under the joint command of Konishi Yukinaga and Kato Kiyomasa. Hideyoshi's decision to split the command between two men who disliked each other was a serious mistake, but the Koreans and Chinese were also riven by political and personal disputes. These internal clashes among all the players added tremendously to the complication of the ensuing events.

The Japanese were victorious on land and sea, inflicting thousands of casualties on the Koreans. Pusan fell quickly, and the Korean navy was defeated in several engagements, though these were less one-sided than the land battles. The Korean navy's cannon and arrow fire left thousands of Japanese dead. Korean resistance melted away as government officials and army commanders fled. Although some local resistance was temporarily successful, the Japanese were soon in control of much of southeastern Korea. In most instances the Japanese outnumbered the Koreans, as at a battle at the Han River near the city of Chungju. The Korean commander, Sin Yip, chose to meet the Japanese army on flat ground, where he felt his cavalry would overwhelm the arquebus-armed Japanese, rather than defend the Chiryong Pass. Quite apart from his misguided underestimation of Japanese soldiers and their firearms, his decision to fight on open ground with his back to a river when slightly outnumbered, 19,000 to 16,000, was ill-advised. Japanese cannon and arquebuses forced Sin into a desperate charge that failed. Chungju fell on 7 June. Had Sin succeeded, and there is no guarantee that a different strategy would have worked, he might actually have checked the Japanese invasion.

Chungju's fall convinced the Korean king to flee his capital at Seoul, while dispatching the crown prince and his younger brother out to rally the populace. The Japanese deliberations on the best approach to Seoul, and over the speed of their advance, were rendered moot when the city was abandoned. After occupying Seoul on 11 June, the Japanese concluded that they could now disperse their forces to take control of Korea, while other units continued to chase the Korean king. The king reached Pyongyang on 17 June.

Hideyoshi prepared another 60,000 troops for Korea in July figuring that, although the Koreans had been defeated, the Ming army would soon arrive. His admonitions to his commanders to remain linked up for mutual support was unrealistic given their dispersion across the countryside. Moreover, all Korean resistance had not stopped, and Japanese units were forced to travel in large groups and stay in fortified positions because of incessant Korean ambushes. The Korean king was anxious that Ming help arrive and considered actually fleeing into Chinese territory.

Wanli was clear that the Korean king should stay in Korea while the Ming army was mobilized, and he immediately made funds and food available to the army as it formed up. The situation in Korea appeared dire, as the Japanese captured Pyongyang on 20 July after an initial setback; but the Japanese were badly overextended and anxious about the arrival of the Ming army. On 16 June, Admiral Yi Sun-sin destroyed 26 Japanese ships near Okpo, and sank dozens more on the following day. Admiral Yi struck again on 8 July, sinking 13 more Japanese ships. Under good leadership, it was clear that the Koreans could defeat the Japanese at sea. At the Battle of Tangpo, Yi recorded the first use of the "turtleboats," an oared ship with a covering of armored plates and spikes, and armed with cannon. The Japanese fleet was destroyed, and a further 21 ships sunk the next day. Yi continued his rampage, sinking another two dozen ships a few days later. In sharp contrast to their land forces, the Korean navy under Admiral Yi was well-equipped with cannon and gunpowder weapons, and it was much more skilled than their Japanese counterparts. Korean and Chinese ships were much more maneuverable and much better designed than Japanese ships.

Yi Sun-sin's victories endangered the entire Japanese expeditionary force, and the Japanese naval commanders concentrated at Pusan were anxious to find and destroy the Korean navy. On 14 August Yi annihilated the Japanese fleet at the Battle of Hansan Island. Of 82 Japanese ships, only 14 escaped. Shortly thereafter, Yi completely destroyed a Japanese fleet of 42 ships at Angolpo. His final action of the year was the destruction of more than a hundred Japanese ships in Pusan harbor in a furious engagement on 29 September. But rather than attempt to destroy the remaining Japanese fleet, Yi held back. He was concerned that if the Japanese army were cut off in Korea they would be even more cruel to the populace.

Japanese efforts to win over the people had generally failed, and with the exception of a few collaborators, Japanese rule was resisted. As the overextended Japanese army was registering the impact of Yi Sun-sin's naval victories, and realizing that, despite their battlefield victories over the Korean army, the populace was not simply accepting Japanese control, the first Ming troops arrived in July. The first Ming foray of 3,000 troops was almost completely annihilated by the Japanese, startling Wanli and his court into more aggressive action. Song Yingchang estimated that the campaign would require 72,000 firearms of different sizes, as much gunpowder and shot as was available, 27,000 bows and crossbows, millions of arrows and crossbow bolts, and tens of thousands of troops.[20] Diplomatic negotiations were also opened with the Japanese, though these would prove fruitless and often comical over the coming years, as neither side negotiated in good faith, frequently lied to each other, and entirely excluded the Koreans from the talks.

Ming preparations proceeded apace, and Li Rusong was finally able to depart Ningxia for the Korean front. Korean partisans were registering small but important victories over the Japanese, even forcing the Japanese to abandon the city of Kyongju. Brutal Japanese reprisals further stiffened Korean resistance. Li Rusong entered Korea with about 40,000 troops in January of 1593, a far smaller force than planned for and with a far smaller percentage of good soldiers. Li was finally prepared to attack Pyongyang in February, where a combination of cannon fire and brutal street fighting drove the Japanese out in a single day's fighting on 8 February, killing more than 12,000 Japanese soldiers. The Japanese had never experienced such an intensity of firepower, and after the Battle of Pyongyang, which permanently blunted the Japanese invasion, they relied upon ambushes and hit-and-run tactics rather than face the Ming directly. Kaesong was liberated on 19 February and the Japanese reeled back to Seoul.

It was now Li Rusong's turn to overextend himself, and at the Battle of Pyokchegwan he was nearly killed as he led his men into an ambush. His small cavalry detachment of 3,000 men advanced ahead of his artillery and he found himself receiving arquebus fire from high ground. He tried to effect a fighting retreat, but was only saved by the arrival of a relief force. Casualties were similar on both sides, perhaps 500–600 each, and although Li Rusong's spirits were somewhat dampened, this merely slowed the Ming advance. A subsequent night raid burned a large Japanese storehouse, administering the *coup d'grâce* to the Japanese position in Seoul. That city was abandoned on 18 May 1593, and all Japanese forces withdrew to positions around Pusan.

At this point Chinese and Japanese negotiators began intense talks to resolve the situation. The Ming initially withdrew most of its troops from Korea, leaving behind a small force to train the Korean army. Neither side understood the other's position, which was partly the fault of the negotiators, who lied both to their own leaders and their interlocutors, and partly the result of the vast chasm that separated the Chinese and Japanese leaderships' respective understanding of the situation. Oversimplified, Hideyoshi thought he was the glorious victor, and the Ming court thought he was a criminal and a failure. The talks were further undermined by Japanese officers on the ground who opposed a peace, leading to the massacre of 60,000 Koreans at Chinju on 27 July. The talks would continue for three years without resolution or much understanding by either side.

By 1596, the bizarre course of negotiations came to a close when Chinese envoys arrived in Japan to invest Hideyoshi with his titles. Unfortunately, Hideyoshi thought he was to be made emperor of the Ming, and the patents provided invested him as king of Japan. Enraged, Hideyoshi ordered a second invasion of Korea. The second Japanese invasion was a pointless affair since all of the Japanese commanders and even Hideyoshi knew that they could not conquer Korea in the face of the Ming army.

About 200 Japanese ships landed in Korea on 1 March 1597 to bolster the Japanese forces and defensive positions already there. As the Ming anxiously mobilized troops and supplies to respond to the invasion, the Japanese army engaged in an orgy of destruction while it built up its forces. The Japanese proceeded much more cautiously this time, reducing the city of Namwon and its Chinese garrison after a brutal four-day siege in September and defeating the Korean navy, no longer under Yi Sun-sin, who had fallen foul of court politics, as well. The Japanese march on Seoul was blocked at the Battle of Chiksan, where the Chinese ambushed the Japanese vanguard on 17 October. Although the Japanese lost only 500 or 600 men, and the Chinese were unable to follow up their pursuit, Seoul was never again threatened and the Japanese fell back. Just as importantly in the eyes of some historians, Yi Sun-sin was reinstated on 13 September.

Yi Sun-sin's return was felt almost immediately as he destroyed a Japanese fleet of over a hundred ships near Chindo Island on 2 November. In the days that followed, the Japanese fought well on the defensive, inflicting several tactical defeats on the Ming and Korean forces, particularly at Ulsan, that did little, however, to reverse the tide of the campaign. Wanli and his court were now also concerned with the rebellion of Yang Yinglong in Sichuan, since the reassignment of generals and commanders to Korea had allowed Yang to revitalize his uprising. A large Chinese navy with big ships and heavy cannon arrived in 1598, along with more troops and supplies. While the Japanese dug in and waited for the Ming–Korean offensive, Hideyoshi consulted with his generals and concluded it was time to withdraw. His death in September was therefore not even the proximate cause of the end of the campaign since he had already decided to withdraw. Even so, several more battles took place before the Japanese army left Korea. The decisive battle was a naval engagement. At the Battle of Noryang Straits on 14 December over 200 Japanese ships were sunk, though Yi Sun-sin was killed during the battle. Hideyoshi's irrational dream was brought to a close, at least for the next 400 years.

Yang Yinglong[21]

The third of Wanli's Three Great Campaigns had to wait for the conclusion of the war in Korea before beginning in earnest. By that time the rebellion of Yang Yinglong, a leader of aboriginal tribesmen in the southwest, had grown beyond any hope of local control. Yang's rebellion had been festering for over a decade, but his apparent rehabilitation on two occasions and the campaigns against Pubei and the Japanese had given him the time to develop into a major military problem. When the court was finally able to turn its attention to the far southwest of the empire, it had to overcome a near-independent kingdom with an army of nearly 100,000 Miao tribesmen. The term "Miao," as used by the Ming authorities, covered an enormous range of aboriginal people, but the grievances of those fueling Yang's rebellion appeared to be the same – the encroachment of Han Chinese settlers and the Ming state into their lands.

In 1599, the court ordered all of the victorious generals of the Korea campaign to go to Sichuan and crush Yang Yinglong. Li Hualong, who was placed in overall command, requested large numbers of firearms and considerable funds so that he could build up an army. Yang Yinglong, for his part, was limited in what he could do, for although the high mountains and deep jungles of his territory provided him with some protection from the Ming army, any foray into Sichuan would risk either the disintegration or destruction of his poorly trained and ill-disciplined army. By late 1599 and early 1600 the Ming army was beginning to skirmish with Yang's forces on the outskirts of his territory. Yang himself had served in the Ming army before, so he knew what it was capable of. He could not make up for his lack of firearms, but he did recruit more men, reaching nearly 150,000 by the end of 1599. The real number and quality of these troops is, however, open to question.

Li Hualong's plan called for eight columns of about 30,000 men each to attack Yang from all directions, a far larger combined force than the Ming had mobilized in Korea. Most of the Ming troops were also aboriginal people. The attack began on 26 March 1600, and proceeded slowly and methodically. Superior firepower defeated the Miao rebels time and again, overcoming stockades erected throughout the difficult passes. The march was a series of small clashes and ambushes of hundreds of men that the Ming army won, pushing the Miao back and taking the critical Sangmu Pass on 20 April. Yang Yinglong himself was defeated in a nighttime raid and forced to withdraw to Hailongtun in the mountains, his final redoubt.

The final advance on Hailongtun began on 6 June from all directions. All of the outer positions around Hailongtun had been reduced by 28 June, leaving Yang with about 17,000 men and a month's food. Heavy rains delayed the final assault, which carried the fort on 15 July. Yang killed himself.

Wanli's active participation in military affairs was not matched in the civil sphere. With the great campaigns over, the emperor withdrew into his back palace more and more (though this had begun long beforehand) and virtually stopped meeting with his officials. Wanli entered a bitter stalemate with his own government, as his officials opposed his will and he lost the energy to overrule them at every step. This was indeed ironic for an emperor who proved so decisive in military affairs, supporting successful generals in the face of criticism, overcoming institutional bottlenecks and freely disbursing huge sums of money as needed. But his government was deeply riven with factions, and where he could see the point of deciding policy issues when presented with a variety of opinions, deciding political winners and losers was less compelling. Hongwu's system required the emperor to make all major decisions, however, and civil officialdom demanded that Wanli make the political choices that so concerned them. When he refused to, government operations at the highest level ground to a halt.

The military establishment went into sharp decline after the Three Great Campaigns, no longer fostered and protected by the emperor. When the Jurchen arose in Manchuria to threaten the dynasty soon after Wanli's death, the best commanders the court could call upon were the same men who had served Wanli. No new generation of commanders had emerged, and Wanli's successes were idiosyncratic. It was Wanli that made the system work, often in opposition to his own government's advice. Without an emperor strong in military affairs, however, the dynasty was doomed.

Notes

1 Zhang Tingyu et al. (eds), Mingshi, Taibei: Dingwen shuju, 1994, p. 295, translated in Kenneth Swope, "The Three Great Campaigns of the Wanli Emperor, 1592–1600: Court, Military, and Society in Late Sixteenth-Century China," Unpublished Ph.D. dissertation, University of Michigan, 2001, p. 7.

2 For the Tumu Incident, see F.W. Mote, "The T'u-mu Incident of 1449," in Frank A. Kierman and John K. Fairbank, Chinese Ways in Warfare, Cambridge, Mass: Harvard University Press, 1974, pp. 243–272.

3 The first time being Emperor Hui of the Western Jin on 9 September 304. See David Graff, Medieval Chinese Warfare, London: Routledge, 2002, p. 46.

4 Henry Serruys, "Sino-Mongol Relations during the Ming," Melanges Chinois et Bouddhiques, 18 (1975), vol. 2, p. 8 cited in Mote, "Tumu," p. 250.

5 Mote, "T'u-mu," p. 253.

6 Ph. de Heer, The Care-taker Emperor, Leiden: E. J. Brill, 1986.

7 Arthur Waldron, The Great Wall of China, Cambridge: Cambridge University Press, 1992, p. 100.

8 Ibid., p. 105.

9 The slow rate of fire left infantry arrayed in the field extremely vulnerable to fast-moving cavalry. Kenneth Chase has persuasively argued that it was this limitation that diminished the returns on firearms development in China. Small incremental improvements did not increase the effect of hand-held firearms enough to redress the battlefield imbalance of power with respect to the steppe. Consequently, the Chinese government did not emphasize firearms development. See Kenneth Chase, Firearms: A Global History to 1700, Cambridge: Cambridge University Press, 2003.

10 I use this term generically to refer to the hand-held guns, rather than specifically to distinguish the weapons used from muskets.

11 Albert Chan, *The Glory and Fall of the Ming Dynasty*, Norman: University of Oklahoma Press, 1982, p. 54.
12 Ibid., pp. 57–59.
13 Kwan-wai So, *Japanese Piracy in Ming China During the 16th Century*, Ann Arbor: Michigan State University Press, 1975, pp. 15–36.
14 Ray Huang, *1587, A Year of No Significance*, New Haven, Conn.: Yale University Press, 1981, pp. 170–171.
15 For a survey of Chinese naval warfare, see Peter Lorge, "Water Forces and Naval Operations," in David A. Graff and Robin Higham (eds), *A Military History of China*, Boulder, Colo.: Westview Press, 2002, pp. 81–96.
16 Brian Moloughney and Xia Weizhong, "Silver and the Fall of the Ming: A Reassessment," *Papers on Far Eastern History*, 40 (September 1989), pp. 51–78, cited in Kenneth Swope, "The Three Great Campaigns," p. 14.
17 Swope, "Three Great Campaigns," p. 19.
18 Ibid., pp. 89–156, for the account of Pubei's rebellion.
19 Ibid., pp. 157–383, for the account of the Japanese invasion of Korea and the Ming–Korean response to it.
20 The precise mixture of firearms is unclear. Since more firearms than bows or cross-bows were ordered it may well be that this was a supplemental budget to increase the preexisting weapons already held in the armory or distributed to the troops in the field. Song Yingchang may well have expected that he would not receive anything near his estimated requirements.
21 Swope, "Three Great Campaigns," pp. 386–453, for the account of the campaign against Yang Yinglong.

CHAPTER SEVEN

A people created for war,
1610–1683

> We have exterminated the bandits and pacified the disorder,
> establishing our capital at Yanjing . . . Our state does not rely on
> military force. It solely tries to transform through virtue, imperi-
> ally ruling the myriad locales. From now on, Yanjing will be the
> place where we have established out dynasty. How, then, could
> we return once more to the east and not establish a capital here.
>
> *Shizu Shilu*, the Veritable Records of Shizu's reign[1]

Wanli's strong military performance during his Three Great Campaigns was
eclipsed by the last decade of his rule, when imperial indolence and self-
imposed isolation from the government, coupled with the rising threat of the
Jurchen in the steppe, provided the prologue for the Ming's destruction. It is
probably not appropriate to assign too much blame to Wanli for the fall of the
dynasty in the 1630s and 1640s, or at least no more blame than any other
emperor who left the government's failing institutions unchanged. Wanli's
invigoration of the Ming military in the face of protest by his civil officials and
subsequent retreat from court demonstrate how the poisoned political atmos-
phere of the court and government had congealed into an almost completely
catatonic system by the late sixteenth century. Wanli's successful military commanders were undermined or sidelined almost immediately after the campaigns
were over, some even before, leaving very little to show in long-term development of the army from their efforts. While the army itself had changed from a
mostly hereditary, financially independent force into a paid, professional force,
now heavily dependent upon firearms, the officer corps remained dependent
on hereditary leaders. These hereditary military officers were not the families of
the early Ming, but they were the lineages that the court looked to for generals
from the late sixteenth century until the end of the dynasty. Like so many
dynasties before it, the Ming had great difficulty cultivating military talent
institutionally.

The political and military problems of the late Ming became a crisis with the
rise of the Jurchen, the same semi-nomadic steppe people who created the Jin
dynasty in the twelfth century. After their initial political consolidation as the

Later Jin, they changed their ethnic designation to "Manchu" in 1636. The creation of the Manchus as a people, polity and military force was a remarkable political achievement, made even more dramatic by their exploitation of Ming weakness to conquer China. Manchu success demonstrated the power that a relatively small, but politically unified and militarily effective, group could wield even over the vast territory and people that would become the Qing empire. The power of their unity was amplified by good leadership that judiciously applied force to only those regional powers who opposed them, while accepting and essentially confirming the preexisting power of those who accepted them. Manchu success was based upon their desire to rule and exploit China, not transform it.

While it was the Manchus who created the Qing dynasty and empire out of the ruins of the Ming, they were not the only problem facing Wanli's successors. Peasant rebellions in the late Ming severely taxed the political resources of the court, particularly in concert with the Manchu problem on the border. The rebellions were a difficult military problem, but not insoluble. On several occasions government forces nearly wiped out the most important rebel leaders and their bands of followers before pulling back from a purely martial solution. The rebels regrouped and continued their depredations, badly undermining the dynasty's attempts to deal with the Manchu threat. It was the court's internal political problems that prevented the dynasty from adopting a reasonable military policy. The Ming emperor and his court were incapable of responding to either the rebellions or the Manchus effectively, let alone both at the same time. Wanli in his younger days did better. It was not a question of resources but of leadership.

Even had the requisite leadership existed on the throne, the corrupt and sclerotic Ming bureaucracy sat atop a society in the midst of economic crisis. It is even more remarkable under these circumstances that it took so long for the Manchus to conquer the Ming, a process of decades rather than years, or that the Ming army was almost able to destroy the peasant rebellions. Despite all the signs of senescence, the Ming empire in the seventeenth century was still wealthy and powerful; its fall was not inevitable. Moreover, the Manchus had to acquire cannon in sufficient numbers, as well as the trained men to use them, before their raids could be transformed into campaigns of conquest. Ming fortifications armed with cannon were a formidable obstacle to Manchu incursions, and even in the field cannon substantially multiplied the power of Ming armies. This initial technological superiority did not provide enough of an advantage to overcome poorly conceived plans and weak leadership, and the Manchus were eventually able to obtain enough firearms to even the contest. Even so, Beijing was first captured by a peasant rebel army tens of thousands of men strong. The Ming dynasty's fate was decided on the battlefield, regardless of the underlying social and economic factors, and not just from the perspective of the Manchus.[2]

The rise of the Manchus[3]

The Jurchen's never had as close a relationship, hostile or friendly, with the Ming as the Mongols had. Jurchen leaders accepted Ming titles to facilitate commerce, but no real obligations were incumbent upon them in return. For most of the Ming dynasty the Jurchen were not perceived to be a significant threat to the dynasty or its interests. In the late fifteenth century they learned how to make iron weapons from captured artisans using smuggled iron (both China and Korea prohibited trading raw materials like iron to the steppe, or teaching tool making), and at the very end of the sixteenth century they acquired mining and smelting skills. Nurhaci, the Jurchen leader who would create the Manchus as a people, employed hundreds of foreign artisans to manufacture weapons and armor, in addition to native artisans. By the late sixteenth century the major Jurchen leaders had walled settlements.

In the 1580s power began to shift among the Jurchen tribes, moving away from confederation under the leadership of the chieftain sanctioned by the Ming. A Ming force intervened to attack that chieftain's rival and restore the status quo, in the process also killing a father and son of the Aisin Gioro lineage. The Ming recognized Nurhaci, the eldest male orphan of the son, as the legitimate inheritor of his father's title. Nurhaci immediately set out to revenge himself upon the man who had advised the Ming commander to intervene, effecting his death three years later and establishing himself as a successful leader. In 1589 the Ming officially designated him commander-in-chief of the Yalu region, acknowledging his actual strength. His rise to power did not go unchallenged. A two-year conflict with other Jurchen tribes concluded with Nurhaci's decisive victory at Jaka on the Hun River in 1593. After allying with the Western Mongols, he destroyed or incorporated most of the remaining Jurchen tribes over a 20-year period.

For Nurhaci to become more than a powerful tribal chieftain, however, he had to politically and socially reorganize the Jurchen into a less family-, clan- and village-centered society. He accomplished this by placing all his Jurchen followers into "companies" (Manchu: *niru*) of 300 households, which, after 1601, were grouped into ten battalions of five companies to form "banners" (Manchu: *gusa*) that served as military and social units.[4] The original four banners (red, blue, white and yellow) were expanded to eight in 1614 by adding four bordered banners. It seems unlikely, however, that the banners were actually at their full, theoretical strength. In a similar vein, a Manchu script was invented in 1599 to further enhance the ethnic and cultural standing of the Manchu as a people and polity. Mongolian had been the lingua franca of steppe diplomacy for several centuries, and this was part of Nurhaci's successful efforts to transfer the mantle of Mongolian imperial legitimacy to himself.[5] He was in fact hailed as khan by a group of Mongols in 1607. In 1616, Nurhaci established the Later Jin dynasty, both to indicate his maturing political ambitions and to further elevate his own authority over the still-powerful Jurchen and Mongol tribal chiefs.

Despite his years of campaigning to establish his preeminence as leader and efforts to improve industrial production, Nurhaci's economic base was still weak. Ming intervention in steppe affairs, not the least of which being the attack which killed his father and grandfather, provided him the gravamen of any dispute with the Ming he chose to invoke. Nurhaci began his expansion by attacking the trading city of Fushun on 9 May 1618. He offered the garrison generous terms of surrender, and they duly capitulated after the first assault on the walls. The officers and soldiers were then incorporated into the Manchu army, with their commanding officer becoming a Jin aristocrat and marrying one of Nurhaci's granddaughters. A 10,000-man relief column sent to save Fushun was routed.[6]

The Ming court was shocked by these events and launched a massive military response the following year. An army of about 90,000 men left Mukden (Shenyang) on 5 April 1619 in four columns to converge on Nurhaci's capital ten days later. Coordination was poor, and three of the columns were defeated in detail, the first near Sarhu, close to Nurhaci's capital, 14 April; the second at Sanggiyan Hada on 15 April; and the third at Dungge-Gau on 17 April. The overall commander fell back with his army intact, but, having lost 45,000 men, was soon executed.[7] Having neglected the northern defenses for so long, and unwilling to disburse the funds or wait for the military establishment to be rebuilt, the court placed any general in an impossible situation. Factional politics, particularly the rise of the Donglin Academy partisans, prevented rational policy formulation. Kaiyuan fell to the Manchus on 26 July, followed by Tieling on 3 September. The impressively fortified Shenyang then fell, as did Liaoyang on 13 May, after a force it sent out was crushed in the field. Another Manchu offensive in 1621 conquered Liaodong, allowing Nurhaci to move his capital to Liaoyang.[8]

With every southern advance, however, Nurhaci had to contend with growing internal political problems. On the one hand he had to overcome Jurchen resistance to leaving their accustomed lands and shifting from their tribal institutions to Manchu imperial institutions. On the other hand he had to digest a growing Chinese population whose customs conflicted with Jurchen practice. Conflicts between Jurchen overlords and their subject Chinese people were often violent, with the Jurchen treating the Chinese as chattel, which they sometimes were, having been captured in war and enslaved, and the Chinese occasionally murdering the outnumbered Jurchen living in their midst. It took considerable effort to resolve these conflicts, which was one of the factors slowing the Manchu advance south after the capture of the city of Guangning in 1622. Nurhaci paused while he dealt with these political issues, and assessed the major fortified cities he now faced.

Factional warfare within the Ming court continued unabated, preventing any firm decision by the half-wit Tianqi emperor (if he was even capable of making a decision of any kind) concerning northern border policy. The only positive step taken was the introduction of Portuguese cannon to some of the northern garrisons. Factional politics had left the forward Ming outpost of Ningyuan virtually abandoned when Nurhaci attacked it on 19 February 1626. Ably commanded and defended, and equipped with Portuguese cannon in addition to more venerable poliorcetic resources, Ningyuan not only held out for six days but forced Nurhaci to lift the siege with heavy losses. Nurhaci himself may have been wounded during the fighting. He died later in the year on 30 September 1626.[9]

Nurhaci's death, economic problems in Manchu territory, and the momentarily effective Ming defenses at Ningyuan opened a window of opportunity for peace negotiations. Hung Taiji, Nurhaci's successor, actually proposed peace conditions to the Chinese commander at Ningyuan, Yuan Chonghuan, in 1627 but his demands were far too one-sided to be entertained. Since the Manchu leader was unwilling to give up any captured territory, Yuan could be forgiven for seeing this as more a temporary expedient by Hung Taiji to gain food and money than a genuine opportunity for a lasting peace. Unfortunately, this was not the reason Yuan did not continue negotiations – even after Hung Taiji sent a second, less overbearing, set of proposals. The Tianqi emperor had died and, coupled with his successful defense of Ningyuan, Yuan's political position had dramatically improved. He resolved to pursue an aggressive border policy aimed at recapturing the territory lost to the Manchus. Yuan ordered abandoned outposts reoccupied and their defenses upgraded. While Hung Taiji digested this response to his peace overtures, Yuan was received by the new emperor, Chongzhen, promoted to minister of war, and given full authority to carry out his promise to recover all the lost territory within five years.[10]

In 1629, Yuan Chonghuan decided to eliminate a local warlord adventurer named Mao Wenlong, whose activities on the Korean, Manchu and Chinese borders against the Manchus won him much moral and material support from the Ming court. Mao's virtual execution in July was ill considered and poorly timed. Not only did it add force to rumors that Mao knew that Yuan was negotiating with the Manchus, but Yuan's supporters at court were also losing their hold on power. When Hung Taiji bypassed Ningyuan and raided all the way to the walls of Beijing in November, Yuan was disgraced. He was dismembered in the marketplace the following year on 22 September for unauthorized truce negotiations with the Manchus. The rest of his family were killed, enslaved or exiled, thus permanently dampening any further discussion of negotiations in the court.[11]

Although it is doubtful whether Hung Taiji would have accepted a permanent political settlement of his relationship with the Ming dynasty in the 1630s, the unwillingness of the court to consider even the temporary expedient of a truce with the Manchus hobbled the Ming army's efforts to suppress the empire's growing rebellions. Factionalism was intense, and any suggestion of negotiating with the Manchus was viciously attacked. Manchu raids now penetrated deeply into north China, though without cannon and troops trained in siege warfare, these *chevauchées* demonstrated the limits of the Manchu military as much as the Ming defenses. Caught between internal rebellion and external raids, the "righteous" literati of the south now controlling the government refused to allow their own taxes to be increased and utterly failed to formulate a responsible set of policies.[12] Their regionalism and ideology hamstrung the court, and Chongzhen was incapable of resolving these problems.

Late Ming rebellions

Soon after Chongzhen took the throne in 1627 scattered rebellions broke out in Shaanxi. These uprisings were caused by poor economic conditions, compounded by increased taxes to pay for the war with the Manchus and long-term government misrule. A drought in 1628 was the proximate cause of the first disturbances, fueled by impoverished farmers and army deserters. Had the government responded promptly and effectively the rebellions would have been quickly suppressed. Later efforts to resolve the situation foundered on the reasonable reluctance of several officials to rely solely on force to eliminate rebel bands. Unfortunately this humanity allowed many rebel groups to surrender when cornered or starving and then return to rebellion when they'd recovered. Manchu raids through the Great Wall in 1629 not only pulled troops away from Shaanxi and Shanxi, but also further fueled the rebellions when some of those troops mutinied.[13]

By 1631 all of the most important rebel leaders who had initiated the uprisings had been killed by government forces, but the rebellion as a whole had grown in size. The many groups were not an organized whole, though they demonstrated a wide variety of military proficiencies, including the use of firearms and knowledge of siege techniques. As the government response in Shaanxi became more effective, and the pickings less good, the rebel bands shifted east into Shanxi and Beizhili (Hebei), actually capturing Zezhou after an eight-day siege. Northeast China now had rebels in its middle and southern parts and Manchus threatening its northern part. These fed off each other as the rebels took advantage of Manchu disruptions and Ming troop movements to prey upon local society. Local officials concentrated on defending cities and important towns, which left the rebels free to roam through the hamlets, villages and lesser towns. The court's response was mixed, with poor coordination and a general refusal to recognize the seriousness of the situation balanced out by the obvious economic threat the rebels now posed to a more vital area. Troops from the border and the Beijing garrison, among other sources, were dispatched to suppress the rebels, though the Beijing troops proved entirely unwarlike.[14]

Overall the imperial army was still better trained and armed than the rebels, and this was made clear in most clashes between the sides. Almost always outnumbered army units routinely defeated rebel bands in the early 1630s, though the occasional rebel victories could be stunning. Local society reacted strongly to roving rebel bands, fortifying settlements, and arming and training militias. Life became increasingly militarized, localized and, perhaps paradoxically, lawless. Finally, an overall commander charged with suppressing the rebels was appointed in 1634 to coordinate efforts across the provinces of Shaanxi, Shanxi, Henan, Huguang and Sichuan. Ironically, the rebels also began to try to coordinate their activities early in 1635, though they were less successful than the government in their efforts. The dominant role played by Li Zicheng at the rebel meeting was a marker of his future importance.

For a time at the end of 1638 and the beginning of 1639 it seemed as if the rebels would be brought under control, as several of the most important had surrendered and been resettled, and others had been nearly destroyed. But most of the surrendered rebels were biding their time and building themselves up, and the Manchus launched a large-scale raid in early 1639 that momentarily captured the provincial capital of Shandong. That summer the rebels returned to their previous activities, capturing several towns. On 24 August, Zhang Xianzhong's rebel army shattered an imperial force 10,000-men strong under Zuo Liangyu at Mount Luoying, killing many of them and their officers.[15]

The disaster at Mount Luoying had tremendous political repercussions, disgracing the supreme commander for rebel suppression and forcing Grand Secretary Yang Sichang to personally take the field in an attempt to save his own career. When Yang arrived at his field headquarters in Xiangyang late in 1639 the rebellion had shifted westward into Sichuan. Yang's plan in 1640 was to encircle and contain the rebels, and then to send in strike forces to destroy each individual band. Zuo Liangyu disobeyed Yang's orders to remain in a blocking position and attacked Zhang Xianzhong's rebel band on 28 March. The rebels were ensconced at Mount Manao, and Zuo managed to send a detachment disguised as rebels into the fortified camp while he lay in wait outside. When the disguised troops started to attack from within, the rebels panicked and tried to flee. Zuo's victory was almost complete, except that the rebel Zhang escaped. This was a great victory, but Yang did not pursue Zhang Xianzhong, and by the summer the rebel leader had reconstituted his army.[16]

A rare moment of alliance between Zhang Xianzhong and two other rebel commanders allowed them to break into Sichuan up the Yangzi River. Once again the rebels were confined into a narrow area, forcing some to surrender, and once again they broke out and continued their activities. Yang Sichang himself reached Sichuan late in 1640, and proceeded to punish the commanders in the Sichuan area severely before taking personal control over directing the suppression efforts. He knew that escalating political attacks at court were gaining force as he failed to yield significant results. His political enemies were well aware, and made the point explicitly to the emperor, that the great success at Mount Manao happened in opposition to his orders. Yang threw all of his forces into the pursuit of the rebels, failing to understand that the rebels' greatest advantage was in their superior mobility. Zhang Xianzhong and his fellow rebels simply outdistanced most of the imperial army.

Having run around the imperial army, Zhang headed back down the Yangzi, crushing the one government force that managed to catch up to him at Kaixian.

Zhang now covered some 365 miles in less than eight days to enter Huguang and capture the city of Xiangyang on 15 March 1641. He took the city by planting disguised agents within it, but the city was really left vulnerable because Zhang had literally arrived before the news of his breakout of Sichuan. He stayed there for two days, looting the government stores and recovering his wives and advisers imprisoned there after the battle at Mount Manao.[17]

Li Zicheng had meanwhile effected the capture of an even greater city, Luoyang. Li had been quiet for some time following his own near annihilation in 1638, but a famine in Henan gave him the opportunity to recruit a large army. He besieged Luoyang on 7 March 1641, taking the city when government troops mutinied over poor rations and two junior officers surrendered to Li. As had happened at Xiangyang, the rebels murdered the resident imperial prince and looted the city. The main rebel army under Li Zicheng soon left the city, which was quickly retaken by government forces. When Yang Sichang heard of the fall of first Xiangyang and then Luoyang he committed suicide, taking poison on 10 April 1641.[18]

Having captured Luoyang, Li Zicheng began to act in a somewhat less bandit-like way, taking measures to alleviate the suffering of the poor and promoting some measures of social justice. He had even left behind a subordinate to hold Luoyang, rather than merely abandoning it; but that proved a futile gesture. Li now moved on to attack Kaifeng. Despite confusion within the city, a strong defense was eventually mounted that drove Li off after seven days. Li was himself wounded by an arrow in the eye, and it took him several months to recover, during which time his army did little campaigning. Government forces failed to pursue him, while the local officials and commanders turned to political infighting.

Li Zicheng spent the summer not only recuperating but also absorbing other rebel leaders and their bands into his army. His recent successes convinced many leaders to subordinate themselves to him, and by the autumn of 1641 he resumed action with greater forces at his disposal than he had ever previously possessed. A government army was soon trapped and destroyed, followed by successful attacks on Xiangcheng, Nanyang and most of southwestern Henan's important towns. Li started back toward Kaifeng again in 1642, along the way failing to capture Yancheng, commanded by Zuo Liangyu, and retaking Xiangcheng. He commenced his second siege of Kaifeng in mid-January, reasonably certain that no government armies threatened his rear. Li's initial attempt to overtop the walls by building a tower with cannons on it higher than the city wall was successfully countered by the defenders who constructed an even higher tower with cannons overnight. A subsequent attempt at escalade got only a few rebels onto the wall where they were captured and killed. Li then tried digging through the walls, which were some 120 feet thick at the base and covered with brick. Within a week 36 holes, each big enough to hold 100 men, were dug, and more of the wall was soon pulled down. But the city defenders drove the rebels from the breaches. On 11 February Li had gunpowder packed in the holes with his troops ready to rush in. The explosion blew out, rather than in, killing and wounding many of Li's troops, but doing little damage to the wall. Li lifted the siege and withdrew the following day.

His second siege of Kaifeng was a learning experience, and as Li Zicheng campaigned to the city's south and east for the next three months he was clearly thinking through his errors. When he attacked the town of Guide, for example, he successfully used gunpowder charges to breach its wall. Li came to understand that siege warfare, unlike his previous style of campaigning, was a systematic discipline requiring patience. He built up supplies during the winter of 1641 and spring of 1642 determined to starve the city into submission. The third siege of Kaifeng began in May, with the rebel army entrenched around the city. Li defeated two government relief armies, which effectively isolated the city. The Ming court failed to do anything substantive. The siege dragged on through the summer and into the autumn, when desperation and privation on both sides convinced first the defenders and then the rebels to break the Yellow River dykes near the city. A second break on 8 October let free the river with a roar, inundating the city. Li Zicheng withdrew without any valuable plunder, having inflicted several hundred thousand deaths from starvation or flood.

With Kaifeng and the area around it absolutely devastated, Li moved back toward Nanyang, where he defeated the remaining government forces in Henan in a series of battles. Li then chose to expand his area of influence rather than deepen it in Henan, and in so doing probably missing a real opportunity to transform his roving army into a political force with a real economic base. Here he again demonstrated the conceptual weakness of his background, just as he had in his initial attempts to capture Kaifeng. Li was in the process of learning how to become a political leader as he continued his military activities. He drove into Huguang almost unopposed, capturing cities and towns barely defended by disorganized, demoralized and incompetently led government forces. As in Henan, Li held these settlements only briefly before moving on. When he turned his attention north and attempted to return to Shaanxi, however, stout resistance by well-led, competent troops utterly frustrated him. Politically, Li consolidated his position to advance his now imperial ambitions by assassinating some of his subordinate rebel leaders.

In early 1643 Li Zicheng established a rudimentary administration at Xiangyang, finally taking real steps toward his longer-term imperial aspirations; he proclaimed himself Prince of Xinshun on 27 April. Li next planned to move into Shaanxi and Shanxi in order to create a base for an attack on Beijing. He was temporarily pre-empted by a southward drive into Henan by Sun Quanting, who had built up a strong army in Shaanxi. Against Sun's better judgment, the court had ordered Sun to destroy Li Zicheng in Henan, an area now an agriculture wasteland far from his supply base in Shaanxi. On 20 October Sun won a crushing victory over Li at Ru sub-prefecture in Henan, followed by several smaller successes. Supply problems and internal splits began to erode Sun's strength, and he was soon forced on the defensive. Two months after his campaign began, Sun was retreating back into Shaanxi *sans* much of his army. Shaanxi was now open to Li, and he marched in after sweeping aside the remnants of Sun's army (Sun died in battle at Weinan).[19]

In Shaanxi Li began to create some level of real control over the province. On 8 February 1644 (the first day of the lunar new year) he proclaimed a new dynasty, Dashun, with himself elevated to the title of Prince of Shun.[20]

The fall of Beijing

Li Zicheng was already moving east into Shanxi as he established his new dynasty, and most government resistance rapidly collapsed. The provincial capital of Taiyuan fell almost immediately after it was attacked on 16 March, when a section of wall was brought down with cannon fire and a defending officer surrendered. Li's army met almost no resistance as it marched east, with even a major city like Datong surrendering without a fight on 7 April.[21] In Beijing the court's complete political breakdown was evident in the emperor's inability to even decide to flee. Politics and symbolism convinced him that fleeing his capital would effectively destroy the dynasty, yet Chongzhen did not see that the dynasty could only be preserved if he survived the fall of Beijing. He even rejected the idea of sending the heir-apparent to Nanjing.[22]

Desperate attempts to raise money and prepare Beijing's defenses fell short. Some money was raised, the imperial treasuries being short of funds, but many wealthy people could not overcome their own greed even in such a crisis. They must have been unable to accept the possibility that the city might fall. Border generals like Wu Sangui were ordered to return and defend the capital, but only left their posts facing the Manchus reluctantly. Li Zicheng's army reached the outskirts of Beijing on 23 April, where the Three Great Camps, set up so long ago to train the Ming army, surrendered. Li's envoy discussed terms less than surrender with the emperor, though nothing came of this. No one in the bureaucracy could even formulate a response to the situation, much less a plan. The eunuch in charge of the city's defense opened a gate to Li Zicheng's army on the night of 24 April, and the imperial city was soon surrounded. Chongzhen hanged himself on Coal Hill the next morning.[23]

The creation of the Manchus and the Qing dynasty

Hung Taiji had commenced raiding into Ming territory in 1629, and continued a regular series of incursions through the 1630s and the beginning of the 1640s without actually destroying the Ming border defenses. The most important result of the 1629 raid was the capture of Chinese cannon founders capable of manufacturing Portuguese pieces, and gun crews. In early 1631 the first group of 40 new cannon had been cast in Later Jin territory; Chinese troops were incorporated into the Later Jin army primarily as siege units equipped with cannon. Hung Taiji also began the gradual process of imperializing his rule through the imposition of Chinese government institutions and diminishing the power of other high-ranking Manchus.[24]

In the autumn of 1631 Hung Taiji besieged the fortress of Dalinghe and its surrounding strongpoints. The new cannon were critical in reducing the fortifications, and even more critical in a battle of 19 October against a Ming relief army twice the size of the Jin force. Cavalry charges were important, but it was the cannon and arquebuses used on both sides that were truly central to the contest. Jin casualties were heavy as they directly assaulted infantry armed with firearms, but with the help of their own cannon firing into the Ming ranks, they won. The siege continued until 21 November, when Dalinghe surrendered.[25]

Hung Taiji changed his dynasty's name to "Qing" and his people's ethnonym to "Manchu" on 14 May 1636, reflecting continuing military success and ambitions for future conquests.[26] He was ambivalent about the increasing sinicization that the imperial enterprise brought, fearing the loss of Manchu culture, particularly its martial vigor, but recognized the political and administrative value of a bureaucratic system. The banner system occupied a strange place in an imperial Chinese administration, privileging a distinct hereditary group of Manchus, Mongols and Chinese, each in their own eight banners, over a theoretically meritocratic, literate, professional bureaucracy. It would nevertheless continue mostly intact until the dynasty fell in 1911.

Manchu campaigns were not universally successful, however, and they were beaten back from Jinzhou in 1639 and 1640. Hung Taiji had by that time conquered Mongolia and Korea, taken full control over the Amur Basin, and secured a good section of the coastline. The Manchu emperor personally took the field to force the issue of Jinzhou in 1641. On 24 September a disastrously organized Ming relief force was attacked in its camp and scattered, leaving 53,783 corpses behind. Subsequent Ming relief attempts foundered for lack of troops and low morale, with the nearby fortress at Songshan falling by treachery on 18 March 1642, and the city of Jinzhou surrendering on 8 April.[27] Manchu raids continued into Ming territory through its tottering northern defense line. When Li Zicheng's army approached Beijing in 1644, border generals like Wu Sangui were ordered to the capital with their forces. Wu abandoned Ningyuan and marched toward Beijing via Shanhaiguan but, whether because of intentional slowness or simply the unexpected speed of Li Zicheng's advance, was only halfway between Shanhaiguan and the capital when the city fell. Uncertain about what to do, Wu fell back to Shanhaiguan.

Wu Sangui and the Battle of Shanhaiguan

Li Zicheng's attempts to win over Wu Sangui failed, forcing Li to march on Shanhaiguan to destroy what was the strongest Ming army threatening his position at Beijing. Wu Sangui, for his part, was then forced to turn to the enemy he'd been fighting for so many years for help – the Manchus. The timing for the Manchu court could not have been better, as they had already resolved to invade the Ming, rather than merely raid it, and dispatched an army to that end before Wu's emissaries arrived. The Manchu army diverted from its original route of march and headed for Shanhaiguan. The Qing court was now ruled by the 6-year old Shunzhi emperor, who had taken the throne on 8 October 1643, under the regency of Dorgon and Jirgalang.

Wu Sangui believed that he could entice the Manchus to help him defeat Li Zicheng with the offer of a share of the booty looted by the rebels and the cession of additional territory north of the Great Wall. But the Qing campaign paradigm had changed to conquest, and their expeditionary army was under new orders not to loot or abuse the population. Furthermore, Wu's withdrawal from Ningyuan had already left the territory he proposed to cede to the Qing in their hands. With Li Zicheng's army approaching Shanhaiguan, Wu had no choice but to surrender to the Manchus and join their campaign to avenge Chongzhen, rather than harnessing them to his own purposes.

The Manchu army under Dorgon was 60 miles north of Shanhaiguan when Li Zicheng arrayed his 60,000 men near the fortress complex on 25 May 1644. Wu tendered his submission to Dorgon by courier and started to deploy his army of about 50,000 men by the Sha River west of Shanhaiguan. Dorgon force-marched his army to Shanhaiguan, arriving a few miles away on the night of the 26th. While the battle opened near the Sha River with Wu Sangui's army making repeated direct assaults on Li Zicheng's army, Wu personally surrendered to Dorgon. A sandstorm blew in covering the approach of the Manchu cavalry as they circled around Wu's right flank to attack Li's left flank. The rebel army was completely shattered and reeled back to Beijing to victimize the capital before abandoning it.[28]

The Qing conquest

Dorgon's army swept into Beijing unopposed on 5 June to find a shocked population expecting Wu Sangui. Wu, however, had been dispatched to pursue and destroy Li Zicheng by Dorgon. The real work of conquering China was just beginning for the Manchus, and despite the weakness of the Ming state and the chaos wrought by the late Ming rebellions, a considerable amount of military resistance remained to be overcome. It was only in 1662 that the last Ming emperor was captured and strangled, and the territory of the Ming dynasty brought under firmer control. In some places the control was quite strong and in others quite weak, but the execution of the Yongli emperor rendered all future claims of upholding the banner of Ming resistance tenuous or moot. A new Qing ruler took the throne in 1661, the Kangxi emperor, who would reign for six decades. The Kangxi emperor presided over the final resolution of two problems that developed out of the first stage of the Qing conquest: the disposition of the satrapies in southern China controlled by Wu Sangui, Geng Jingzhong and Shang Kexi, and the naval power based on Taiwan created by Zheng Chenggong (Koxinga).

Chinese armies under Chinese generals, rather than Manchu banner forces, carried out much of the Qing conquest of China. The banner army that Dorgon led in 1644 was perhaps 100,000-men strong, completely inadequate to take and hold extensive territories or very many cities. Northern China was still disturbed by bandits, anti-Ming rebels, Li Zicheng's remnant Shun forces, and even the odd Ming loyalist band. Unlike the Ming government, however, Qing forces were prepared to exterminate these groups and any others that disturbed the peace or resisted Qing authority, preferring to err on the side of killing too many rather than too few. Dorgon was forced to relent on the surprisingly emotional issue for the Chinese of adopting the Manchu haircut, with the front of the head shaved and a queue at the back. Although Dorgon felt strongly about the issue, he reluctantly backed down when it became clear that it would incite tremendous and widespread resistance.[29] In the early stage of the Qing conquest it was important to ease any obstacles to what might still be construed as collaboration.

While some Qing armies concerned themselves with rooting out local troublemakers in north China, others focused on destroying the remaining structures of Ming power that still controlled most of the Ming empire. The latter process required a combination of force against Ming armies or loyalists and the co-opting of local elites into the new dynasty. In Shandong province, for example, local elites were eager to join a new government that would restore order and confirm them in their dominant positions. The Manchus were pleased to engage the Shandong elites, and Shandong men served the early Qing administration in large numbers.[30] Dorgon was also sensitive to the need to reopen roads and transportation so that food and money would flow to Beijing. He therefore expended great effort in restoring safe communications, something the late Ming administration had been unable to accomplish.

Very early on, Qing authorities physically separated bannermen from the subject population. Separate cities were built, sometimes within existing cities, even as the conquest was progressing. Most Chinese troops were incorporated into Green Standard armies that restored order in the countryside. These forces were under the command of provincial governors and tightly constrained in the ambit of their activities. After peace was restored most of these *ad hoc* measures solidified into regular practice.

The end of Li Zicheng

Li Zicheng and his shattered army managed to outrun Wu Sangui and return to Shanxi, before quickly moving on to Shaanxi where he began to rebuild his base and fortify his position in anticipation of the coming attack. Former Ming generals who had welcomed Li into Shanxi now turned on his forces there, tendered their submissions to the Manchus, and commenced new careers exterminating the Shun forces for the Qing dynasty. With Wu Sangui now back in Beijing, however, the Qing forces on the ground in Shanxi were unable to drive the Shun garrison out of Taiyuan. Disturbances broke out in many areas that had initially gone over to the Qing in Shandong and Hebei, preventing Dorgon from sending more troops into Shanxi. It was not until late 1644 that these uprisings were sufficiently settled that the Manchus could turn their attention to Li Zicheng.

Three Manchu banner armies attacked Li Zicheng, accompanied by Chinese troops. Taiyuan fell quickly in November after bombardment by Chinese banner units with Portuguese cannon, and the resulting pursuit by banner and Chinese forces destroyed the Shun hold in Shanxi. The other two armies drove into Shaanxi from the north and south. By the end of January 1645 the bannermen of the northern army (which Wu Sangui and Shang Kexi were attached to) broke through Shun defenses and marched on Yan'an. The southern army waited a month for heavy cannons to come up before assaulting strongly defended Tong Pass, one of the strategic keys to China. Fierce resistance initially turned back the Manchu assault on 7 February, inflicting heavy casualties, before devastating fire from the Portuguese cannon overwhelmed the defenders. The way now lay open to Xi'an, Li Zicheng's capital. Li was unable to defeat the Manchu cavalry in the field and abandoned Xi'an after looting it and putting it to the torch. Despite his complete strategic defeat, he retained an army tens of thousands of men strong as he fled to Huguang. The Manchus relentlessly pursued him south, defeating him time after time. Some time in September of 1645 he died after being attacked in the Jiugong mountains by local militiamen.[31]

The Qing–Southern Ming war

Ming forces did attempt an organized resistance from south of the Yellow River, with some of the commanders even conceiving of retaking north China from the Manchus. These hopes collapsed quickly as assassination, personal jealousies and internal political conflict undermined the Southern Ming war effort. The Ming court, now based in Nanjing, tried to coordinate the remains of the regular army, local militias, local strongmen and bandits of all stripes with little success. Moreover, the Nanjing court was still uncertain about whether it should attempt to defend the territory it still held, fall back to a more defensible position, or formulate an offensive strategy. Some ardent loyalists believed that if the Ming attacked the Manchus the people of north China would rise up in support. Even some of the more aggressive commanders knew that this was unlikely even if such an offensive could be launched.

In 1645 two Southern Ming generals responsible for the northwestern defense line submitted to the Manchus. This not only opened the way across the Yellow River but also added tens of thousands of good troops to the Qing cause. These generals and their troops then led the Qing army into southern China. With the generals on the border defecting, plans for an offensive strategy were impossible. Confusion at the Nanjing court was also losing it the support of local strongmen in the territory it held. Defection fed on defection, nurtured by political infighting. Li Zicheng's old nemesis, Zuo Liangyu, led his army and navy down the Yangzi toward Nanjing to settle political scores, but died of natural causes along the way. His unruly troops continued on their way, however, forcing the Nanjing regime to divert troops to defend itself against them. Zuo's army was defeated and driven back, though insufficient force was available to destroy it, and it surrendered en masse to the Qing. Ironically, many of the officers and men would later acquit themselves extremely well in Qing service.

Defections continued to erode the northern defenses and increase the size of the Manchu army throughout 1645. The Manchu southern drive halted briefly before the walls of Yangzhou where the commander, Shi Kefa, refused repeated entreaties to surrender. The actual siege began on 13 May, with a massive assault on the walls on 20 May. Qing casualties were extremely high as the defenders' Portuguese cannon raked the massed infantry. Qing cannon concentrated on the northwest corner of the city, and the Qing infantry were already overcoming the walls by sheer weight of numbers when, whether by design or accident, the main gate of the city was thrown open. Shi Kefa attempted to commit suicide by slitting his own throat, but did not cut deeply enough and was captured. He still refused to submit and was executed. The Manchu commander ordered a massacre of the city's inhabitants for five days, though the atrocities continued for ten days. The lowest estimate is that 20,000 to 30,000 people were killed, the highest 800,000.[32]

The Qing army's southern progress continued, and by 1 June it had crossed the Yangzi. The current Ming emperor fled Nanjing, to be progressively abandoned by his entourage and eventually fall into Manchu hands on the 15th. Yet even before the emperor's capture, Nanjing had surrendered to the Manchus on 8 June. A large number of local elites committed suicide with the fall of the Ming dynasty, but most did not, nor did they actively resist the new regime. Although collaboration was ethically distasteful, it was also the most practical response to the situation. The Qing authorities now struggled to assume control by enlisting cooperative local power-holders, smashing bandits and loyalist groups to reestablish order, and pursuing the last fragments of Ming authority in southern China.

A succession of Ming courts cropped up in the south, while uprisings of sometimes only vaguely loyalist bands arose throughout the empire. The Manchus had effectively destroyed Ming imperial authority and now had to reassert imperial authority under the Qing dynasty. Local uprisings were put down with immense brutality, with directed massacres against cities and towns that resisted Qing forces, and mass slaughter of captured rebels. These bitterly fought campaigns continued for many years after the fall of Nanjing. Sometimes what had formerly been a minor bandit problem became a loyalist rebellion. As time went on and the Manchus remained in China, the devastating suppression of rebellion and cooptation of local elites concerned with social order gradually brought peace. In the south, three Chinese generals, Wu Sangui, Shang Kexi and Geng Jingzhong, were sent to stamp out the fleeing Ming court and conquer the area for the Qing. It was Wu Sangui who captured the last Ming emperor in Burma in 1662 and had him strangled upon his return to Yunnan. The three generals' reward for conquering the south were virtual fiefs in their former theaters of operation: Wu Sangui held Yunnan and Guizhou; Shang Kexi, Guangdong; and Geng Jingzhong, Fujian. These separate kingdoms could not continue without slighting the power of the emperor. Matters came to a head in 1673 when Shang Kexi asked the Kangxi emperor leave to retire from his post and to be replaced by his son, Zhixin.

The Revolt of the Three Feudatories

The emperor accepted Shang's resignation, but rejected the idea of passing his control of Guangdong to his son. Wu Sangui and Geng Jingzhong then tendered their resignations, forcing the Kangxi emperor to either confirm their positions as hereditary or precipitate a war. Both sides were clear about what was at stake. After some deliberation, the emperor, supported by the Board of Revenue's declaration that it had enough money in the treasury to support a ten-year war and his grandmother's advice, accepted Wu's and Geng's resignations. Wu initiated his rebellion on 28 December 1673 under the banner of the Zhou dynasty. He quickly seized most of Hunan early the next year, while nearby Guangxi entered a sort of quasi-rebel state, overturning Qing authority but not quite joining Wu. Geng Jingzhong waited until 21 April 1674 to rebel, quickly overwhelming loyal Qing forces in Jiangxi and Zhejiang. The Kangxi court feared a link-up between these rebels and the Zheng regime on Taiwan (see the next section), but this failed to come off.[33]

The court began mobilizing troops in April, bringing together an army that would ultimately number 200,000 bannermen and 400,000 Green Standard soldiers. But events continued to go against the Qing in the last half of 1674 and beginning of 1675. First, a general in Sichuan rebelled and allied himself with Wu Sangui; next a provincial commander in Shaanxi mutinied when ordered to attack Sichuan in 1674, taking over eastern Gansu early the next year; then in 1675 there was a brief uprising of Chahar Mongols; and by early 1676 Shang Zhixin accepted the title of Prince of Fude from Wu Sangui, placing Guangdong in open rebellion. For all of his military strength, however, Wu and his rebels could not claim the affections of most of the Chinese population. Wu was an early and active Qing turncoat, rendering his reestablishment of Ming customs a pointless and even macabre gesture. The Kangxi emperor controlled far greater economic resources than Wu and, as importantly, rejected any question of retreat or acceptance of Wu's regime in the south. Even in the darkest hour of the rebellion the Kangxi emperor proved an intelligent and strong leader.

Wu's armies initially enjoyed a superiority in the quality and number of their weapons, having early on started to cast cannon and swords. Qing government resources, and the enlistment of the reluctant Jesuit father, Verbiest, soon produced more and better weapons. Once again, field commanders clamored for heavier cannon, finding them decisive in battle. As the imperial armies became better armed, as well as better paid, Wu's battlefield advantage diminished, despite extremely mediocre Qing generals. Wu could not advance north, and once Green Standard forces recaptured eastern Gansu in July of 1676, Sichuan became vulnerable, and the Qing western flank was secured. Meanwhile the Qing attack on Fujian was beginning to gain ground, as inadequate supplies weakened Geng's authority. He surrendered in November while he could still gain some advantage for doing so.[34]

Qing armies continued their advances toward Wu Sangui's positions in Hunan, where Wu declared himself ruler of the Zhou in March of 1678. His official reign was short, however, and he died from illness on 2 October 1678. It would not be until 7 December 1681, however, before the last vestige of the Revolt of the Three Feudatories was crushed in Kunming, Yunnan.[35]

Shi Lang and the conquest of Taiwan

The great maritime hero Koxinga/Coxinga, Zheng Chenggong (1624–1662), was the son of a Chinese merchant and pirate and a Japanese mother. His father fought the Manchus as a Ming loyalist after the fall of Nanjing, but surrendered to them in 1646 when they attacked Fujian. Zheng Chenggong disagreed with his father's decision and became an implacable foe of the Qing. In addition to his base in Fujian, Zheng captured the islands of Jinmen and Xiamen, and launched naval attacks on the Qing coastline. Zheng's attacks, beginning in 1655 moving north up the coast, culminated in his attack on Nanjing in August of 1659. Though he disposed of 400 ships and a reported 250,000 men, Zheng cautiously laid siege to the city. Although he had some cannon, his siege craft was poor, perhaps the result of his men's indiscipline. A sally by a small force of veteran Manchu cavalry drove Zheng's men back from the city, and a larger combined charge of infantry and cavalry before dawn the following day caused widespread panic. Zheng and his men retreated to their ships and the safety of the ocean.

Zheng was forced to seek a safer and more extensive base as the Qing dislodged him from the mainland. In 1661 he forced the Dutch out of Taiwan, making him a particularly great nationalist hero for modern Chinese because he defeated a Western power.[36] Zheng died the next year, leaving his maritime trading and pirating empire to his son Jing. Zheng Jing tried to take advantage of the Revolt of the Three Feudatories to get a foothold on the mainland, but was unable to establish a stable relationship with Geng Jingzhong. Besides, Geng and the rebellion's fate rendered the issue moot. The Kangxi emperor now saw that a defensive policy *vis-à-vis* the Zheng regime was unacceptable.

The Qing captured Zheng Jing's bases on Jinmen and Xiamen in 1680, though this was mostly due to a secret agreement with the defenders to surrender. There was a brief lull in Qing activity with respect to Zheng Jing while the final acts of the Revolt of the Three Feudatories was played out. Zheng Jing himself died in 1681, leaving control to his son Keshuang. Shi Lang, a former Zheng Chenggong supporter who had submitted to the Qing in 1646, was put in charge of the campaign to capture Taiwan. Admiral Shi spent two years gathering ships, training men and fighting political battles (in which the emperor ultimately supported him). In July of 1683 he set out, fighting a week-long battle to capture the Pescadores. Victory in that battle brought about Zheng Keshuang's submission, though with very favorable terms. Although the Kangxi emperor originally downplayed the capture of Taiwan, stating that "Taiwan is outside the empire and of no great consequence,"[37] he was later convinced to incorporate Taiwan into the Chinese empire for the first time because leaving it unoccupied would have invited the return of the Dutch. And for the first time in Qing history there were no threats to the dynasty's hold over China.[38]

Notes

1 *Shizu Shilu*, 5:59b, translated in Frederic Wakeman, *The Great Enterprise*, Berkeley: University of California Press, 1985, p. 451.
2 See Dorgon's comments in 1645, in Frederic Wakeman, *The Great Enterprise*, p. 18.
3 Gertrude Roth Li, "State Building before 1644," in *The Cambridge History of China*, Volume 9: *Part 1, The Chi'ing Empire to 1800*, Cambridge: Cambridge University Press, 2002, pp. 9–72, for the discussion that follows.
4 Ibid., p. 34.
5 Ibid., p. 28.
6 Frederic Wakeman, *The Great Enterprise*, pp. 59–62.
7 Ibid., pp. 62–63.
8 Ibid., pp. 63–64.
9 Ibid., p. 83.
10 Ibid., pp. 82–86.
11 Ibid., pp. 127–131.
12 Ibid., p. 134.
13 James Bunyan Parsons, *Peasant Rebellions of the Late Ming Dynasty*, Tucson, Ariz.: University of Arizona Press, 1970, pp. 1–21.
14 Ibid., pp. 26–29.
15 Ibid., pp. 68–69.
16 Ibid., pp. 69–75.
17 Ibid., pp. 75–81.
18 Ibid., pp. 81–82,
19 Ibid., pp. 90–113, 117–120.
20 Ibid., p. 123.
21 Ibid., pp. 125–126.
22 Frederic Wakeman, *The Great Enterprise*, pp. 240–257.
23 It is more accurate to say at the base of Coal Hill. A visitor to the Forbidden City who starts at the top of Coal Hill, as the author did, will be very disappointed to be directed ever downward to a tree at the very bottom. pp. 257–266.
24 Ibid., pp. 167–170.
25 Ibid., pp. 170–190.

26 Ibid., p. 206.
27 Ibid., pp. 211–224.
28 Ibid., pp. 310–313.
29 Ibid., pp. 420–422.
30 Ibid., pp. 424–436.
31 James Bunyan Parsons, *Peasant Rebellions*, pp. 161–167; Frederic Wakeman, *The Great Enterprise*, pp. 501–508.
32 Frederic Wakeman, *The Great Enterprise*, pp. 546–563.
33 Lawrence D. Kessler, *K'ang-hsi and the Consolidation of Ch'ing Rule, 1661–1684*, Chicago, Ill.: University of Chicago Press, 1976, pp. 80–82.
34 Kangxi ordered Geng drawn and quartered in 1682 for the murder of provincial governor Fan Chengmo during the rebellion.
35 Lawrence D. Kessler, *K'ang-hsi*, pp. 83–89.
36 There is a statue of Zheng receiving the surrender of the Dutch at the site of the remains of the Dutch fort in Tainan, Taiwan.
37 Lawrence D. Kessler, *K'ang-hsi*, p. 94.
38 Ibid., pp. 90–94.

CHAPTER EIGHT

The Old Man of Ten Complete Military Victories, 1684–1795

With southern China finally settled, and the issue of Taiwan resolved, the Kangxi emperor turned his attention to the north and west. The Qing emperor was 30 years old in 1684, firmly in control of his government, and confident of his abilities after crushing the Revolt of the Three Feudatories and quashing the Zheng regime on Taiwan. His empire was as large or larger than any other Chinese empire in history, but developments in Central Eurasia drew the Kangxi emperor, as well as his son and grandson, into a prolonged war that ultimately expanded his territory even further. As Peter Perdue put it, "The conquest of Central Eurasia was the second stage of the Manchu 'Great Enterprise,' following directly on their establishment of control over Han China."[1] Vast amounts of blood and treasure were expended over the course of seven decades to defeat the Zunghar Mongols decisively, but there were sound strategic reasons for at least some of the effort.

Qing China confronted two powers in Central Eurasia: Russia and the Mongols. Russia complicated dealings with the Mongols because it could supply them with food and weapons for their internal struggles, or even in conflicts with China. It was therefore crucial for the Kangxi emperor to neutralize the Russians before attacking the Zunghars. It was also important to stabilize bilateral relations with Russia, since it was beginning to push its territorial claims toward Chinese territory. A short war resolved both of these problems in Qing favor, opening up lucrative trade for the Russians. The Kangxi emperor then had a free hand to deal with the Zunghars.

Although the Kangxi emperor was successful in eliminating, at least briefly, the Zunghar threat by force of arms, his son, the Yongzheng emperor, was too fiscally conservative to wholeheartedly adopt such an active military policy. Negotiations were a much cheaper way of removing military threats. The Yongzheng emperor nevertheless intervened in Qinghai, annexing it after a successful campaign, and launched a campaign against the Zunghars that went badly. It fell to the Yongzheng emperor's son, the Qianlong emperor, to improve the Qing military supply system to the point where the Qing army could exploit political weakness among the Zunghars and destroy them as a military threat. Logistics was the key to mastering the steppe threat, and it was only by learning how to translate China's immense wealth and resources into a powerful and enduring military reach that the Qing was able to subdue the Mongols.

In 1792 the Qianlong emperor wrote a record of the Ten Complete Military Victories of his reign to celebrate his own accomplishments. Though there had been many military successes, and the Qing empire was larger than any "Chinese" empire before it, some of the victories the Qianlong emperor referred to were actually failures. The Qianlong emperor's political claims had not been completely supported by his military power, and his failure to discover or admit this to himself was an example of an emperor believing his own rhetoric. But the Qing empire in 1792 was one of the greatest empires of that time in territory, wealth and stability, and it is both teleological and Eurocentric to attempt to find future failure intrinsic to that accomplishment.

The Qianlong emperor's military problems were not much different than his grandfather's. Even during the Kangxi reign period the Manchus' military prowess was declining rapidly. As they settled into a peaceful empire, the skills of riding and shooting were hard to maintain. Cavalry was also less effective in much of southern and western China. Just as Chinese armies under Wu Sangui and other Chinese generals were used to conquer the south, so it was again that Chinese armies led the way in putting down Wu's southern rebellion. The Green Standard armies outnumbered the banner armies (200,000 to 350,000 banner troops in 1685 to about 600,000 Green Standard, down from 900,000 during the Revolt of the Three Feudatories), and played a much more active role in the day-to-day functions of keeping the peace. Banner forces were mostly posted in the north and around Beijing, though about 30,000 remained in the south scattered in garrisons as a threat to any future uprising. Firearms battalions were added to each banner in 1683, though these were manned by Chinese bannermen unable to ride horses.[2] The Qianlong emperor's great military achievements demonstrated that the problems of a peacetime army could be overcome with sufficient imperial leadership and will, but also that it did not work without the emperor's direct involvement.

As a conquering ethnic group, the Manchus had a vested interest in not interconnecting the subject population of the Chinese very tightly, or creating any organization outside the emperor's direct control that united personnel across the empire. Banner units were considered completely loyal, even if not always effective, and Green Standard units somewhat loyal, though also not always effective. The same was true of the officer corps (the Kangxi emperor had initially employed Manchu generals during the Revolt of the Three Feudatories, but gradually shifted to Chinese generals who performed better). There were thus political as well as financial and ideological reasons for not maintaining the Qing army at a high level of readiness and integration. Like the Ming army, it required both time and the personal intervention of the emperor to override the internal security breaks on its smooth functioning. By campaigning actively against the Zunghars as a possible threat, the Qianlong emperor was able to develop the logistical capabilities of his army without compromising his overall security. In social and institutional terms, the networks created to supply the army in Central Eurasia were temporary; the vast distances spanned more than overwhelmed any resulting integration of newly annexed territory. The Qianlong emperor's campaigns, even the actually successful ones, did not build an integrated nation; if anything, they further attenuated the already loose regional ties within the Qing empire.

The Kangxi emperor's Russian campaigns[3]

Russian probes into the Amur River region had begun in the 1650s, when the Manchus were preoccupied with establishing real control over their Chinese empire. Qing–Russian diplomacy stumbled along ineffectively until a Russian trade mission reached Beijing in 1669. Though allowed to trade, the Russian government would not realize until after a second mission the following year that it had made contact with the Chinese emperor, rather than a tribal leader. The Kangxi emperor soon figured out that the incursions in the Amur River region were connected to the Russians, and alerted the regional military governor to keep a close watch on their activities. A 1676 Russian diplomatic mission also ended badly, with the emperor insisting that the tsar had to return certain fugitives and send a better envoy before good relations could be established. The mission did convince the Kangxi emperor to put his forces on the border on a more active military footing, shifting Mongol tribes away from the border and organizing the local population for possible military recruitment.

The emperor proceeded cautiously, gathering intelligence, including a "hunting trip" by several Manchu commanders in 1682, about the Russian positions, particularly around the city of Albazin. Although diplomacy was still his preferred method, the emperor knew that war was likely and began a build-up of men and supplies in the theater. Dutch cannon were brought up, and the river system exploited to transport three years' provisions to the front. An early suggestion simply to starve the Russians at Albazin and Nerchinsk by destroying their crops in the surrounding fields was held as a fall-back plan if Albazin could not be captured. The emperor originally intended to attack in 1684, but the local commander balked, and the opportunity was missed. The emperor's threats to the Russians still having been ignored, Albazin was captured by a new commander in June of 1685 after a three-day siege. The fort was destroyed, but for some reason the crops were not destroyed or harvested and carried back to the Qing storehouses. The Qing army then withdrew.

The standing crops allowed the Russians to return to Albazin and rebuild its fort soon after the Qing army left. In 1686 the second siege of Albazin lasted from July until November, when the emperor lifted the siege and accepted the offer of peace talks. The Kangxi emperor wanted to settle his border problem with the Russians in order to keep them from assisting the Mongol leader of the Zunghars, Galdan. Actual talks took some time to organize, but concluded in

1689 with the Treaty of Nerchinsk, the first treaty between a Chinese dynasty and a Western power based upon equal diplomatic status. This freed the Kangxi emperor's hand to deal with Galdan's growing threat.

The Kangxi emperor's campaigns against the Zunghars, 1690–1697[4]

Galdan had been subjugating Mongol tribes since the 1670s, taking control of all of eastern Turkestan by 1679. The Kangxi emperor, then occupied with the Revolt of the Three Feudatories, reluctantly sanctioned these activities by confirming the title awarded to Galdan by the Dalai Lama. Galdan next attempted to extend his rule over the Eastern Mongols, the Khalkhas, in the 1680s, forcing a confrontation with the Qing. The Kangxi emperor recognized the clear threat that a united Mongol confederation under an ambitious leader posed to his empire's interests in Central Eurasia. In July of 1690 the emperor personally took the field to chastise Galdan, but he soon got sick and returned to Beijing while his army carried on. The Qing army was extremely limited in its reach as it carted cannon and provisions with it into the steppe. Galdan, overconfident after a crushing victory over the Khalkhas, strayed within the limited compass of Qing operations and suffered a severe mauling at Ulan Butong on 3 September. Qing cannon were extremely effective, but Arni, the commanding general, was in no position to follow up the battle with a vigorous pursuit. Somewhat less than 200 miles from Beijing, Arni was near the end of his supply lines. Unable to do more militarily, Arni accepted negotiations conducted by the Dalai Lama's envoy.

The Kangxi emperor was not pleased with Arni's decision to negotiate, since Galdan was allowed to escape – but he had had little choice given the means at his disposal. Ulan Butong had been an atypical battle in the steppe, and both sides knew it. Galdan rebuilt his forces 1,500 miles away from Beijing, far beyond the reach of any Qing army. The Kangxi emperor pushed for improvements in the army's supply system in order to extend its reach; even so, he was forced to depend upon Galdan moving much closer to Qing territory if he wanted to get to grips with him. Galdan's food supplies in Zungharia were precarious, and poor harvests forced him east in 1695, stopping at the Kerulen and Tula rivers. The Kangxi emperor seized the opportunity to pounce upon Galdan's 20,000 men, sending three armies of 35,000 men each some 700 miles into the steppe. Once again the emperor personally took part, driving his armies near or past their logistical limits. Just as before, he was lucky that as Galdan fled one army he ran into another. Galdan's army was decisively crushed at Jaomodo on 12 June 1696, though he escaped.

Smaller detachments were sent in pursuit of Galdan, keeping him on the run until a close adviser poisoned him on 4 April 1697. The Kangxi emperor's determined pursuit of Galdan may well have been, as Peter Perdue has argued, unnecessary for his immediate strategic purposes after 1690, but it did reflect a desire to resolve military problems permanently. That pursuing such a course also enhanced his glory, not that it needed much enhancing in 1690, was also consistent with the Kangxi emperor's Manchu background. A purely defensive stance with respect to the steppe might well have been cheaper, but this would have left the initiative in the hands of Galdan. Having been forced to be reactive for so much of his reign, it is therefore not surprising that the emperor was a bit overeager to take and keep the initiative against Galdan.

The Yongzheng emperor's campaigns against the Zunghars[5]

Galdan's death did not destroy the Zunghar polity, and after some good initial relations with the Qing court the Kangxi emperor had been forced to send two armies to drive the Zunghars out of Tibet in 1717. The Yongzheng emperor (r. 1723–1735) placed cost cutting ahead of campaigning, and pulled Qing troops back from their forward positions on the frontiers. Just as his father before him, however, a conflict on the border drew him into Mongol politics, this time in the Kokonor region of Qinghai. The rivalry of two Mongol leaders, one backed by the Qing court, erupted into open warfare when the Qing-supported leader began to expand his territory. The other leader responded by attacking various Kokonor Mongol groups, who then fled to Qing territory for protection.

Although the Yongzheng emperor's superb general Nian Gengyao advised against involvement in the struggle, the emperor overruled him. After a perfunctory diplomatic suggestion to submit to the Qing that was rejected, Nian was soon ordered to take the field. A rumor that the refractory Mongol leader would invite the Zunghars into Qinghai no doubt added some urgency to the situation, and reminded the emperor of the problem of the still unvanquished Zunghars. In the event, the Zunghars did not get involved, and General Nian dislodged the offending Mongols in less than a month. Nian's victory was celebrated far out of proportion to its significance, demonstrating that in spite of his interest in financial austerity the Yongzheng emperor was still interested in military glory. Qinghai itself was put under direct Qing administration for the first time. Despite this, Nian fared poorly, being allowed to commit suicide in 1726 after being accused of a variety of crimes.

In 1727 the Qing concluded a new treaty with Russia at Kiakhta, firming up the already solid diplomatic relationship, and a new leader, Galdan Tsereng, took over control of the Zunghars. The Qing court demanded that Galdan Tsereng have no formal relations with Tibet and hand over a fugitive leader of the earlier Kokonor power struggle as the price for peaceful relations. These demands were patently unreasonable, and giving such concessions to the Qing would have made Galdan Tsereng look weak. Whether the Yongzheng emperor overestimated Qing power or was simply manufacturing a *casus belli* is unclear, but in 1729 he vowed to destroy the Zunghars. He faced the same logistical problems his father had, but compounded by his earlier pull back of troops from the frontier.

The two expeditionary armies were recalled soon after they set out in 1629, when an envoy from Galdan Tsereng arrived offering to concede on the issue of handing over the fugitive leader. By the time the army commanders had returned to Beijing Zunghar raids in Qinghai and Turfan cast serious doubts on the sincerity of Galdan Tsereng's intentions. The attacks were beaten back, and the campaign begun again the following year. Yue Zhongqi, the commander of the western army, had made a realistic, and therefore expensive proposal to invade Western Mongolia that the emperor rejected based on cost. The actual campaign was therefore carried out in a rather inadequate way, given the goals and obstacles the Qing army faced. Furdan, the commander of the northern army, built a fort at Khobdo, deep in Mongolia. In 1731 he was lured out of the fort with 10,000 men by deceptive intelligence that convinced him that the Zunghars were no longer concentrated in a single force. His first encounter on 30 July went well, and he drove off a force of 2,000 Zunghars. Three days later, however, he was surrounded at Hoton Nor, a small lake, by the main Zunghar army of 20,000 men. Furdan broke out on 27 July, returning the 125 miles to Khobdo with only 2,000 men.

Furdan's disaster would have been more significant had it not occurred so far from Qing territory, and had not Galdan Tsereng suffered a crushing defeat the next year at Erdeni Zhao by the Khalkhas. The Yongzheng emperor was not temperamentally suited to military campaigns – operations that required spending immense resources for uncertain and dubious outcomes. He treated his successful commanders badly, shirked responsibility for his own mistaken military judgments and had unrealistic expectations for campaigns. Chastised by the defeat at Hoton Nor, the Yongzheng emperor abandoned further adventures, leaving his son, the Qianlong emperor, the question of what to do about the Zunghars.

The Qianlong emperor

The Qianlong emperor ruled for the longest period in Chinese history. He "retired" as emperor in 1796 so as officially not to exceed the length of his grandfather's 61-year reign, but continued to rule in fact until his death in 1799. In 1792 he congratulated himself on the Ten Complete Military Victories of his reign: two campaigns against the Jinchuan tribes in Sichuan, three against the Zunghars, crushing restive Turkic Muslims in Xinjiang, putting down a rebellion in Taiwan, an extended war against Burma, a similar conflict with Vietnam, and driving the Gurkhas out of Tibet. Not all of these campaigns were actual victories, and some were more significant than others, but the sense of power and prestige that the Qianlong emperor's long rule evoked was not mere show. China at the end of the eighteenth century was a vast, wealthy empire led by an assured and generally competent ruler. It was not well-integrated, however, making its whole actually less than the sum of its parts. Just as Qianlong's "humble" style-name "The Old Man of Ten Complete Military Victories" disguised, intentionally or not, a less than perfect military record, so too did imperial ideology as a whole paper over the fundamental disunity of the Qing realm. Indeed, Chinese imperial rhetoric was not always used in parts of the empire like Manchuria, Tibet, Mongolia, or Xinjiang, where the emperor was described in more locally specific cultural terms and language. The Qing empire was not just China.

Unlike most culturally Chinese emperors, the Qing emperors maintained a consistent interest in the steppe and Central Eurasian world through at least the end of the Qianlong reign. They were, after all, Manchu, although the cultural distinctiveness of that term had diminished considerably among those who had lived among the Chinese for over a century. The complexity of that identity and its significance is best demonstrated in the Qianlong emperor's three campaigns against the Zunghars. He was, as I have just discussed, more concerned with Central Eurasia than any "purely" Chinese emperor would have been, and perhaps more interested in military glory. Thus driven finally to crush the Zunghars, the Qianlong emperor imposed his will on the Qing military and forced it to develop an unprecedented logistical system that would allow it to project power deep into Central Eurasia. This was not typical steppe or Manchu warfare, but rather a previously unimagined extension of Chinese warfare.

Before turning to the Qianlong emperor's military campaigns, it is important to note the many other cultural and political activities of his very long reign. Perhaps the most notorious matter was the literary inquisition that grew out of the Qianlong emperor's literary collection project, the Complete Library of the Four Treasuries. While collecting and editing the enormous work, some 3,470 works reproduced as a set with 36,000 folio volumes (collected between 1773 and 1775, with the finished work produced in 1782), the books were also examined for treasonous or offensive (to steppe people) language. Many books were destroyed or altered, and many authors executed and their families severely punished for sometimes only marginally problematic writings.[6] In politics, the Qianlong emperor's reign saw the expansion of the Grand Council system begun by his father during the war against the Zunghars. The Grand Council was a tool of imperial centralization that allowed the emperor to bypass the official bureaucracy for many decisions, particularly in prosecuting wars.[7] The military activities of the Qianlong reign must be read against this backdrop of increasing imperial centralization and ideological control.

The Qianlong emperor's campaigns against the Zunghars[8]

A leadership struggle among the Zunghars, beginning in 1745, gave the Qianlong emperor an opening to intercede and ultimately destroy them as a polity. In 1753, Prince Amursana fled to Qing protection after Prince Dawaci drove him out. Both princes had allied together to overthrow the previous khan, and now Dawaci took that title for himself. The Qianlong emperor seized the chance to install a Zunghar leader beholden to the Qing and backed Amursana in his bid to overthrow Dawaci. Two armies, one of 20,000 men and the other of 30,000 men, would advance into Zungharia in 1754. A magazine system connecting China with the oases of Turkestan stocked six months of supplies for the West Route army of 20,000 troops. Military farms around Hami and Barkul, the jumping off point for the second army, were also an important grain source. It cost almost ten times the purchase price of grain to transport it to Hami, but the imperial treasury was comfortably able to afford the massive costs of the campaigns.

The Qing expeditionary army was composed of bannermen and Mongol cavalry, accompanied by banner firearms. The cavalry–firearms combination was extremely effective. Once the Zunghar forces were brought to bay by the cavalry, the slower-moving firearms could be brought up to destroy them. As the campaigns progressed, however, tens of thousands of Green Standard infantrymen were also brought up, increasing the Qing army's firepower and ability to hold territory. Every Qing victory convinced subordinate tribes to go over to the Qing, and the Zunghar empire unraveled. Dawaci was quickly driven out in 1754; he fled to Russia and was handed over to the Qianlong emperor. Amursana was installed as khan, but soon asserted his own independence. Having participated in the attack on Dawaci, the Zunghar leader was well aware of the Qing army's capabilities and limitations. Amursana's betrayal was a surprise, catching the Qing army without adequate logistical support. The second campaign, beginning in late 1755, turned on the reestablishment of Qing supply lines. Once these were straightened out, the Qing army defeated Amursana, who fled to Russia in 1757. A smallpox epidemic then killed nearly half the Zunghars, and was followed by the imperially ordered extermination of the rest of the population. The Qianlong emperor finally and permanently settled the Zunghar problem by genocide.

The Qianlong emperor's Zunghar campaigns, and the linked campaign against the Turkic Muslim Khojas from 1757 to 1759, were a major turning point in steppe-Chinese history. This was the first time that a logistic system had been created that allowed a Chinese empire to fight a sustained war far into the steppe and bring the enormous material wealth of China to bear in a devastating way. The campaign against the Khojas was a series of sieges in Turkestan won by Qing armies supported by a reliable transport system. The limited resources of the steppe had always constrained the actors involved, making it difficult to strike at widely dispersed populations or limited pieces of strategic territory (like pasturage). Qing China's vast economy was harnessed by an effective government bureaucracy actually able to access that wealth. This was all driven on by an emperor prepared to insist on results. The ultimate value of the campaigns is less clear. By finally destroying the Zunghar state the Qianlong emperor dramatically increased Qing prestige and power in the steppe. The campaigns demonstrated yet again what the imperial Chinese state and military could do under an assertive emperor. Generals and officials opposed the campaigns, they did not all go well, and there were many setbacks, but the emperor persisted. Although firearms were important in Qing warfare, it is clear that it was logistics that so radically changed the basis of the Chinese empire's relationship with the steppe. This was a human, rather than a technological revolution.

The first Jinchuan war, 1747–1749[9]

Western Sichuan was controlled by hereditary chieftains with only the vaguest connections to the Qing government. These non-Han peoples were widely dispersed in mountainous terrain, where one of their main distinguishing features from the Qing court's perspective was their constant internecine fighting. For the first century of Qing rule the dynasty's actions were confined to mediating the fighting and gradually encroaching on the chieftains. Its basic policy with respect to the different groups was to prevent them from uniting into a threat. When one of the chieftains successfully began to conquer and incorporate other tribes in early 1747, and to challenge Qing authority directly, the Qianlong emperor sent armies into the area to suppress the chieftain.

The initial Qing efforts were defeated with heavy losses. Progress into the mountains was blocked by literally hundreds of stone towers and other fortifications, while the restricted terrain made it impossible to bring superior numbers to bear. Qing supply lines were vulnerable and guerrilla warfare further reduced Qing striking power. The Qianlong emperor mobilized over 200,000 men for an invasion in the middle of 1748. Well supplied with arquebuses, cannon and food, the Qing army shifted the conflict to a war of attrition. It became obvious to the tribesmen that they would eventually lose in the face of such overwhelming material and military resources, and they entered peace negotiations. The Qianlong emperor was willing to accept this political victory since it reinforced the idea of the Qing's great military power. The peace would last for two decades.

Burma, 1765–1769[10]

The Qianlong emperor's campaign against Burma (Myanmar) was actually a failure, a fact the emperor was well aware of but that was actively edited out of the historical records. It was wrong-headed from the beginning, having been prompted by an overreaction by the emperor to suspicions about his border officials. The Burmese thought it was due to the death of a Chinese merchant in a brawl. Despite a long history of diplomatic relations, the Chinese court knew very little about what was going on in Burma. Burma bordered on the province of Yunnan, which was not itself under regular central government control before the Yuan dynasty. Yunnan was loosely controlled during the Ming, and the border region between it and Burma was filled with autonomous local chieftains. The Yongzheng emperor instituted tighter control over Yunnan, but this was relaxed under the Qianlong emperor.

In Burma, Aung Zeya overthrew the Toungoo dynasty (1468–1752) and established his own Kon-baung dynasty in 1752. Local chieftains along the Qing–Burma border resisted the new dynasty, prompting the third Kon-baung king, Hsinbyushi (r. 1763–1776) to force them into submission in 1765. This led to a clash with Qing troops that sparked the war. The Chinese governor-general of Yunnan and Guizhou, Liu Zao, had been in the area since 1757, but was unaware of the dynastic change in Burma. He initially reported the disastrous clashes between the Green Standard troops and the Burmese as three great victories, before later admitting the truth. The Qianlong emperor demoted him, whereupon Liu committed suicide, confirming his guilt in the emperor's eyes. The emperor now escalated the war because Liu's suicide aroused his suspicions about what was really going on.

When Liu's replacement, Yang Yingju (d. 1768), arrived, peace had already been restored. Yang was under considerable pressure to produce results, and launched several incursions that also ended disastrously. He reported defeats as victories, all the while suffering horrendous casualties from tropical diseases. The emperor dismissed reports of 90 percent casualties from illness. Yang's lies were uncovered, and he was brought back to Beijing to commit suicide by the emperor's order. The Qianlong emperor now mobilized an army of Manchu bannermen under a Manchu general to invade Burma. Mingrui (d.1768) drove deep into Burma planning to capture its capital at Ava. Hsinbyushi focused on attacking Qing communications, rather than confronting the main army. Mingrui and his army were cut off while besieging Wanding. Already decimated by disease, and attacked from several directions, Mingrui committed suicide. Of his 10,000-man army, only about two dozen returned.

The Qianlong emperor now placed one of his most trusted men, Fuheng (d. 1770), in charge. Fuheng pursued a relentlessly aggressive policy, planning a three-pronged invasion for the fall of 1769. The invasion started out in October at the height of the epidemic season (Fuheng had downplayed warnings about disease). Almost immediately, disease began to take its toll. Fuheng advanced as far as Kaungton, a heavily fortified town on the Irrawaddy River, where intense fighting and disease caused thousands of Qing casualties over the month-long siege. A truce was worked out by the generals of both sides, against the vehement opposition of Fuheng, and the Qing army withdrew in December. Neither court fully accepted the truce; the Qianlong emperor determined to launch another campaign in 1770, but this was soon downgraded into minor border harassment by small numbers of troops. The outbreak of the second Jinchuan war in 1771 shifted attention away from Burma. The Qianlong emperor maintained a trade embargo for the next 20 years before diplomatic relations were finally restored. The Qing claimed final diplomatic victory, though this was also a fiction.

The second Jinchuan war, 1771–1776[11]

By 1770 another chieftain in western Sichuan began to dominate his fellow leaders, stimulating the same response from the Qianlong emperor as 20 years before. Once again, however, the initial Qing efforts failed as the stone forts and difficult mountain terrain blunted the power of the Qing army. In the interim, the tribesmen had learned that logs and packed earth provided a much stronger defense against cannon than bare stone. The effects of their artillery now diminished, units were trapped in the mountains and took heavy casualties. In 1773 a large Qing force of 16,000 men was trapped and destroyed, leaving only 500 survivors. The Qianlong emperor refused an offer of negotiations after this defeat, insisting that the tribesmen surrender. Here we see the emperor's basic position that he only negotiated peace when he was winning. He would not negotiate to extricate himself from a failed campaign; this was the source of so much difficulty in bringing the Burma war to a real political resolution.

Once again, the Qianlong emperor sent an army of 200,000 men into the Jinchuan area, this time armed with larger cannon cast by Jesuits on site. Rather than attempt to drag these large cannon through the mountains, the materials for manufacturing them were brought up and the weapons made near a given fort. Although effective, the cannon were considerably more dangerous to use and unreliable. The packed earth and logs were blasted through, thus restoring the previous balance of attack and defense. And also as before, the conflict shifted to a war of attrition as the vast Qing army used most of its force to protect its own supply lines, while sending out banner troops to attack those of the Jinchuan tribesmen. The head of the Jinchuan chieftains was captured in 1776 and executed in Beijing. As in the Zunghar campaigns, superior logistics and firepower enabled a determined Qing army methodically to reduce an enemy.

Taiwan, 1787–1788[12]

The background to Lin Shuangwen's rebellion in Taiwan is somewhat unclear. Lin was a member of the Heaven and Earth Society, and although the society was strongly implicated in the uprising as far as the Qing authorities were concerned, it does not appear that his actions were part of the society's program. Lin was a local tough, and in the wake of an unrelated "secret" society incident in a nearby district, the authorities decided that Lin was a potential threat to local order. The local population in Daliyi did not cooperate, so Qing troops tried to force them to do so by arresting innocent people and burning a few houses. This was apparently standard practice in the extremely violent world of late eighteenth-century Taiwan. Soldiers beat at least two society members to death.

Lin organized an attack on the town of Dadun on 17 January 1787, followed on the next day by attacks on Zhanghua and Lugang, and culminating in the capture of Zhuluo a week later. Whatever the incoherence of Lin's initial intentions, he realized that once his actions brought about the deaths of Qing government officials he had no choice but to rebel. Soon after Lin's central Taiwanese uprising there was a nominally related southern Taiwanese uprising as well.

Taiwan in the late eighteenth century was a fragmented and only vaguely governed place, riven with violent intercommunity fighting. Migrants from different parts of Fujian clustered together for the most part, clashing amongst themselves and also with the aboriginal inhabitants. The rebels' armament reflected the mostly low-level violence of the area, consisting of swords and spears, with the odd fowling gun. They obtained some arquebuses and cannon after defeating the local imperial soldiers, but were woefully under-equipped to face a properly mobilized imperial army. Some efforts were made to obtain more gunpowder locally to address this weakness, with limited results.

The initial Qing response in March recovered some towns and cities without seriously threatening the rebellion. Lin went over to the attack while further imperial forces were slowly dispatched, but he was unable to retake any of the positions held by the imperial army. Bogged down before Zhule (present-day Jiayi), the rebellion lost momentum. In September 100,000 imperial troops landed and quickly crushed the rebellion. Lin was captured and executed in Beijing.

Vietnam, 1788[13]

Like the Burmese campaign, the Qianlong emperor's intervention in Vietnam was also a failure subsequently cast as a victory. The Nguyen family overthrew the Le dynasty in 1788, and when the royal family fled to China and asked for Qing help, the Qianlong emperor agreed to restore their throne. The campaign that followed was notable only because one of the three Qing forces was transported by sea. The other two armies marched overland from Yunnan and Guangdong. By December of 1788 the Qing army had captured Hanoi and restored the Le dynasty. During the Chinese new year celebrations a month later, however, the Nguyen attacked and drove the Qing army and the Le dynasty out. The Qianlong emperor then accepted the Nguyen usurpation.

The Gurkhas, 1790–1792[14]

In the 1760s the Gurkha king conquered all of Nepal, placing the mostly Buddhist population under his Hindu rule. In 1768 he made Katmandu his capital and began to look for ways to expand his territory. His southern border with India brought him in touch with the British East India Company, whose support for a venture into Tibet was assumed by the Gurkha rulers. A Nepalese army invaded southern Tibet in 1788, looted the great monastery of Shigatse and attacked Lhasa. The Manchu Qing officials in Lhasa had no military forces at their disposal, and so withdrew to Qing territory with the Dalai Lama and the infant Panchen Lama. Once he received word of the incursions (1788–1789), the Qianlong emperor immediately dispatched forces from Sichuan to drive them out. It took considerable effort to march those forces to Lhasa, and by the time they arrived the Gurkhas had already withdrawn. The commanders duly reported that they had successfully driven out the Nepalese, adding one more lie to the Qianlong emperor's Ten Complete Military Victories.

When the Gurkhas invaded again in 1791, the Qianlong emperor punished the commanders of the previous "campaign" and sent an army of about 10,000 men under Fukang'an and Hailancha to drive the Nepalese out. The army marched into Tibet from Qinghai during the winter of 1791–1792, finally engaging the Gurkhas in the summer. Three months of successful campaigning drove the Gurkhas out of Tibet and back to Nepal. While the Qianlong emperor was writing his record of Ten Complete Military Victories, Fukang'an and Hailancha were still fighting in Nepal. It was only in 1793 that the Gurkhas surrendered as the Qing army neared Katmandu. The emperor was justifiably premature in describing the second campaign as a victory; his description of the first campaign as a victory was an utter fraud.

The Ten Complete Military Victories

The Qianlong emperor's clear fraud in delineating his ten great victories has been taken by some historians as an apposite analogy for his reign as a whole. Great achievements in some areas created complacency about fundamental failures in others. The grandeur of the High Qing is thus portrayed as a façade masking the real decline of the empire.[15] Although the Qianlong emperor's self-serving catalogue of victories was certainly predicated on falsehood, it was no worse than the imperial propaganda of many other emperors, or even many other aspects of dynastic self-legitimation. Imperial rhetoric was characteristically hyperbolic. The Qianlong emperor's record of military accomplishment was a public statement that reinforced his prestige and legitimacy. Very few people apart from the emperor knew the entire truth of his claims, and even those who did were unlikely to discuss the facts widely. Most of the government and virtually all of the elite strata of society who cared to acquaint themselves with such imperial pronouncements would have had no reason apart from pure cynicism to doubt the emperor's claims.

It is instructive that a man who had reigned for nearly six decades felt it necessary, or at least helpful, to gloss over his failures and trumpet a perfect military record. There was certainly a large measure of ego involved, as it is clear that the Qianlong emperor took victories and defeats personally. But ego alone does not explain his inclusion of campaigns that were either outright failures or non-events. The records of the Burmese war were censored very heavily, but those of the Vietnamese intervention and the first Gurkha campaign were not. Moreover, the suppression of Lin Shuangwen's rebellion was an internal matter.

Rebellions were usually regarded as evidence of a ruler's failings, even if successfully put down, rather than events worth boasting about. There were other rebellions during the Qianlong reign that were similarly suppressed, yet the emperor did not include them. Perhaps Taiwan was a distant frontier in the emperor's mind, and so deserving of inclusion. Generally, the Qianlong emperor must have included campaigns that were actual failures in his list because to exclude them would be to admit that they were not complete successes.

The Qianlong emperor had spent his entire reign creating and manipulating imperial symbols to enhance his own power. It was the emperor who proposed the Complete Library of the Four Treasuries project and then brought it into being despite official disinterest. The Qianlong emperor ruled through the Grand Council virtually in opposition to the government bureaucracy. He jealously guarded the power the government officials wanted to take from him. The emperor fought for centralization, but could not reasonably, even with his Grand Council, make all the day-to-day decisions necessary to run the government. Some power had to be left in the hands of the government bureaucracy. The emperor's ability to contend with that bureaucracy was determined by his prestige; the Qianlong emperor never forgot that even after more than half a century on the throne. Although his position or legitimacy was not in question in 1792, his power with respect to the government was. His reign was secure, but only prestige allowed him to rule.

In 1793, Lord George Macartney was allowed an audience with the Qianlong emperor. Macartney was sent to China by the British government to convince the emperor to allow a British ambassador to reside in Beijing, to end the Canton trading system, to open up more ports for trade and to establish fair tariffs.[16] He was fortunate to arrive in the year that the emperor was celebrating his eightieth birthday, and so was given an audience under the Qing rubric of a foreign envoy coming to congratulate the emperor. Macartney was frustrated in all of his goals, and returned with the Qianlong emperor's famous edict to George III that stated: "We have never valued ingenious articles, nor do we have the slightest need of your country's manufactures." Joanna Waley-Cohen has demonstrated that the edict was a statement for public consumption rather than a declaration of policy or an explanation of court attitudes.[17] Generations of historians have used the edict as an exemplar of Chinese cultural conservatism, chauvinism and resistance to science and technology. But both the Ming and the Qing dynasties had eagerly exploited European developments in firearms, astronomy and math, just to name a few important areas. Taken together, the Qianlong emperor's record of his military feats and his edict to George III show a ruler acutely aware of the powerful effect of official and elite opinion. Even for an emperor, all politics was really domestic.

Despite the obvious mendacity of parts of the record, the Qianlong emperor had some very real military accomplishments. His conquest of the Zunghars was predicated on a revolutionary development in warfare: the mastery of a logistic system that allowed the full weight of Chinese wealth to overwhelm steppe warfare. This fact belies the idea that eighteenth-century China was militarily or even institutionally stagnant at a fundamental level. Strong emperors like the Kangxi, Yongzheng and Qianlong emperors could make institutional changes and drive the bureaucracy to function, but it took immense effort. When imperial will was lacking or faltered, the in-built inertia of the government took over and reduced operations to their more regular, anemic state. The conquest of the Zunghars was thus as much a political and bureaucratic triumph as a military one. With the Zunghars eliminated, and the Gurkhas driven off, Qing influence over the Tibetan Buddhist establishment was assured. This was another tool in the control of Central Eurasia as most of the Mongols were Tibetan Buddhists.

The emperor's real and ideological control of his subjects was more and more attenuated as the eighteenth century progressed. It seems as if it was only in the area of military and foreign policy that an emperor could exercise power fairly freely, at least within the limits of his army's reach. The Qianlong emperor's effort to extend his army's functional zone of operations was a direct extension of his own power over a greater area. It was easier to overcome fierce military resistance to the Qing army on the frontiers than to push imperial power down into local Chinese society. Members of the local elite class staffed the imperial government, and their loyalties, with very few exceptions, remained local. It is perhaps in this sense that the Qianlong emperor could regard his suppression of Lin Shuangwen's rebellion as a notable success. At least in Taiwan he was able to overcome local resistance to the exercise of imperial power; he would have been hard pressed to have accomplished the same feat on the mainland.

The elaborate and highly developed system of Confucian scholarship, coupled with a strong gentry identity, prevented the government from ever fully controlling the ideological levers of Chinese society. Educated men claimed for themselves the right to judge the actions of the emperor and the government, and to pass moral judgments as the keepers of the cultural flame. Although many emperors contested this claim, it remained an active ideological brake on complete imperial domination. Indeed, once success in the civil service exams became a remote possibility for the overwhelming majority of educated men, the ability to enforce some measure of ideological conformity by demanding the fluent reproduction of accepted interpretations under pressure diminished considerably. The Qianlong emperor was, by some measures, the most powerful emperor in Chinese history, but his control of Chinese society was extremely limited.

During the Qing conquest of Ming China, the Manchus struck a deal with local elites that allowed them to rule the empire in return for non-interference in local affairs. This was a pragmatic decision that accorded with developments in Ming local society, and it is possible that no imperial Chinese government would have been able to have changed the course of centuries of institutional development. When we consider the difficulties that the Qing government initially had in imposing the Manchu haircut on the Chinese population, with resistance so strong that Dorgon was forced to back down temporarily, it is not surprising that it was reluctant to reach down into local society unless absolutely necessary. The Qing government would have had to change course sharply and force its way into local society for the Qing empire to evolve into a coherent nation.

Strong rulers like the Kangxi or Qianlong emperors might have been able to have radically changed the imperial government's relationship with local society and knit the territory and populace of their empire into a more cohesive polity, but they had little reason to do so. The emperor's power would have been diminished, not enhanced, if the Qing empire as a whole, or even a part of it, had been more united. The Yongzheng emperor had created the Grand Council to circumvent his own bureaucracy, and the Qianlong emperor expanded it for the same reason. Qing emperors had enough trouble with the gentry class at the local level (resisting new cadastral surveys for tax purposes, for example), and within government when the exam system kept individual members of the elites in competition with each other. Factional politics and corruption made government officials vulnerable in the struggle for power, protecting and enhancing the emperor's position. Legitimacy at the local level did not make gentrymen a threat to imperial power, precisely because the government was not directly involved at that level. Conversely, local legitimacy did not provide imperial legitimacy or access.

Whatever the underlying structural problems in Qing society and government, the Qianlong emperor could take credit for some extraordinary military accomplishments. The territorial claims that some of his truly successful campaigns enforced remain part of modern China today. It is true that he did not build or even make a start on building a modern nation-state with all the attendant military, technological and economic power. The creation of the Qianlong emperor's military machine was not part of a state-building process, and did not contribute to that intentionally or otherwise. He conquered to extend his influence and increase his own prestige, not to deepen them institutionally. Conquest was primarily about the Qianlong emperor's personal power, not the state's, and so the heights of power he attained did not continue for long after he died. With the retrospective decline of Qing power from the Qianlong emperor's peak, it seems as if the longest-ruling emperor in Chinese history took his power with him to the grave.

Notes

1 Peter Perdue, "Three Qing Emperors and Their Mongol Rivals," in Nicola di Cosmo (ed.), *Warfare in Inner Asian History*, Leiden: E.J. Brill, 2001, p. 371.
2 Lawrence D. Kessler, *K'ang-hsi and the Consolidation of Ch'ing Rule, 1661–1684*, Chicago, Ill.: University of Chicago Press, 1976, p. 108.
3 For the Kangxi Emperor's Russian campaigns, see Ibid., pp. 97–103.
4 For the Kangxi emperor's Zunghar campaigns, see Peter Perdue, "Three Qing

Emperors," pp. 373–377, and Jonathan D. Spence, *Emperor of China*, New York: Vintage Books, 1988, pp. 17–22.

5   For the Yongzheng emperor's Zunghar campaigns, see Peter Perdue, "Three Qing Emperors," pp. 377–387.

6   R. Kent Guy, *The Emperor's Four Treasuries*, Cambridge, Mass.: Harvard University Press, 1987.

7   Beatrice S. Bartlett, *Monarchs and Ministers: The Rise of the Grand Council in Mid-Ch'ing China, 1723–1820*, Berkeley: University of California Press

8   For the Qianlong emperor's Zunghar campaigns, see Peter Perdue, "Three Qing Emperors," pp. 387–390.

9   For the first Jinchuan war, see Paul Lococo, Jr, "The Qing Empire," in David Graff and Robin Higham (eds), *A Military History of China*, Boulder, Colo.: Westview Press, 2002, pp. 130–131.

10 Ibid., pp. 129–130; Alexander Woodside, "The Ch'ien-Lung Reign," in Denis Twitchett and John K. Fairbank (eds), *The Cambridge History of China*, Volume 9: pp. 263–268.

11 Paul Lococo, "The Qing Empire," pp. 131–132.

12 David Wright, "Rebellion in Taiwan," *Insight*, vol. 4, no. 1 (Fall 1987), pp. 1–4, pp. 16–19, for this account of Lin Shuangwen's rebellion. I am grateful to Professor Wright for making a copy of his article available to me on very short notice.

13 Jonathan Spence, *The Search for Modern China*, New York: W.W. Norton and Company, 1990, p. 111, for this account of the Qianlong emperor's Vietnam war.

14 Ibid., pp. 111–112.

15 Frederich Mote, *Imperial China, 900–1800*, Cambridge, Mass.: Harvard University Press, 2003, p. 940.

16 The Canton system restricted foreign merchants to trading with a specifically designated group of Chinese merchants, who were in turn responsible for the conduct of those foreign merchants while in China. This control mechanism also limited where foreigners could trade.

17 See Joanna Waley-Cohen, "China and Western Technology in the Eighteenth Century," *American Historical Review* (December 1993).

Conclusion

The Qianlong emperor's last year of official rule was in 1795, and he retired the following year as an act of filial piety to his grandfather, the Kangxi emperor. It was not appropriate for a grandson to show up his grandfather by ruling longer than that hitherto longest of reigns. Like many of the Qianlong emperor's gestures it was partly genuine and partly imperial theater. His reign did, in fact, end, but he ruled until he died in 1799. In terms of Confucian ideology it was a magnificent affirmation of the family values that were the bedrock of Chinese society and the Qing state. The Qianlong emperor was not, however, simply a Chinese emperor; he ruled the Qing empire that contained explicitly non-Chinese groups, like the Manchus, the Mongols, the Tibetans and the Xinjiang Muslims, apart from many smaller ethnic minorities. A Manchu himself, the Qianlong emperor was acutely aware of his own ethnicity, and lamented the loss of Manchu culture among his compatriots in China. Though sinified, the Manchus in China remained a privileged group set apart from their Chinese neighbors. And the Qing emperors continued to address their different subjects in different languages using different imperial rhetoric. The Qing dynasty was a multi-ethnic empire not fully synonymous with "China," and it is therefore not surprising that people ruled as non-Chinese groups under such a dynasty would not ultimately identify themselves as ethnically Chinese.

The Qing empire was fragmented not only between ethnic groups but also within those ethnic groups. Central Eurasian steppe peoples like the Mongols were rarely a unified polity, making it difficult to forge a long-term, stable relationship with them. Yet the Chinese population of the Qing empire was also fragmented, mostly geographically. The Qing government was very concerned to maintain its monopoly as the only institution that crossed those geographic boundaries and tied the empire together. This was not a new phenomenon, however, and earlier dynasties had been similarly concerned about larger social or religious networks that might develop into politically active organizations. The few networks that managed to do so could become extremely powerful, like the Donglin Academy and its later echo the Fushe Society, during the Ming dynasty, whose members could dominate the civil service exams and control a large number of government posts. Not only did these networks not truly serve the interests of the dynasty in which they operated, they also directly threatened the power of the throne.

Notwithstanding Ouyang Xiu's justification of parties of good men in the eleventh century, few emperors tolerated the existence of a single, dominant group within their governments or empires. Unable to keep all of officialdom from grouping together, the only response was to play groups off against each other. It was easier to keep general order within the empire by sanctioning local power while crushing any attempt to expand that power. Dynasties accepted the fact that they could not push imperial power down to the lowest levels without the medium of the local elites to transmit that power. Since the local elites were also the pool of talent drawn upon to staff the imperial government, they could be placed in competition with each other to serve that state, and thus kept from uniting against the throne. All of these considerations of loyalty and power required constant attention, lest they cease to balance each other out and either cause a functional breakdown, a rebellion, or both. A government that was not sufficiently cohesive could not carry out its duties, but one that was too united could resist the imperial will.

The demands of political power in pre-modern China limited the nation-building an emperor could engage in without destabilizing his own dynasty. Mobilizing large armies for campaigns against steppe people or other threats created a tool that could cut both ways. It was much safer to keep only the minimum amount of forces at hand for routine threats, and form expeditionary armies on an *ad hoc* basis when required. This was true in other spheres of government activity as well, and explains why imperial governments could perform astonishing feats of organization on occasion without effecting long-term improvements in operations. The drawback of such inbuilt inefficiency was that a threat might become critical before an effective response could be put together, or a weak emperor might fail to provide the leadership necessary to respond effectively. It was a hard balance to maintain, and during times of peace military preparedness tended to suffer badly. It took the Song dynasty several years to mount an effective response to the Tangut invasions in the 1030s and 1040s, for example, but the Song court was overwhelmed by events in the 1120s before it could put its army in order.

Imperial Chinese dynasties did not try to build a modern nation-state, or even a solid precursor to the nation-state. Within severe technological con-straints, a relatively small bureaucratic superstructure maintained nominal authority over a vast empire. This was only made possible by placating local elites, limiting elite cooperation through the exam system, and ruthlessly sup-pressing any non-governmental organization that spanned localities. One of the greatest fears of the Qing government in dealing with Lin Shuangwen's rebel-lion was that the Heaven and Earth Society that he belonged to was also established on the mainland. While late nineteenth- and twentieth-century writers lamented the inherent weakness that the Qing dynasty bequeathed "China" as it confronted the modern West and modernizing Japan, this structural frailty, the tenuousness of the connections within society and between society and the state, was not unique to the Qing. All imperial Chinese dynasties accepted or fostered this frailty in order to preserve their own rule.

While imperial courts from the Song to the Qing were concerned with limiting the reach of military and social groups, commercial organizations developed relatively unimpeded. Commercial networks gradually spanned the empire, or at least the profitable parts of it where most people lived, and took control over important resources like food. The Qianlong emperor's ability to supply his armies during the Zunghar campaigns grew out of the highly commercialized Qing economy. Both wealth and transport networks were available to the imperial state as never before. Merchants do not appear to have been much of a threat to the imperial state, however, for several reasons. First, as merchants became wealthy enough to take their place as local elites, they conformed to elite practices and came under state controls over the elites. Education led to exam-taking and other politically and culturally constrained behaviors. Second, despite instances of merchants disposing of considerable military resources, commerce depended upon the state to maintain peace and security. Unrest of most kinds was harmful to business. Third, wealth allowed a merchant to buy titles and exemptions from the state, and to participate in corruption to his advantage. There was no need for a powerful businessman to oppose a powerful institution if he could buy its services. Fourth and finally, business and wealth could continue under a new regime, making active participation in political affairs not only dangerous but unnecessary as well.

War and society

I have argued throughout this book that successive Chinese dynasties used the military to keep the empire separated into small enough groups that no one of them could threaten the throne. This ran in parallel to political and administrative efforts, and was further supported by the increasing importance of local power from 900 to 1795. Wars did not knit the empire together except at the highest political level, and entry into this imperial forum was tightly controlled. Chinese dynasts built their empires by destroying regional powers and accommodating local ones. The empire was not a homogenized nation tightly connected by shared social or cultural ties. Elite culture was shared, drawing from a canon of philosophical, literary and historical texts, but most of the population spoke mutually unintelligible dialects, had no contact with anyone beyond perhaps the nearest market town, and practiced only vaguely similar cultures. The very different environments that Chinese farmers worked in across the empire, for example, resulted in very different agricultural lifestyles. The apparent unity of Chinese culture and empire, as displayed in the written record, obfuscates the very real differences among most of the population. This has been further amplified by the efforts of modern nationalists to lay historical claims to "natural" polities encompassing vast territories and peoples.

These differences across China do not repudiate the political claims of its imperial dynasties any more than differences across any other invoked polity, but they do emphasize the importance of military force in constituting dynastic territories. There was no "China" without war. Even more significantly, "China" could only be formed by protracted, successful military and political campaigns stretched over decades. Every dynasty was marked by the course of these conquests, and configured by the foundation built by the dynastic founder, his family and his officials, both civil and military. All of the dynasties considered in this book – Liao, Song, Jin, Yuan, Ming and Qing – were different at fundamental and functional levels, while also partaking in some measure of the tradition of Chinese imperial ideology (which itself changed over time). These political and institutional structures, in turn, affected the development of Chinese society without making complete breaks at every change of dynasty. Much was retained, and the limited reach of imperial power at the local level insulated most of the population from the winds of dynastic fortune.

The fundamental similarities of imperial power formation and retention beneath the surface differences are instructive. The first step before attempting to conquer an empire was to create a disciplined, unified political organization. This political organization was usually synonymous with a military one, and it may well be that the enormous attention civil–military relations have enjoyed is something of a false dichotomy, or at least belongs more to considerations of established governments. The basic political issue for all emperors or would-be emperors was loyalty. Effectiveness was of secondary importance; incompetence could be tolerated while disloyalty could not. Both military and administrative effectiveness were far more critical in creating an empire than in maintaining one. And where administrative skills were reasonably widespread, capable generals were always in short supply, even among the steppe peoples.

Effective generals were the most problematic figures in imperial China. All emperors stemmed from the pool of capable military leaders, and all founding emperors had to assemble a small group of good commanders around them for a dynasty to succeed. Generals really were the arbiters of dynastic fortune in ways that civil officials were not, since the only crises that threatened dynastic survival were military ones. Good generals had to be found, but also controlled, honored, and not allowed to get too arrogant. Many good generals were killed by their emperors shortly after a dynasty became stable, and some were even killed when they did not pose a real threat to the throne. A proven general by his very nature was a political hazard. If a previously successful general were sent out on a misguided campaign and thus failed, the blame would naturally fall on the official or emperor who conceived of the plan. A general was then usually killed to take the blame for the failure. Alternatively, a successful general might be killed to keep him from receiving his political due, or to allow an emperor or statesman to monopolize the glory. Being a general in imperial China was never an easy or secure job, even if the dangers and uncertainties of the battlefield could be successfully negotiated.

On the civil side of the dynastic equation, serving in the central government became increasingly hazardous over the last thousand years of imperial Chinese history. There was only one instance of outright political assassination during the three centuries of the Song dynasty, but over the course of the Yuan, Ming and Qing dynasties there was a dramatic increase in violence at court, and indeed even in the presence of the emperor himself. Officials could be flogged in front of the emperor, sometimes even tortured, and executions, imprisonment and exile to distant frontiers was not uncommon. At the same time, the exam system came to be seen as a highly unreliable route to power. More and more widespread access to education increased the pool of exam-takers, without a commensurate increase in exam degrees or government positions. Thus it was not only more dangerous to serve in the highest ranks of government, it was harder and harder to even get in the door. Local power and local service were much more reliable and much safer.

Successive imperial governments tolerated and even encouraged some aspects of local autonomy, like community compacts to maintain the peace, for example, as long as the authority of the government was explicitly accepted. Since there was seldom any profit to be had in opposing the government, no one within the mainstream of society, particularly elites, had any reason to do so. Even Lin Shuangwen was not originally inclined to rebel against the Qing government, despite being a marginal member of society in a marginal part of the empire. It was only when the government's heavy-handed tactics in attempting to arrest Lin forced him to respond violently, and resulted in the death of government officials, that he had no choice but to rebel. Lin knew that killing government officials dramatically escalated the stakes to a point where the Qing court would have to respond. The Qianlong emperor's overreaction to the rebellion because of its connection to the Heaven and Earth Society was indicative of a certain imperial mindset. Surely no local thug would be stupid enough to rebel against the government on his own; nor would ordinary farmers disgruntled enough or organized enough. A larger conspiracy had to have been behind it, even though none of the confessions extracted afterward supported that conclusion.

With most of society theoretically unarmed and untrained in warfare, the imperial army had two main functions after the initial establishment of the dynasty: internal security and external defense. That, at least, was the rhetorical construction of the army's function. In practice, the imperial army was also sent on campaigns of conquest whose only real purpose was military glory for the emperor. Even the supposedly weak and civil-focused Song dynasty sent a successful expedition to conquer the West River region in the early 1070s as a first step in a larger strategy to destroy the Tanguts. Although the Song court had good reason to want to destroy the Tanguts, and so the West River campaign might reasonably fall under the rubric of border defense, the campaign was clearly expansionistic and assuaged the injured military feelings the court had been nursing for decades. Unfortunately, it was very difficult for any army to fulfill all of these functions – conquest, security and defense – without significant time to retrain and reorganize between tasks. Some Mongol Yuan forces never really shifted out of conquest mode even while in garrison, limiting their security functions only to the most serious challenges to government authority. This made some sense for the imperial government, but left local order in the hands of local elites. Overall, imperial Chinese armies could perform many tasks extremely well if given the time and leadership to prepare.

Local Chinese society was also more militarized than the imperial government thought it was supposed to be. The significant gap between the imperial army's policing responsibilities and its ability to carry them out left individuals and groups no choice but to learn to defend themselves. Bandits were a constant problem, and in north China, depending upon the period, raids by steppe bands were also a regular threat. Martial arts, both for personal defense and as part of community militias, became widespread in many areas. Although frequently prohibited, weapons were available and owned by ordinary subjects. Certain professions developed their own security forces to protect the transport or storage of their goods, or the transaction of their services. In times of crisis the state was even willing to draft these forces for its own defense, like the Tea Merchant's Army in the Southern Song. This is not to say that Chinese society was highly militarized, but rather that weapons and martial skills were available despite government attempts to limit the means of violence to the imperial army or sanctioned forces.

The relationship between the means and methods of warfare and society in China between 900 and 1795 was complex. There is no sense that changes in military technology suddenly or even slowly changed society, or that changes in society changed the military. This does not mean, however, that the military was isolated from society. When we consider that even during the Qing dynasty, when part of the army was explicitly separated from the rest of Chinese society by its ethnicity, the majority of the imperial army was still Chinese, drawn from the ordinary farming population as Chinese armies always had been. China was not a distinctively non-military society in any quantifiable sense, though the rhetoric of the elites actively sought to downplay the importance of the military. This was partly because they reasonably thought that society should not be ruled by force or war glorified, but also partly because their own positions depended upon their control of force. Local gentry directly controlled significant means of violence and could rely upon imperial armies to put down rebellions trying to overturn the existing social order. In essence, the military and society in China were so tightly intertwined that attempting to separate them is not realistically or heuristically sustainable.

The years 900 and 1795

Over the course of 900 years China changed in many ways, while retaining an imperial system that grouped vast territory under a single dynastic government.

Over time, the empire became wealthier, the emperors became more autocratic and the power of local elites increased. Nowhere else in the world was such a large territory and great population so consistently grouped under a single political regime. The period between 907 and 979 was the last moment of a real multi-state system before the chaotic warlord period in the early twentieth century. Chinese empire building was bloody, expensive and took decades to effect, but it was successful with a regularity unmatched anywhere else. The empires formed were usually stable for several centuries despite often being corrupt, inefficient and incompetent. Contrary to our expectations, then, it may be that corruption, inefficiency and incompetence actually sustained Chinese empires during their rule. A failed government allowed commerce to develop, despite nominal ideological resistance, and left society to function as it could. Imperial armies were concerned with the requirements of imperial rule, not enforcing imperial justice or laws throughout society. Local elites readily accepted ineffective government since that left power in their hands.

Chinese society in 1795 was wealthier and more populous than in 900, and far more sophisticated at all levels. Everything from agriculture to medicine to education was more developed, with far greater specialization in both the intellectual and commercial spheres. Yet none of these advances overturned the idea of empire, or changed the general trajectory of greater local autonomy and increased imperial autocracy. The Qianlong emperor's armies were far more powerful than anything fielded during the tenth century. Not only did they dispose of immense firepower through gunpowder weapons, they were also almost logistically unrecognizable. The defeat of the Zunghars was revolutionary in terms of the military, and thus political, reach of the Qing empire, permanently altering the perception of what a Chinese empire could accomplish with respect to the steppe. It was the commercialization, the economic development, of the Qing empire that created the preconditions for that revolution, not a technological breakthrough. Technological advances had been continuously absorbed into Chinese society for centuries and subsumed within its cultures without rewriting the paradigms. The resilience and persistence of Chinese elite and local culture up until 1795 is astonishing.

The persistent empire

If only the idea of Chinese empire had come down through history like that of Mauryan, Gupta, Egypt, Persia and Rome then it could have been placed with those other imperial ideas in the realm of political rhetoric, useful for inciting nationalism or assuaging injured patriotic feelings. In China, however, reality accorded with the idea of empire in a substantive way. Granted, imperial ideology did not match empirical reality exactly, but there were empires in fact as well as name. These empires were vast polities controlling immense wealth and resources; they functioned in messy reality and not abstract ambitions. They were formed and maintained by warfare. Without war there was no China, only

Chinese cultures and Chinese peoples. Chinese empires were human institutions that could be staffed or ruled by non-Chinese yet not invalidate imperial ideology.

The persistence of the Chinese empire demonstrated the flexibility of the idea. Rather than a rigid system requiring strict territorial boundaries and fixed power relationships between the central government and its subject populace, the Chinese imperial system allowed for widely varying borders and almost any relationship between central court and subjects short of outright opposition. The adept use of war and violence, coupled with political theater, established and maintained a balance of power between center and periphery. Although a unified polity existed in the rhetorical realm, a generally fragmented polity obtained throughout the actual realm. Commercial networks did not create political ties or generate cohesive nationalities any more than they did across the kingdoms and states of South Asia, Europe or the Middle East. Elite culture was similarly incapable of constructing a real nation because the elites themselves were so firmly tied to their localities. They could and did travel and associate themselves with dynasties and concepts of transcendent Chineseness, but this did not prevent the majority of them from abandoning one dynasty for another, or placing their own local interests above their government's. While modern commentators might see this as selfishness, at the time it was simply a reasonable reaction to events. To the elite, if they thought about it at all, "China" did not reside in a particular dynasty, it was the dynasty that occupied China. What that was specifically, outside of the canon, history and shared customs of the Chinese elite, was unclear. But since many were quite willing to serve and to live under non-Chinese rulers, their commitment to China as a nation was idiosyncratic at best.

Loyalty in Chinese political ideology, derived from the Confucian canon with the odd bit of Legalist thinking thrown in, was always directed at specific people: to one's ruler, parents, older brother, or friend, not to a political institution or a people. For the elite this meant that their political aspirations were tied to the imperial structure if they wished to move out of their locality. But if one had not served in government in any capacity, or even received an exam degree from a dynasty, then it was really a matter of choice whether one owed that ruling house one's loyalty. As the population grew (from perhaps 60–80 million in 900 to perhaps 300 million in 1795),[1] and the elite population along with it, and local power became more and more important, a smaller and smaller percentage of the population actually owed a given dynasty its loyalty. The military was also tied to the dynasty, but most soldiers focused their loyalty on their commanders first, and then the government. With the possible exception of certain distinct ethnic minorities, loyalty to a people or a concept of nation did not exist. A Chinese empire demanded a very limited amount of loyalty from a small number of its subjects, and simple obedience enforced by the military from the rest. This was why empires could be formed at all, and why the idea and system could persist; but it was also why they collapsed as well.

For most people, for most of Chinese history, the political power that concerned them was local. Barring the transit of imperial armies through their area, imperial power was distant and even abstract. Although Chinese empires maintained immense armies in absolute number, imperial soldiers shrank as a percentage of the population over the nine centuries covered in this book. Local forces maintained order or not, or enforced the will of the local elites, without much reference to the imperial court. Imperial courts husbanded their political and military resources in preparation for crises, but were reluctant to expend them on truly extending their power into the countryside. Farmers were expected to farm, pay their taxes and perform corvee labor, but not participate in politics or war. They and most local elites had little at stake in any particular dynasty. This condition supported the imperial system without building a national polity. China in 900 or 1795 was an empire, not a nation.

Note

1 It is extremely difficult to estimate China's population before the twentieth century, and scholars differ, sometimes quite broadly, on their figures. The range I have provided in the text is in keeping with a survey of several sources. See Ping-ti Ho, *Studies on the Population of China, 1368–1953*, Cambridge, Mass.: Harvard University Press, 1959; Yuesheng Wang, "A Study on the Size of the Chinese Population in the Middle and Late Eighteenth Century," in *Chinese Journal of Population Science*, vol. 9, no. 4 (1997), pp. 317–336; C.Y. Cyrus Chu and Ronald D. Lee, "Famine, Revolt, and the Dynastic Cycle: Population Dynamics in Historic China," in *Journal of Population Economics*, vol. 7, no. 4 (1994), pp. 351–378; J.D. Durand, "The Population Statistics of China, AD 2–1953," in *Population Studies*, vol. 13, no. 3 (1960), pp. 209–256; Huanyong Hu (ed.), *The Population Geography of China*, Shanghai: East China Normal University Press, 1984.

Index

Routledge History

Medieval Chinese Warfare
David Graff

'This is an important addition to the rapidly growing literature in English on Chinese warfare.' – The Journal of Asian Studies

Shortly after 300 AD, barbarian invaders from Inner Asia toppled China's Western Jin dynasty, leaving the country divided and at war for several centuries. Despite this, the empire gradually formed a unified imperial order. Medieval Chinese Warfare, 300–900 explores the military strategies, institutions and wars that reconstructed the Chinese empire that has survived into modern times.

Drawing on classical Chinese sources and the best modern scholarship from China and Japan, David Graff connects military affairs with political and social developments to show how China's history was shaped by war.

Hb: 0–415–23954–0   Pb: 0–415–23955–9

Modern Chinese Warfare
Bruce A. Elleman

Why did the Chinese empire collapse and why did it take so long for a new government to reunite China? *Modern Chinese Warfare, 1795–1989* seeks to answer these questions by exploring the most important domestic and international conflicts over the past two hundred years, from the last half of the Qing empire through to modern day China. It reveals how most of China's wars during this period were fought to preserve unity in China, and examines their distinctly cyclical pattern of imperial decline, domestic chaos and finally the creation of a new unifying dynasty.

Hb: 0–415–21473–4   Pb: 0–415–21474–2

Available at all good bookshops
For ordering and further information please visit
www.routledge.com

Routledge History

Warfare in World History
Michael S. Nieburg

'Neiberg has produced one of the best surveys available.' – Jeremy Black, *European History Quarterly, vol. 33, no. 4, 2004*

Despite the catastrophic effect of war, wars have also proved to be instrumental to long-term change in world history. This text is the first of its kind to survey how warfare has developed from ancient times to the present day and the role it has played in shaping the world we know. The periods discussed include:
- the pre-gunpowder era
- the development of gunpowder weapons and their rapid adoption in Western Europe
- the French Revolution and the industrialization of warfare
- the First and Second World Wars
- the Cold War and the wars of liberation fought across the Third World

With in-depth examples illustrating the dominant themes in the history of warfare, *Warfare in World History* focuses not only on the famous and heroic, but also discusses the experiences of countless millions of unknowns who have fought in wars over time.

Hb: 0–415–22954–5   Pb: 0–415–22955–3

Introduction to Global Military History
1775 to the Present Day
Jeremy Black

'A lucid and succinct account of military developments around the modern world that combines a truly global coverage of events with thought-provoking analysis. By juxtaposing the familiar with the previously neglected or largely unknown, Jeremy Black forces the reader to reassess the standard grand narrative of military history that rests on assumptions of western cultural and technological superiority. .. It should have a wide market on world history courses that are increasingly common parts of American, British and Australian university programmes.' – Professor Peter H. Wilson, *University of Sunderland*

'Jeremy Black does an admirable job in distilling a tremendous amount of information and making it comprehensible for students.'
– Professor Lawrence Sondhaus, *University of Indianapolis*

' An excellent book. Too often, in military studies and histories, the land, air, and maritime aspects are dealt with in separate books. This work integrates all aspects of conflict in a reasonable manner.'
Stanley Carpenter, *Professor of Strategy and Policy, US Naval War College, Newport, Rhode Island*

Hb: 0–415–35394–7   Pb: 0–415–35395–5

Available at all good bookshops
For ordering and further information please visit
www.routledge.com

Routledge History

Rethinking Military History
Jeremy Black

'Jeremy Black has exercised his formidable powers of historical dissection, critical analysis, and creative cogitation to produce an exciting book...it should spark constructive debate about how historians may better practise their craft' – Theodore F. Cook, *William Paterson University of New Jersey*

'Jeremy Black provides timely arguments against a narrowly technological perception of military history, shaped by Western experience. His survey of five centuries of global warfare shaws the shortcomings of this perspective and the necessity to uinderstand the political and cultural aspects of warfare' – Jan Glete, *Stockholm University*

'Formidable' – Paul A. Fideler, *Lesley University*

This must-read study demonstrates the limitations of current approaches, icnuding common generalisations, omissions, and over-simplifications. Engaging theoretical discussions, with reference to specific conflicts, suggest how these limitations can be remedied and adapted, whilst incorporating contributions from other disciplines. Additional chapters provide a valuable and concise survey of the main themes in the study of military history from 1500 to the present day.

Hb: 0–415–27533–4   Pb: 0–415–27534–2

Available at all good bookshops
For ordering and further information please visit
www.routledge.com